Coercive Power in Social Exchange describes the progression and results of a decade-long program of experimental research on power in social exchange relations. Exchange theorists have traditionally excluded punishment and coercion from the scope of their analyses; Molm examines whether exchange theory can be expanded to include both reward and coercive power. Working within the framework of Emerson's power-dependence theory, but also drawing on the decision theory concepts of strategic action and loss aversion, Molm develops and tests a theory of coercion in social exchange that emphasizes the interdependence of these two bases of power. Her work shows that reward power and coercive power are fundamentally different, not only in their effects on behavior but also in the structural incentive to use power and the risks of power use. When exchanges are nonnegotiated and secured by the "shadow of the future," rather than by binding agreements, dependence both encourages and constrains the use of coercion.

COERCIVE POWER IN
SOCIAL EXCHANGE

STUDIES IN RATIONALITY AND SOCIAL CHANGE

Editors: Jon Elster and Michael S. McPherson

Editorial Board:
Fredrik Barth
Amartya Sen
Arthur Stinchcombe
Amos Tversky
Bernard Williams

Linda D. Molm
University of Arizona

COERCIVE POWER IN
SOCIAL EXCHANGE

CAMBRIDGE
UNIVERSITY PRESS

PUBLISHED BY THE PRESS SYNDICATE OF THE UNIVERSITY OF CAMBRIDGE
The Pitt Building, Trumpington Street, Cambridge CB2 1RP

CAMBRIDGE UNIVERSITY PRESS
The Edinburgh Building, Cambridge CB2 2RU, United Kingdom
40 West 20th Street, New York, NY 10011–4211, USA
10 Stamford Road, Oakleigh, Melbourne 3166, Australia

© Linda D. Molm 1997

First published 1997

Printed in the United States of America

Typeset in Times Roman

Library of Congress Cataloging-in-Publication Data
Molm, Linda D.
Coercive power in social exchange / Linda D. Molm.
p.   cm. – (Studies in rationality and social change)
Includes bibliographical references (p. 293) and index.
ISBN 0–521–56290–2. – ISBN 0–521–57461–7 (pbk.)
1. Social exchange.   2. Power (Social sciences)   3. Retribution.
I. Title.   II. Series.
HM291.M638   1997
303.3—dc20   96–8679
                                                      CIP

*A catalog record for this book is available from
the British Library.*

ISBN 0–521–56290–2 hardback
ISBN 0–521–57461–7 paperback

Contents

Figures and Tables

Figures

Tables

Preface and acknowledgments

The product of nearly a decade of theoretical and empirical work on power in social exchange networks, this book describes the progression of a theoretically driven, cumulative program of experimental research, begun at Emory University in the mid-1980s and completed at the University of Arizona. During that 10-year period, many of the results of the individual experiments in the program were published in journals, the typical outlet for experimental research.

As the program progressed and both empirical findings and theoretical knowledge began to cumulate, however, I became more and more frustrated with the impossibility of conveying the substance of the whole in a series of pieces, each of which had to stand more or less on its own. The logic and significance of each successive experiment depended substantially on what had gone before and, as that earlier body of work became larger and larger, the journal format could no longer accommodate what I wanted to say. This book has given me that opportunity.

In writing this book, I had two different, but related, objectives. One was to compare reward-based and coercive forms of power in social exchange relations: how they are different, why they are different, and the implications of those differences for both theory and social relationships. The results of this analysis offer important insights and challenges for both social exchange theory (which traditionally has ignored the role of punishment and coercion in social relationships) and theories of coercive power (which traditionally have ignored the capacities of actors, in most relations, to reward as well as to punish each other).

My second objective was to show how a cumulative program of experimental research can be used to build and test theory. I wanted to show the process – not merely the product – of theory development, and to convey the sense of discovery and puzzle solving that accompanies this kind of work. Consequently, rather than starting with the theory that was the final product of this effort and then reporting a series of experiments that test and support it, the book follows the structure of the work itself. It describes the development of a theory of coercive exchange over time, as successive experiments tested predictions, raised new questions, and gradually shaped and refined my understanding of coercive processes in exchange relations.

The book is intended for several audiences. Because it draws on work from a variety of disciplines, it should appeal to sociologists, psychologists, economists, and political scientists who are interested in issues of power, exchange, decision making, and coercion. I intend it for both professionals and graduate students in those fields. Those who are primarily interested in the conclusions of the research, rather than in the methods and data analysis, can follow the substance of the empirical chapters (Chapters 5–9) by reading the "implications" and "conclusions" sections that accompany each of the experiments and skipping over the design and analysis sections. On the other hand, those same design and analysis sections, plus the fairly lengthy treatment of the relation between theory and experimental design in Chapter 4, should make the book useful for graduate courses on research methods.

Experimental work relies, more than some kinds of research, on sizable contributions of both financial support and research assistance. I would like to thank, first and foremost, the National Science Foundation for supporting this entire research program through three grants (NSF SES-8419872, SES-8921431, SES-9210399). I would also like to thank Emory University and the University of Arizona for providing the experimental laboratories in which the research was conducted, and the University of Arizona for providing sabbatical time in which to write the book. Without the generous support of NSF and the universities, the work could not have been carried out.

Numerous students served as research assistants on the project. Three graduate students, who were in charge of coordinating the laboratory experiments and supervising a team of undergraduate experimenters at various times during the project, deserve special mention: Suni Lee at Emory University, and Phillip Wiseley and Theron Quist at the University of Arizona. Their professionalism, skill, and dedication to the project were essential to its success. All three also contributed to the intellectual enterprise, most notably Theron Quist and Phillip Wiseley, who were coauthors on the two justice articles on which Chapter 8 is based. Three other graduate students, Sally Fago, Daniel Jones, and David Richmond, were involved in the project for shorter periods of time, but made valuable contributions nonetheless. David Richmond also drew the computer-generated figures for the book. And Gretchen Peterson, a new participant in the project, created the index. Undergraduate students at both universities served as excellent, professional experimenters during the project: Cathy Amoroso, Amanda Gibson, Lynn Motley, Peggy Bausch Ransom, Connie Siegel, and Kent Stock at Emory, and Lawrence Ducchesi, Anne Lane, Nancy Morris, Lisa O'Laughlin, and Angelina Quesada at Arizona.

William Dixon aided the project in many ways, always as a supportive partner, but also as a valuable source of statistical and computing advice. I particularly thank him for his help with the design and execution of the logit analysis in Chapter 5.

Jon Elster, Edward Lawler, and Michael Macy provided valuable comments on an earlier draft of the manuscript. Their suggestions made the final product a much better one. I remain entirely responsible for its shortcomings, of course.

Finally, I would like to thank the reviewers and editors of the journals in which articles from this project appear. Although the material in the book has been extensively revised, it has benefited from their advice. The following chapters draw, to varying degrees, on several of these publications:

Chapter 5:

Linda D. Molm. 1988. "The Structure and Use of Power: A Comparison of Reward and Punishment Power." *Social Psychology Quarterly* 51: 108–122.

1989. "An Experimental Analysis of Imbalance in Punishment Power." *Social Forces* 68:178–203.

1989. "Punishment Power: A Balancing Process in Power-Dependence Relations." *American Journal of Sociology* 94:1392–1418.

1990. "Structure, Action and Outcomes: The Dynamics of Power in Exchange Relations." *American Sociological Review* 55:427–493.

Chapter 7:

Linda D. Molm. 1997. "Risk and Power Use: Constraints on the Use of Coercion in Exchange." *American Sociological Review*. In press.

Chapter 8:

Linda D. Molm, Theron M. Quist, and Phillip A. Wiseley. 1993. "Reciprocal Justice and Strategies of Exchange." *Social Forces* 72:19–43. 1994. "Imbalanced Structures, Unfair Strategies: Power and Justice in Social Exchange." *American Sociological Review* 59:98–121.

Chapter 9:

Linda D. Molm. 1994. "Is Punishment Effective? Coercive Strategies in Social Exchange." *Social Psychology Quarterly* 57:75–94.

1. Introduction and overview

Over the course of a 15-year period, a group of social exchange theorists (Blau 1964; Emerson 1962, 1972b; Homans [1961] 1974; Thibaut and Kelley 1959) developed a theory of power that differed markedly from prevailing conceptions in the social sciences. Their view of power derived from exchange theory's emphasis on the ties of mutual dependence that underlie all social structures. People depend on one another for much of what they value and need in social life, and they provide these benefits to each other through the process of social exchange – offering, for example, status in exchange for leadership, loyalty for friendship, patronage for political support, and esteem for advice.

Not only does mutual dependence bring people together, however; it also provides the structural basis for power: one actor's *dependence* is the source of another's *power*. To the extent that dependence is mutual, actors in social relations have power over each other. And, to the extent that their dependencies are unequal, their relation will also be unequal, in terms of the benefits that each contributes and receives. More powerful, less dependent actors will enjoy greater benefits at lower cost.

When compared with more traditional conceptions of power as coercive (e.g., Bierstedt 1950; Weber 1947), the exchange theorists' view of power is strikingly benign. Common stipulations in definitions of power, such as intentionally imposing one's will on another, overcoming resistance, and making others behave contrary to their own interests, are notably absent. Emerson (1962, 1972b), for example, argued that power exists in all social relations, even intimate ones; that its use involves no necessary intent to harm, coerce, or even influence; and that both parties in a power relation – the powerful and the weak – will act out their respective roles even if they have no awareness of power governing their interaction. The mechanism underlying this process is not coercion, but simply the same laws that govern economic exchange: when demand is high and supply is scarce (the conditions that create dependence), one pays more for the things one values.

Emerson's (1962, 1972b) development of the exchange conception of power, commonly referred to as "power-dependence theory," strongly influenced the way that sociologists and other social scientists think about power. Two of his central ideas are now widely accepted among those who study power: that dependency is the source of one actor's power over another, and that power is an attribute of a relation, not an actor. Although power-dependence theory has its roots in social psychology, this conception of power has been applied at virtually all levels of analysis and in diverse substantive areas. Research based explicitly on Emerson's theory or on other dependency theories has studied power in families (e.g., McDonald 1980; Scanzoni 1972), in communities (e.g., Galaskiewicz 1979; Marsden and Laumann 1977), in international relations (e.g., Keohane and Nye 1977), and both within and between organizations (e.g., Bacharach and Lawler 1980; Hickson, Hinings, Lee, Schneck, and Pennings 1971; Jacobs 1974; Mindlin and Aldrich 1975; Pfeffer and Salancik 1978).

While exchange theory broadened the scope of power in one respect, however, it narrowed it in another. Rather than extending the more traditional conception of power as coercive to *include* power derived from dependence on others for rewards (what I will call "reward power"), exchange theorists instead excluded coercion from the theory and from its analysis of power. They argued (or sometimes simply assumed) that relations based on exchange were distinct from those based on coercion, and that a theory of exchange must be restricted to voluntary, mutually rewarding interactions. The study of coercive power was left to other theories – social psychological theories of conflict (e.g., Deutsch 1973; Tedeschi, Bonoma, and Schlenker 1972), political theories of deterrence (e.g., Morgan 1977; Schelling 1960), and macro theories of the state (e.g., Weber 1947).

Early on, however, Heath (1976) contended that the exclusion of coercion from exchange was an unnecessary restriction. He argued that voluntary (mutual reward) exchanges and coerced exchanges are fundamentally the same and that both could be explained by exchange principles. Actors give rewards to another in exchange for something they value, either reciprocal rewards or the removal of punishment or threat of harm. Those who control rewards or punishments for others have power over them, derived from others' dependence on them for obtaining things they desire or avoiding things they dislike. Thus, conceptually, the two bases of power are mirror images of each other.

Although numerous authors have distinguished between reward and coercive power and theorized about differences in their effects, systematic investigations comparing these two bases of power are almost nonexistent. Reward power and coercive power are typically addressed by different theories and studied in isolation from one another. Even when researchers study both, they usually measure or manipulate them in noncomparable ways.

As a result, many questions have not been answered, or even asked: Do structures of power that are comparable in all respects *except* the base of power have similar effects on exchange? What are the dynamics of their interaction with each other? Are their causal mechanisms similar, or must different theories be employed to explain their effects? Can any *single* theory explain both? In particular, can exchange theory's analysis of power-dependence relations be extended to include both?

These are the questions that occupy this book. It is the product of nearly a decade of studying and theorizing about power in exchange relations. The research in this volume represents the first systematic, cumulative investigation of social exchange networks in which *all* actors have *parallel* forms of *both* reward and coercive power over one another. This feature of the project also provides its underlying rationale: reward power and coercive power do not exist in isolation, nor are they used in isolation. In virtually all social relations, actors have the potential to exercise both forms of power; social interaction is a mix of "carrots" and "sticks." This project takes account of that reality, by analyzing both forms of power within a single theoretical framework and systematically comparing their effects in social relations that are governed by both.

The theoretical framework

My analytical framework derives from Emerson's (1972a, 1972b) theory of power-dependence relations. His approach to social exchange, more than any other, has shaped contemporary work in the field for the past two decades. The earlier exchange theories stimulated lively debates and created interest in the approach, but it was Emerson's more rigorous formulation that provided the impetus for sustained, systematic research programs, including many that focus primarily on the study of power in exchange networks (for reviews, see Berger and Zelditch 1993; Cook 1987; Emerson 1981; and Molm and Cook 1995). The exchange tradition that Emerson initiated has three main characteristics. First, its objective is the continued development and test of an *abstract theory* of power and exchange. Power-dependence theory encompasses exchange at different levels of analysis and in different substantive settings. The actors who exchange valued resources can be individuals, groups, or organizations (but only when those collective entities act as a single actor, in exchange with other actors external to the collectivity), and their exchanges might occur in families, work settings, international relations, and the like. Rather than developing separate theories of exchange and power in each of these settings, exchange theory abstracts their common, theoretically relevant elements and addresses the relations among those elements.

Second, exchange theory is based on an *instrumentalist model of human behavior*. Its focus is the benefits that people obtain from and contribute to social interaction, and the costs they pay and impose in the process. Assumptions about actors' behavior are derived from either learning or rational choice theories. Emerson chose the former because it required fewer assumptions about actors' cognitions or motivations. I also use a learning model, but extend it to include assumptions about strategic action. The focus of exchange theory is not the choices that individuals make, however, but the relations between actors and the patterns of social interaction that develop.

Third, although there are many applications of exchange principles in natural settings such as families and corporations, *basic research using experimental methods* to test and extend the theory dominates the field. Experiments on social exchange are typically conducted in standardized laboratory settings that aid the cumulation of results across experiments and facilitate theory development.

This work is part of that tradition and it shares all three characteristics. My analysis of power and exchange is abstract (although I use numerous examples of exchange in substantive settings to illustrate my points), I test theoretical predictions in laboratory experiments, and I assume that actors are motivated by the costs and benefits of their actions and relations.

My work differs from most current research on power in exchange relations in two respects, however. First, while many researchers study exchange in bargaining settings in which actors formally negotiate agreements (e.g., Cook, Emerson, Gillmore, and Yamagishi 1983; Lawler 1992; Markovsky, Willer, and Patton 1988), I study exchanges that are nonnegotiated – exchanges in which actors do not bargain about the terms of the exchange, and do not know whether or when others will reciprocate their rewarding acts. Their relations develop gradually, as actors respond to each other's sequential actions and, over time, form patterns of exchange that are mutually beneficial. Second, because of my assumption that such processes take time and require learning, I study exchange relations over a more extended period than do most bargaining researchers. Actors in my experimental networks interact with the same partners over the course of several hundred exchange opportunities, rather than several dozen. Altogether, the experimental data for this project represent 1,800 hours of interaction, recorded over nearly 200,000 exchange opportunities.

This work also departs, in an important way, from most approaches to the study of coercive power. Coercion is often conceptualized as a political tool whose strength rests on either the legitimate authority of the state or the physical might of the military. In contrast, I study coercive power as part of everyday life. Its use is not restricted to actors in particular positions of power or authority, nor does it necessarily involve the use of physical force or extreme deprivation. People can coerce with angry silences and cutting words, with opposing votes and unpleasant work assignments, as well as with weapons and prisons. In this research, coercive power is used – or not used – by actors seeking to improve their outcomes in social relations that offer the potential for both reward and punishment.

The research program

Although this book is primarily a study of exchange and power, it has an underlying subtext: the value of systematic, cumulative experimental research. The theoretical story it tells is the product of a lengthy series of experiments, conducted over many years, and the inductive and deductive theory construction that they facilitated.

Because most experimental research is published in journal articles, it is difficult to get a sense of how experimentation is used to build and test theory (see, however, Berger and Zeldrich 1993). The systematic cumulation of knowledge that is the hallmark of basic experimental research is apparent only in a program of research, not a single experiment. One aim of this book is to show the progression of such a program. The five empirical chapters in the book (Chapters 5 through 9) present results from 15 experiments, conducted over an 8-year period, at two different universities. In the course of this research, I studied over 900 exchange networks and nearly 100 different experimental conditions. All of the experiments were conducted in a standardized laboratory setting specifically designed for the project.

In this book, I attempt to show both the puzzle-posing and puzzle-solving aspects of experimental research. Although experiments must be conducted within a setting that meets certain conditions assumed by a particular theoretical tradition, their value is not confined to the important role of testing deductively derived hypotheses. Experiments also contribute inductively, to the modification and extension of theory, by challenging theoretical assumptions and posing empirical puzzles. These must be solved theoretically before new hypotheses can be tested, deductively, in subsequent experiments.

This project depended vitally on that kind of interplay between deduction and induction. I began deductively, by testing whether power-dependence theory could be extended to coercive power without modification. I compared the effects of equivalent variations in structures of reward and coercive power, operationalized by actors' dependence on each other for monetary gains or losses. Some differences were expected, but the actual results were highly surprising: the structure of coercive power had almost no effect on exchange. Actors with greater power to coerce obtained no advantage in exchange, nor did coercion lead to mutual aggression and the escalation of conflict. Even when coercion offered a means to balance an unequal exchange relation, punishment was rarely used and its use declined over time. Successive experiments repeatedly confirmed these findings. Some variations in the structure of power had small effects, but the dominant finding was the robustness of the original results: coercive power simply made little difference.

These puzzling results provided the impetus for the next phase of the project, in which I developed and tested a theory to explain why the two bases of power have such different effects in exchange relations. At stake were two major questions. First, do reward power and coercive power operate in fundamentally different ways, and, if so, what principles explain those differences? Second, what are the implications of those differences for the objective of incorporating coercive power within the scope of exchange theory? Were the exchange theorists right, after all, in excluding coercion from exchange?

The pattern of results of the first experiments, while weak and inconsistent, offered some theoretical clues. First, they suggested that the weak effects of coercive power do not stem from the ineffectiveness of coercion per se, but from actors' infrequent use of their power to coerce. The link that Emerson assumed, between the structural potential for power and the actual use of that power, was failing to hold for coercive power. Second, they suggested that the key to understanding the infrequent use of coercion lay in analyzing the costs and benefits of power for the *power user*.

The theory development of the second phase unfolded in several stages: first, showing that some of the fundamental principles of Emerson's theory do not apply to coercive power; second, incorporating assumptions from theories of choice and decision making to explain the strategic use of power; third, analyzing how the structure of power encourages or constrains strategic power use through its effects on risk and fear of retaliation; and, fourth, examining how norms of fair exchange contribute to, and reinforce, structural determinants of risk. The fifth and final task of this phase consisted of testing the effects of coercive power when it is used, consistently and contingently.

Contributions

The outcome of this work is a theory of coercion in exchange that has important implications for both exchange theory and theories of coercive power. First, it provides a new understanding of the limitations of exchange theory's structural approach to power. I show that the use of coercive power is not structurally induced in the same way as reward power, and I explain, more generally, the conditions that limit the scope of a purely structural theory of power.

Second, I extend exchange theory beyond these boundaries, to the analysis of strategic power use – power that is used purposively, to influence an exchange partner's behavior, and that can be constrained by risk and fear of loss. That task requires introducing theoretical topics that exchange theory has traditionally ignored: the decision-making processes of actors, cognitive biases such as loss aversion that affect perceptions of actual and potential costs and benefits, and the risks of power use by dependent actors. Cook (1991) has suggested that no theory can attempt to bridge the "micro–macro gap" unless it contains both a full conception of agency and a fully developed model of social structure. For the past 15 years, exchange theorists have concentrated on the latter, extending and refining the theory's model of structure while largely ignoring the role of agency. As my work shows, a broader conception of agency can inform our understanding of structure without negating its importance.

Third, the work provides a detailed comparative analysis of the two bases of power that dominate the power literature and social life: reward power and coercive power. I analyze the similarities and differences in their relations between structure and behavior, the conditions that motivate and constrain their use, and their behavioral and affective consequences.

Finally, this book offers a rather different view of coercive power than most previous analyses. I show that in exchange relations, coercive power has significant limitations, imposed by the structure of dependence. It does not dominate interaction, or lead to escalating cycles of conflict, or help powerful actors to subjugate the weak. Reward dependence, not coercive power, emerges as the primary force in exchange relations. Reward dependence motivates exchange in the first place, and it determines the use of *both* reward power and coercive power, albeit through different mechanisms.

Structure of the book

The next three chapters lay the theoretical and methodological foundations for the research. Chapter 2 introduces the basic concepts and assumptions of social exchange theory and its analysis of reward-based power. Emerson's theory of power-dependence relations receives primary emphasis, but I also draw on the contributions of Blau, Homans, and Thibaut and Kelley. I begin by discussing the "building blocks" of exchange theory – actors, resources, exchange process, and exchange structure – and then describe the analysis of power-dependence relations in some detail. I conclude by comparing power-dependence theory's position with the views of other theorists on some of the historical debates over power.

Chapter 3 examines exchange theory's exclusion of punishment and coercive power. I argue that this scope assumption is unnecessarily restrictive, that it ignores much of everyday social interaction, and that it prevents the comparison of power based on both rewards and punishments. I then examine how other theoretical and research traditions – including macro theories of political power, social psychological theories of conflict and bargaining, and psychological studies of punishment – have conceptualized and studied coercive power. Finally, I apply the exchange framework introduced in Chapter 2 to coercive power and analyze the implications of this extension. I conclude by outlining the objectives and scope conditions of the project.

Chapter 4 describes how these theoretical concepts and scope conditions were operationalized in an experimental laboratory designed specifically for the study of exchange and power. I discuss the purpose of experimental research, its use as a tool for building and testing theory, and the advantages of a standardized setting for cumulating knowledge across a series of experiments. I then show in detail the logic that underlies various aspects of the experimental setting I use and their relation to the concepts and assumptions of exchange theory.

Chapter 5 summarizes the results and implications of the five experiments that comprise the first phase of the research. These experiments addressed the basic question with which the project began: can exchange theory's analysis of power-dependence relations be extended, without modification, to coercive power? Can we predict the distribution of exchange from the structure of coercive power in a relation, just as we can predict it from the structure of reward power? The results show that the answer to that question is clearly no. Not only does coercive power fail to produce effects comparable with those of reward power, it has few effects of any kind.

The next four chapters (6 through 9) build and test a theory that explains why reward power and coercive power have such different effects and predicts when their effects should be more comparable. Chapters 6 through 8 examine constraints on actors' use of coercive power; Chapter 9 studies the effects of coercion when it is used, with varying contingency and frequency.

In Chapter 6 I make two arguments: first, that the weak effects of coercive power result from its low use, not from the ineffectiveness of coercion per se; and, second, that the primary reason why coercive power is used so infrequently is that its use is not induced by structural power alone. I show that Emerson's well-known phrase, "to have a power advantage is to use it" (1972b:67), holds only for reward power. The chapter explains why the use of reward power, but not coercive power, is inherent in structural power, and describes an experimental test of that explanation.

Chapter 7 takes up the next question: if the use of coercive power is not structurally induced, but must be used strategically to create contingencies that influence other actors' behaviors, then what conditions constrain or encourage its use? I draw on assumptions about behavior under risk and uncertainty, particularly from the work of Axelrod (1984, 1986) and Kahneman and Tversky (1979), to answer that question. By taking account of principles of loss aversion and preference for the status quo, I show that the use of power in relations of mutual dependence is risky, and that risk constrains strategic power use – particularly coercive power. Coercion increases only when experimental manipulations reduce the risk of losing the partner's reward exchange.

Whereas the theory and experiments in Chapter 7 focus on structural conditions that affect risk, Chapter 8 examines how norms of justice increase risk by prompting affective and behavioral reactions to partners whose use of power violates norms of fair exchange. I compare actors' perceptions of the just use of the two bases of power under different structures of power. The results offer further support for the conclusions of Chapter 7. The use of coercive power is perceived as more unjust than the use of reward power, it is more likely to provoke retaliation and resistance, and these effects are greatest for actors with the strongest incentive to use coercion.

Chapter 9 addresses the final question in the theoretical puzzle: if coercive power were used consistently and contingently, would it be effective? Would the partner's reward exchange increase, or would coercion lead to a cycle of retaliation and mutual conflict that would ultimately lower *both* actors' exchange outcomes? The analyses and experiments in this chapter show clearly that the effectiveness of coercion increases with the consistency and intensity of its use. These findings, which refute the predictions of many theories, support my argument that the weak effects of coercion in exchange are due primarily to actors' failure to use it.

Chapters 10 and 11 summarize the conclusions of the project. Chapter 10 offers a more formal statement of the theory of coercive exchange developed in Chapters 6–9, reviews the logic of its development, and discusses its implications for social exchange theory. Chapter 11 considers the implications of the core empirical findings for social relationships and for structures and settings outside the scope of the project.

2. Social exchange and power

This chapter lays the theoretical groundwork for the project. Here I describe the basic concepts, assumptions, and principles of social exchange theory and its conception of power. My discussion is based primarily on the contributions of Richard Emerson (1962, 1972a, 1972b), whose theory of power-dependence relations provides the framework for this work. I also draw on the insights of Thibaut and Kelley (1959), whose early treatment of power-dependence relations strongly influenced Emerson's subsequent work; of Homans ([1961] 1974), who is considered by many to be the founding father of sociological exchange theory; and of Blau (1964), whose conception of social exchange as *nonnegotiated* – the terms and timing of which are left unspecified – corresponds most closely to my own.[1]

My discussion in this chapter is limited to reward-based exchange, the traditional focus of social exchange theories. In the next chapter I evaluate this restriction and discuss the consequences of removing it for the assumptions and principles introduced here.

The concept of social exchange

The conception of social interaction as social exchange comes, of course, from the example of economic exchange. As anthropologists recognized as early as the 1920s (Malinowski 1922; Mauss 1925), many forms of social interaction outside of the economic marketplace can be conceptualized as an exchange of benefits. "Neighbors exchange favors; children, toys; colleagues, assistance; acquaintances, courtesies; politicians, concessions" (Blau 1964:88). Although Blau's examples include only exchanges

---

[1] For more detailed descriptions and critiques of the various exchange theories, see Emerson (1981), Molm and Cook (1995), and Turner ([1974] 1986).

of like resources, the exchange of different resources – advice for defer-ence, votes for political support, or love for status – is probably more common.

Both economic and social exchange are based on a fundamental char-acteristic of social life: much of what we need and value in life (e.g., goods, services, companionship, approval, status, information) can only be obtained from others. People depend on one another for such valued resources, and they provide them to one another through the process of exchange. Social exchange theory takes as its particular focus this aspect of social life – the benefits that people obtain from, and contribute to, social interaction, and the patterns of dependence that govern those ex-changes.

Historically, social exchange departed from economic exchange in an important way. Whereas classical microeconomic theory typically assumed the absence of long-term relations between exchange partners and the in-dependence of transactions, social exchange theory took as its subject mat-ter and its smallest unit of analysis *the more or less enduring relations that form between specific partners.* Recurring exchanges are necessarily interdependent in these relations, and, as a result, the patterns of interaction and influence between people over time – not simply on one-shot trans-actions – are of central importance to social exchange theorists. This em-phasis on the history of relations and the mutual contingency of behaviors reflects the influence of behavioral psychology, the other discipline that played an important role in the development of social exchange theory. What distinguishes contemporary social exchange theory from both psy-chology and microeconomics, however, is its emphasis on social structure as the framework within which exchange processes take place, and the structural change that results from those processes.

The elements of social exchange theory: actors, resources, structure, and process

The basic concepts and assumptions of social exchange theory can be organized around four main topics: the actors who exchange, the exchange resources, the structure of exchange, and the process of exchange. These are discussed in detail here and summarized in Appendix I (the basic concepts of exchange) and Table 2.1 (the scope assumptions of exchange).

Table 2.1. *The scope assumptions of social exchange theory*

Actors
   Actors behave in ways that increase outcomes they positively value and decrease outcomes they negatively value.

Resources
   Every class of valued outcomes obeys a principle of satiation (in psychological terms) or diminishing marginal utility (in economic terms).

Structure of exchange
   Exchange relations develop within structures of mutual dependence.

Process of exchange
   Exchange transactions
      Benefits obtained from other actors are contingent on benefits given in exchange.
   Exchange relations
      Actors engage in recurring, interdependent exchanges with specific partners over time.

Note: The scope assumptions or conditions of a theory describe the set of conditions under which the theory is assumed to hold; the theory is restricted to social interaction that meets these conditions.

Actors

The *actors* who engage in exchange can be either individual persons or corporate groups acting as a single unit (e.g., business corporations, voluntary associations, international organizations). They can be specific entities (e.g., your neighbor Joe, the Kiwanis Club) or interchangeable occupants of structural positions (e.g., your next-door neighbor, or the president of IBM). Obviously, corporate actors are more complex than individual actors (e.g., groups have their own internal structure and exchange processes) and are therefore distinct in many ways. The two are assumed to be analytically equivalent only when groups act as a single actor, in exchange with other groups or individuals. For example, a community theater group acts as a single entity when it seeks funding from the local government, but not when its members are interacting with one another in the process of planning or rehearsing a production.

Individuals and groups can be collapsed into the single category of "actors" partly because social exchange theory makes few assumptions about the characteristics of actors. Minimal conceptions of actors are typical of theories concerned primarily with the effects of social structure on social interaction (Lawler, Ridgeway, and Markovsky 1993). Social exchange theory assumes only that *actors behave in ways that increase outcomes they positively value and decrease outcomes they negatively value* (Table 2.1).

This scope assumption is deliberately stated very broadly, so that its wording includes both the ''rational actor'' of microeconomics and the ''operant actor'' of behavioral psychology. Actors may behave rationally, by cognitively weighing the potential costs and benefits of alternative choices of exchange partners and actions, based on various kinds and amounts of information, or their choices may reflect only the costs and benefits of past behavioral choices, without conscious weighing of alternatives (Emerson 1987).[2]

Neither model of the actor restricts the theory to selfish behavior or hedonistic desires. Actors may value getting rich or providing homeless shelters. They may value something that benefits only self, that benefits others, or even that hurts others (e.g., the sadist). The theory makes no assumptions about *what* actors value; rather, it assumes that *if* actor A values y, then A will choose behaviors that produce more rather than less of y. (Actors will not necessarily ''maximize'' outcomes, however.)

Different exchange theories have placed varying degrees of emphasis on the assumptions of these two models. Homans, Blau, Thibaut and Kelley, and Emerson all adopted, to some extent, assumptions derived from learning theories. Homans's and Emerson's theories were specifically derived from operant psychology, Thibaut and Kelley combined learning theory with some of the cognitive flavor of decision theories, and Blau adopted an eclectic mix of psychology, economics, and normative sociology.

Despite the fact that none of these theories is based explicitly on the rational choice or expected utility models of microeconomics,[3] it is common to find them described as ''rational choice'' theories. This may simply reflect the failure to distinguish between the assumptions of behavioral theory and microeconomics (i.e., behavioral theory assumes actors respond to the consequences of past behaviors, without conscious calculation; ra-

---

[2] The information that rational actors use to calculate potential costs and benefits of future choices can include the outcomes of past choices; typically, however, it would include other information as well.

[3] Exchange theories that do employ an explicit rational choice or expected utility model include Blalock and Wilken (1979), Coleman (1973, 1990), and Heath (1976). For more restricted applications, also see Bienenstock and Bonacich (1992) and Yamaguchi (1996).

tional choice approaches assume actors cognitively calculate the expected outcomes of future behaviors), but the language used by the early exchange theorists undoubtedly contributed to this view. Blau, Thibaut and Kelley, and even Homans seemed to describe people making conscious choices based upon self-interested deliberation (Bierstedt 1965). Emerson, in contrast, explicitly omitted any assumptions about the cognitions of actors. He proposed that operant psychology provided a broader base for the theory because it allowed for conscious calculation but did not assume it. Omitting considerations of cognitions of actors facilitated the development of a theory that emphasized structure rather than the thoughts or intentions of individuals.

My research integrates some aspects of both models. Like Emerson, I rely primarily on assumptions of learning and adaptation. I assume that actors learn from the rewarding or punishing consequences of their behaviors, regardless of whether they do so consciously or not. But I also analyze exchange strategies, in which actors create contingencies that produce consequences for other actors' behaviors. Such strategies are often purposive, and their analysis requires incorporating some assumptions of decision theorists (see Chapter 7).

Resources

Several concepts are used to refer to aspects of what actors exchange: resources, outcomes, rewards, costs, value, exchange domains. When an actor has possessions or behavioral capabilities that are valued by other actors, they are *resources* in that actor's relations with those others. These possessions or capabilities may be attached to specific actors or to structural positions whose occupants are interchangeable. While economic exchange is normally restricted to the exchange of goods or services for money, social exchange is much broader, including not only tangible goods and services, but actions that produce socially valued outcomes such as status, approval, or companionship, and psychological gratification such as self-esteem and satisfaction. While the resources of economic exchange (e.g., money) are sometimes valued by so many people that we come to think of them as resources in a very general sense, social exchange theory reminds us that resources depend on their value to others and, therefore, they are attributes of *relations*, not actors. What constitutes a resource for an actor in one relation may not be in another. For example, an employee's knowledge of computers might be highly valued by some co-workers but not by others.

Exchanges of tangible resources involve the transfer of a physical good from one actor to another. Many social exchanges, however, involve no actual transfer of resources. Instead, one actor performs a behavior that produces value for another. Such exchanges occur, for example, when a person comments on a colleague's paper or visits a sick friend. In these examples, an exchange action incurs some form of *cost* for the actor who performs it (the time and effort spent reading the paper or visiting the friend) and produces some kind of *outcome* for an exchange partner (advice or companionship).[4]

The costs of performing an exchange behavior can include one or more of the following: opportunity costs, investment costs, the actual loss of a material resource, or costs intrinsic to the behavior itself. The *opportunity costs* of exchange refer to the "rewards forgone" from alternative partners or behaviors not chosen. For example, the opportunity cost of choosing to go to a movie with a friend rather than staying home and reading a book is equal to the rewards that might have been obtained from the evening at home with the book. *Investment costs* are associated with acquiring certain kinds of resources – for example, the cost of learning a skill, or acquiring a high-status occupation. When material resources are exchanged, the actor incurs the *actual loss* of a resource, which is physically transferred to another. Material resources are depleted through exchange, but nonmaterial resources may not be. For example, social approval is not depleted in the way that money or food might be. Finally, there are costs that are *intrinsic* to the performance of some exchange behaviors, such as fatigue, pain, and unpleasantness. All exchange behaviors entail opportunity costs, but the other three categories of cost depend on the exchange resource.

For the analyses in this book, I assume that exchange resources are capacities to perform behaviors that produce valued outcomes for others, rather than tangible goods. Resources are not physically transferred, and resource supplies are not depleted. Such exchanges can still entail investment costs and intrinsic costs, in addition to opportunity costs. To simplify

---

[4] Economists distinguish resources on such dimensions as divisibility, alienability (i.e., whether resources can be transferred), conservation, time of delivery, and absence of externalities. See Coleman (1990) for a discussion of these properties of resources.

the analysis, however, I assume that investment and intrinsic costs are zero, and that the only costs to the actor are opportunity costs. In exchange relations, the exact value of opportunity costs is often unknown. If, for example, an actor has two alternative exchange partners who both control some resource of value to the actor (e.g., advice or approval), then the opportunity cost of exchanging with one of the partners equals the benefits that might have been obtained through exchange with the other. But that benefit depends not only on the value of the resources the other controls, but on the probability of the other's exchange – and that probability is often uncertain.

The *outcomes* of exchange are defined by the value that actors receive from each other in exchange. Outcomes can have positive value (called, in different literatures, rewards, reinforcement, utility, or benefits), or negative value (costs, punishment, disutility, losses). I will generally refer to positive outcomes as *rewards* and negative outcomes as *punishments*, reserving the term *costs* for the costs incurred by an actor in performing an exchange behavior. (At times, though, I will find it convenient to refer to both opportunity costs and actual losses from another's punishment as costs.)

Behaviorists have traditionally defined rewards (or reinforcers) and punishments functionally, by their effects on future behavior: rewards increase the frequency of the behavior on which they are contingent; punishments decrease the frequency of the behavior on which they are contingent.[5] These effects are generally produced by *changes* in the value of the outcomes that the person is experiencing (Van Houten 1983). Rewards are produced by either *increasing* positive value or *decreasing* negative value, and punishments by either *increasing* negative value or *decreasing* positive value. In short, outcomes have no a priori status as rewards or punishers; whether a particular outcome is rewarding or punishing depends on its relation to an actor's current situation. Thus, a move to a small house might be enormously rewarding to a homeless person, but punishing to a formerly rich man whose status and wealth have declined.

---

[5] Because rewards and punishments are *defined* by their effects on behavior, they cannot be used to *predict* behavior. Doing so creates the familiar problem of tautological reasoning. Social exchange theory does not predict the effects of rewards (or punishments) on behavior, but rather the effect of actors' dependencies on one another for outcomes that are known to be rewarding or punishing to the actors. For further discussion of the debate over tautological reasoning in social exchange theory, see Emerson (1972a, 1981).

Withholding potential rewards (rather than removing existing rewards) can also act as punishment, if rewards have been regularly received in the past or were promised in the future (e.g., an expected raise that is denied). An individual who has come to expect rewards experiences their absence as a loss. Similarly, if punishments have been regularly given in the past, or were threatened in the future, then their absence will be experienced as a reward. Thus, rewards and punishments are best conceived as two sides of the same coin, both in terms of their production and their effects on behavior. As I discuss in the next chapter, their potential interchangeability is central to the conception of coerced exchange.

Exchange theorists have traditionally made two assumptions about the outcomes of exchange: (1) that outcomes are rewarding or, at least, that the positive value of an outcome outweighs the negative value (e.g., some loss of face comes with obtaining advice, but the benefits of the advice outweigh the costs); and (2) that all outcomes obey a principle of satiation (in psychological terms) or diminishing marginal utility (in economic terms) (Table 2.1). For example, food is more valuable to a hungry person than to one who has just eaten, and approval is more valuable to a neglected child than to one who is frequently praised. The first assumption – the restriction of social exchange to the exchange of positively valued outcomes – is, of course, the subject of this book, and I will have much more to say about it in the next chapter.

The second assumption is used to define *exchange domains*. An exchange domain is a class of outcomes that are functionally equivalent, in the sense that receipt of one outcome reduces the value of all outcomes within that domain, through the principle of satiation or diminishing marginal utility.[6] For example, both bread and apples reduce hunger and thus may be considered members of the class of "food"; eating more bread reduces the value of both bread and apples. Similarly, if time spent with two different friends fulfills a single need for companionship, then the two friendships occur within the same domain, and time spent with one friend is likely to reduce the value of time spent with the other. If, instead, one friend is a hiking companion and the other a close confidante, then the two friendships may be in different domains, and time spent with one friend will have no effect on the value of the other's companionship.

---

[6] Emerson's concept of exchange domains is similar to the economic concept of substitutability of resources.

The rate of change in value varies for different classes of benefits. Some benefits, like money, diminish in value much more slowly than others because they can be used to obtain many other classes of benefits. (In economic terms, they have "exchange value," not simply "use value.") As we shall see, this characteristic of money makes it very useful as an exchange resource in laboratory experiments.

The *primacy* of an exchange relation refers to the number of exchange domains that the relation mediates. Relations that mediate many domains (e.g., family relations) have high primacy; relations in a single domain (e.g., economic transactions) have low primacy.[7] Despite the importance of this distinction, nearly all research on social exchange, at least in laboratory experiments, has been restricted to exchange relations in a single domain. My research is no exception; the complexities of studying relations with multiple domains would only confuse the issues of interest in this study. But this remains an important topic for future work.

I have already used the term "value" a great deal; let me now define the concept more explicitly. The *value* of exchange outcomes varies both across and within exchange domains. Across different domains, value refers to an actor's preference ordering of those domains (e.g., an actor's relative preference for friendship, money, and status). Within a single domain, value refers to the magnitude of outcomes that an actor potentially can receive in the relation (e.g., the *amount* of valued friendship, money, or status that a relation offers). Both kinds of value can change over time.

Although efforts to develop a theory of value within social exchange have been attempted (e.g., Emerson 1987), values are currently exogenous variables in exchange theory. The theory makes predictions about exchange behavior *given* information or assumptions about what people value. As I will discuss, values enter into predictions of exchange behavior through their effects on actors' dependencies on one another and the structure of exchange relations. The theory has little interest in *what* actors value, per se; instead, it is concerned with the *relations* that are created between actors when they control outcomes of any kind that are valued by one another. Most important, the theory assumes that actors' behavior is unaffected by the domain of value – that is, actors who value money

---

[7] As Molm and Cook (1995) have noted, there is a close correspondence between the theoretical concept of primacy and the more operational concept of multiplexity in the social network literature.

or approval will tend to behave similarly, in the sense that both will behave in ways that produce those outcomes within the constraints of available opportunities (Emerson 1981).

Because this research studies exchange within a single domain, no assumptions about actors' preference orderings across domains must be made. Instead, it is necessary to assume only that actors value outcomes within the domain of interest, so that they will be affected by manipulations of value within that domain. Procedures for meeting that assumption are discussed in Chapter 4.

With actors, resources, and value defined, we can state four assumptions about the behavior of actors in exchange relations (Emerson 1972a): (1) actors initiate exchanges with other actors who control resources they value; (2) those initiations that produce greater value increase in frequency while those that produce lesser value decline; (3) decreases in the value of a formed relation produce behavioral change; and (4) if the value obtained from a relation declines to zero, the relation will eventually end.

These assumptions satisfy the general scope condition of actors who seek to increase rewards and decrease costs (Table 2.1), and provide the basis for deriving predictions about the effects of structure on social exchange.

The structure of exchange

Social exchange relations develop within structures of mutual dependence among actors. Actors need not be equally dependent on one another, nor do they need to rely on others for all outcomes of value. But some degree of dependence of social actors on one another for valued outcomes is one of the central scope conditions of the theory (Table 2.1).

Broadly speaking, this scope condition encompasses relations of direct exchange, generalized exchange, and productive exchange (Figure 2.1). In relations of *direct exchange*, each actor's outcomes depend directly on the other actor's behaviors. A provides value to B, and B to A, as in Homans's ([1961] 1974) classic example of Person and Other exchanging advice and approval. In *generalized exchange*, the reciprocal dependence is indirect: a benefit received by B from A is not reciprocated directly, by B's giving to A, but indirectly, by giving to another actor in the network or group. Eventually, A will receive a "return" on her exchange from some actor in the system, but not from B. In the simple three-actor exchange shown

(a) Direct exchange

(b) Generalized (indirect) exchange

(c) Productive exchange

Figure 2.1. Direct, generalized, and productive forms of exchange

in Figure 2.1b, the indirect reciprocity involves only one additional actor: B gives to C and C to A. In larger systems of generalized exchange, the reciprocal dependency becomes increasingly indirect and in many cases quite diffuse, as examples of giving wedding gifts and reviewing journal manuscripts illustrate.[8] In *productive exchange* (Figure 2.1c), *both* actors in the relation must contribute in order for either to obtain benefits. Neither

[8] My distinction between direct exchange and generalized exchange is purely structural; it refers only to whether actors have the opportunity to reciprocate benefits directly rather than indirectly. Some comparisons of direct and generalized exchange confound this structural distinction with aspects of the process of exchange, such as the timing of reciprocity or the stipulation of returns. For example, Lévi-Strauss (1969) argued that direct exchange relations always involve a quid pro quo mentality, strict accounting, and an emphasis on immediate reciprocity. Similarly, Sahlins's (1972) definition of balanced reciprocity, which is often equated with direct exchange, specified "transactions which stipulate return of commensurate worth or utility within a finite and narrow period" (1972:148). As I discuss later, whether direct exchanges involve these other elements depends on the process of exchange, particularly whether exchange is negotiated or reciprocal.

can produce benefit for self or other through his own actions. Cooperation, or joint action, is required – as, for example, in coauthoring a book or dancing the tango – and separately obtained benefits are impossible.

The work in this book is restricted to structures of direct exchange. Most of the examples that we commonly think of as "exchange" are direct: neighbors who exchange favors, tools, or dinner parties, colleagues who exchange advice for deference, politicians who exchange votes, and so forth. In each of these examples, A does something for B that benefits B, at some cost to A, and vice versa. Direct exchange relations are characterized by actors who act as individuals (regardless of whether they are individual persons or corporate actors), who obtain separate value from exchange, and whose opportunities for obtaining value may conflict.

Although direct exchange relations are very common in social life, they are not synonymous with it. Many forms of social interaction combine elements of two or more of the types of exchange, particularly direct exchange and productive exchange. If, for example, two actors must jointly engage in the same activity (e.g., a dinner together) to provide the context in which direct exchanges of favors, information, or approval can occur, then the structure of their relation is based partly on productive exchange (i.e., both must participate in the joint activity in order for either to receive benefits from the direct exchange). Interactions that combine these different structures are the topic of Kelley and Thibaut's (1978) analysis of interdependence.

My analysis is restricted to relations based solely on direct exchange. These are distinct from relations that involve elements of productive exchange, in an important respect: in direct exchange, it is possible for one actor to obtain benefit from another while engaged in an alternative activity or relation. A wife who does more of the household chores, for example, not only reduces her husband's share of the work but expands his opportunities to obtain benefits from his job or other activities. As we shall see later in this chapter, it is this feature that makes asymmetrical exchange so beneficial for powerful actors.

Exchange networks. Structures of direct exchange can consist of isolated dyads or networks of connected dyadic relations. An *exchange network* is a set of two or more *connected* dyadic exchange relations (Emerson 1972b). Emerson's conception of connections distinguishes exchange theory's analysis of networks from the large body of research on social networks outside of the exchange tradition (see Cook et al. 1983 for a comparison). He defines two exchange relations as connected *only* if the frequency or value of exchange in one relation affects the frequency or value of exchange in another. Common membership, or the mere existence of interaction or communication, is insufficient.

Connections can be positive or negative.[9] Network connections are *positive* to the extent that exchange in one relation increases exchange in the other (e.g., information obtained from exchange in one relation is used as a resource in another exchange relation), and *negative* to the extent that exchange in one relation decreases exchange in the other (e.g., materials obtained from one supplier reduce the need for materials from an alternative supplier). "Mixed" networks consist of both positively and negatively connected relations. If two relations share an actor – for example, A exchanges with both B and C – but A's exchange with B has no effect on A's exchange with C, the connection is null: for our purposes, these two relations do not form an exchange network.

Negatively connected networks are central to the analysis of power, and they have received far more attention from exchange theorists than positively connected networks (see, however, Bonacich 1992; Szmatka and Willer 1993; Yamagishi, Gillmore, and Cook 1988). Negative connections between two (or more) relations (e.g., B–A and A–C) typically occur when B and C both control resources that offer value for A in the same exchange domain (Emerson 1972b; Yamaguchi 1996). Then, B and C are both potential exchange partners for A within that domain. They provide A with *alternative* opportunities for obtaining value in the domain, and they are competitors for the resources that A controls.[10] Suppose, for example, that the exchange domain for A is advice on establishing a new business, and that both B and C are potential sources of advice for A. The more advice

---

[9] Connections can also be bilateral or unilateral. They are bilateral if the effects of exchange in one relation on exchange in another occur in both directions; they are unilateral if they are one way only. The connections in the networks I study are all bilateral.

[10] While Emerson discussed only negative connections created by alternatives within the same domain, negative connections can also be created if the opportunities for exchange with partners in different domains are temporally overlapping. For example, while the opportunities for exchange in work and family settings normally occur at different times, some occupations present opportunities (or demands) for working extra hours that conflict with time that might normally be spent with family. This situation can produce a (partly) negative connection between an individual's exchange relation with his employer and his exchange relation with his spouse – that is, the more time spent with one, the less with the other. See Whitmeyer (1994) for a discussion of other possible sources of negative connections.

A obtains from B, the less A needs to obtain advice (within the same domain) from C. Consequently, the frequency of A's exchange with B and C will be negatively related; that is, A's exchange with B will decrease the frequency of A's exchange with C, and the B–A and A–C relations will be negatively connected.

Positive connections are created when exchange domains are not only different, but the outcome of A's exchange with B is a valuable resource for A in A's exchange with another actor, C. Then, the one exchange facilitates, rather than hinders, the other. For example, A may be a politician who obtains information from corporate executive B that, when passed on to politician C, allows A to secure C's vote on an important bill.[11]

Exchange networks in which all relations are positively connected are empirically rare; more typically, positive connections are combined with negative connections in "mixed" networks (Yamagishi et al. 1988). Power has been investigated primarily in negatively connected networks. The dynamics of power relations are better understood in such networks, and they are the subject of this analysis as well.

The process of exchange

Whereas the structure of exchange describes the patterns of relations among actors, the process of exchange describes how interaction takes place within that structure. *Exchange opportunities* (which may be defined by particular times, settings, or events) provide actors with the occasion to *initiate* an exchange. For example, a neighbor who is going out of town provides the opportunity to initiate an exchange by offering to care for the neighbor's house (with the hope, no doubt, that the neighbor will reciprocate in the future). When an initiation is reciprocated, the mutual exchange of benefits that results is called a *transaction*. An ongoing series of transactions between the same two actors constitutes an *exchange relation*. The distinction between transactions and relations captures two

---

[11] Yamaguchi (1996) has noted the correspondence between power-dependence theory's distinction between negative and positive connections, and the economic distinction between the substitutability and complementarity of goods. Resources in the same exchange domain provide substitutable goods (or outcomes) and create negative connections. Resources in different domains may or may not be complementary; if they are, they create positive connections.

different aspects of the exchange process: the process by which actors exchange resources in a single transaction, and the relations between transactions over time.

Exchange transactions. One of the most basic scope assumptions of exchange theory is that "Benefits obtained through social process are contingent upon benefits provided 'in exchange' " (Emerson 1981:32) (Table 2.1). It is this assumption that provides the bridge from the theories of individual behavior on which exchange theories are based (i.e., microeconomics and operant psychology) to social interaction. Whether the contingencies that are inherent in social exchange are explained by a "norm of reciprocity" (Gouldner 1960) or learning theory (Emerson 1972b), this assumption is necessary to explain why actors ever initiate exchanges: they expect, or have learned, that giving begets reciprocal giving. This assumption does not mean that reciprocity is equal; as I will soon discuss, the use of power necessarily involves a departure from equal reciprocity.

Although some contingency between A's giving to B and B's giving to A is assumed for all social exchanges, that contingency can result from different processes. Transactions in direct exchange relations take two main forms: negotiated and reciprocal (Emerson 1981).[12]

In *negotiated transactions*, actors engage in a joint-decision process, such as explicit bargaining, in which they reach an agreement on the terms of the exchange. Both sides of the exchange are agreed upon at the same time, and the benefits for both exchange partners are easily identified as discrete transactions. Most economic exchanges other than fixed-price trades fit in this category, as well as many social exchanges (e.g., agreements between husband and wife to go to a movie this week and a ballgame the next).

In *reciprocal transactions*, actors' contributions to the exchange are separately performed and nonnegotiated. Actors initiate exchanges (e.g., with an offer of help) without knowing whether, when, or to what degree others will reciprocate. Exchange relations develop over time as beneficial acts prompt reciprocal benefit; for example, a dinner invitation prompts a reciprocal invitation, or favorable treatment by one's employer. Because

---

[12] Emerson's labels are somewhat misleading, for reciprocity is a defining feature of all forms of exchange, whether negotiated or nonnegotiated. In negotiated exchanges, however, one actor's reciprocity of another's benefits is not a separate choice; instead, actors jointly agree to exchange benefits.

the same act may complete one exchange and initiate another, discrete transactions are difficult to identify. Instead, the relation takes the form of a series of individually performed, sequentially contingent acts; for example, you teach your colleague's class when he is sick, he comments on your paper, you help with his committee report, and so forth. The strict alternation of benefits in this example is unrealistic, of course; reciprocity is more likely to characterize the relation over time than on any single set of paired events.

Whether transactions are negotiated or reciprocal affects (1) the amount of information that actors have about potential outcomes from exchange, and (2) the structure of outcomes in the relation between two actors (Molm 1994b). First, when actors negotiate the terms of an exchange, they know what they are getting for what they are giving. If, in addition, they concurrently negotiate terms with several partners, they can compare the relative benefits of alternative exchanges. In contrast, actors who engage in reciprocal exchange know, at most, only the potential value of alternative relations. After repeated exchanges with the same partners, they may be able to estimate the probabilities that alternative partners will reciprocate their exchange, but they must establish such relations without that knowledge. As a result, A initiates exchange with B without knowing either the benefits or the opportunity costs of exchanging with B.

Second, the two forms of exchange create different relations between actors' behaviors and their outcomes. In negotiated transactions, neither actor can obtain benefit without a joint agreement that provides some benefit to both actors. But in reciprocal transactions, actors can obtain benefit without providing anything in return (and, conversely, they can provide benefit without obtaining anything in return). Reciprocity can be immediate, delayed, or nonexistent. In the absence of joint decision making and negotiated agreements, reciprocal exchanges are secured by what Axelrod (1984) calls "the shadow of the future," that is, each actor's stake in an ongoing relationship. Negotiated exchanges, on the other hand, do not require the prospect of future interaction, especially if agreements are binding. Contractual obligations make defections costly in any event.

Reciprocal transactions are uncharacteristic of economic exchanges, at least in industrial societies, but typical of many social exchanges. The flow of mutually beneficial actions between friends, family members, and intimates often takes this form. In close interpersonal relationships, norms tend to curtail the extent of explicit bargaining. But even in relations within the economic or political sphere, unilateral initiatives are common and the expectation of future reciprocity is often left implicit.

The classical exchange theorists were primarily concerned with reciprocal transactions. Homans ([1961] 1974) argued that explicit bargaining is rarely a part of enduring personal relationships, and Blau (1964) proposed that the absence of negotiations is what distinguishes social from economic exchange:

> Social exchange differs in important ways from strictly economic exchange. The basic and most crucial distinction is that social exchange entails *unspecified* obligations. . . . one person does another a favor, and while there is a general expectation of some future return, its exact nature is definitely *not* stipulated in advance. . . . the nature of the return cannot be bargained about but must be left to the discretion of the one who makes it. (Blau 1964:93–94; emphasis in original)

In contrast, most contemporary theorists study exchanges that are negotiated through explicit bargaining. The research programs of Cook, Emerson, and Yamagishi (Cook and Emerson 1978; Cook et al. 1983; Yamagishi et al. 1988), of Willer, Markovsky, and Skvoretz (Markovsky et al. 1988; Willer, Markovsky, and Patton 1989; Skvoretz and Willer 1991), and of Lawler and Bacharach (e.g., Bacharach and Lawler 1981; Lawler 1986) all study negotiated transactions in which actors make strictly binding agreements.[13]

In this book, as in my other research (e.g., Molm 1981, 1985), I return to the forms of social exchange that the classical exchange theorists – Blau, Homans, and Thibaut and Kelley – had in mind. By analyzing exchanges that are reciprocal and nonnegotiated, this work provides some balance to the dominant emphasis on bargaining in recent theoretical and empirical work on exchange. It also provides a useful bridge to research on mixed-motive games, particularly the burgeoning literature on the evolution of cooperation (e.g., Axelrod 1984, 1992; Axelrod and Dion 1988), which also studies how social interaction is established when individuals do not know each other's intentions and cannot make enforceable agreements.

---

[13] Game theorists make a similar distinction between noncooperative games and cooperative games (Heckathorn 1985). In cooperative games, strictly binding agreements are made jointly; in noncooperative games, actors decide on their choices independently, without knowledge of others' choices.

Exchange relations. Whereas the form of individual transactions was Blau's basis for distinguishing between social and economic exchange, the relation *between* transactions was the criterion that Emerson (1972b, 1981) used.[14] Classical microeconomic theory traditionally assumed that actors engaged in sets of *independent* transactions that were aggregated into markets. Although relations between economic exchange partners developed under some circumstances, such long-term relations were usually ignored for theoretical purposes.

Social exchange theory, in contrast, is built on a very different premise: that actors engage in recurring, *inter*dependent exchanges with specific partners over time (Table 2.1). The scope of the theory is restricted to such relatively enduring relations between actors; transactions that occur rarely or only once are excluded. The lack of independence assumed between transactions also means that the unit of analysis in social exchange theory must be the series of interactions that comprises a continuing exchange relation.

When the same actors exchange repeatedly with each other, the assumption that their actions are contingent on one another applies not only *within* transactions (i.e., A's benefits to B are contingent on B's benefits to A), but *across* transactions (e.g., the benefits given and received in an earlier A–B exchange affect A's subsequent behavior toward B). The interdependence of sequential transactions provides the opportunity for actors to influence their partners' behaviors in ways that are impossible when transactions are independent. In isolated transactions, such as the one-shot prisoner's dilemma game, the rational choice is to defect from the exchange and receive benefits from the other without reciprocating. But when the same actors repeatedly interact with one another, they can respond contingently to the other's previous behavior, rewarding desirable actions and withholding rewards for undesirable actions. As a result, it may not be in A's long-term interests to shortchange B. Whether it is depends on their relative power.

---

[14] Yet another criterion that has been used is the kind of benefits exchanged, for example, material or monetary versus social or psychological. Emerson (1981) assumed that differences between kinds of benefits are of little theoretical importance. He also argued that the distinction is rather meaningless, because many benefits have both psychological and material properties.

Power and dependence

The concepts I have just discussed form the building blocks of social exchange theory. But the heart of the theory is its analysis of power. As Homans ([1961] 1974), Blau (1964), and Emerson (1972a) all observed, a striking feature of exchange theory is the attention it directs to power. It was originally Thibaut and Kelley's (1959) insight, however, that the structural condition that provides the basis for social exchange – the mutual dependence of actors on each other – also provides the basis for power. Relations of dependence bring people together (to the extent that people are mutually dependent, they are more likely to form relations and to continue in them), but they also create inequalities in power (unequal dependencies give less dependent actors an advantage in the relation). Emerson built this insight into a theory of power-dependence relations (1962), and later made this analysis the cornerstone of a more general theory of social exchange (1972a, 1972b). Because his theory of power was developed first and then placed within the broader context of social exchange, this portion of the broader framework is often referred to as "power-dependence theory." I will use that label at times as well.

In an exchange relation between actors A and B, A's *power* over B is defined as the level of potential cost that A can impose on B. It derives from, and is equal to, B's dependence on A. Each actor is *dependent* on the other to the extent that outcomes valued by the actor are contingent on exchange with the other. This contingency is primarily a function of two variables, value and alternatives. B's dependence on A increases with the *value* to B of the exchange resources that A controls, and decreases with B's *alternative* sources of the same (or equivalent) resources (Emerson 1972b).[15] These alternatives are typically other potential exchange relations in a negatively connected exchange network – for example, alternative sources of information, friendship, political support, and the like.[16] If, for example, A is a

---

[15] "Availability" refers not only to the number of alternatives that B has, but to the probability that those alternatives will reciprocate exchange. The latter is primarily a function of the alternatives' dependence on other partners. For example, if both A and B have two alternative partners, but B's alternatives can exchange only with B while A's alternatives have other potential partners, then A's alternatives are less "available" than B's. If value is held constant, A's dependence on B is greater than B's dependence on A. In general, alternative partners who themselves have fewer or less valuable alternatives are more available than those who have more or better alternatives.

[16] They can also be nonsocial sources; for example, one may have the choice of obtaining information from a colleague (a social source) or from the library (a nonsocial source).

potential political supporter for B, then B's dependence on A (and A's power over B) increases with the value that B places on A's support (based, say, on A's financial resources or political clout), and decreases with the availability to B of other potential supporters.

There are several important implications of this conception of power. First, *power is an attribute of a relation*, not an actor, derived from an actor's control over resources that are valued by another actor. Because the value of resources is relation-specific, and because some actors have more alternatives for acquiring valued resources than others, it is meaningless to speak of "powerful persons." A may have power over B, but not over C.

Second, *power is a potential*, inherent in the structure of mutual dependencies created by the differential access that actors have to others who control resources they value. The definition of power as a potential is essential to a structural theory of power; only by defining power as a potential can it be treated as an attribute of an actor's position in a structure of dependence relations. As I will discuss, structural power is distinct from the behavioral process of using power and the exchange outcomes of power use; how structure affects behavior is one of the central questions of exchange theory and of this book.

Third, *power is nonzero-sum* (Lawler 1992). Because each actor's power is defined by the other's dependence, an increase in one actor's power does not imply a decrease in the other actor's power. There is no a priori relation between the two. Both actors might increase their power over each other, both decrease their power over each other, one increase while the other remains constant, and so forth. As a result, it is both possible and necessary to distinguish between the *average power* and *power imbalance* in a relation.

Average power and power imbalance

Power in the A–B relation is jointly determined by B's dependence on A and A's dependence on B. Because the two actors' dependencies on each other can vary independently (power is not zero-sum), we can distinguish between two theoretical dimensions of power in the relation: average power and power imbalance (Lawler 1986; Molm 1987a).

The *average power* of an exchange relation, defined as the average of two actors' dependencies on each other, is a measure of the absolute strength of the actors' power over each other. Emerson proposed that it is also a measure of the *cohesion* of the relation – that is, the higher the absolute dependence of two actors on each other, the more likely the relation is to form and survive, even in the midst of conflict and power imbalance.[17] This holds true of friendships, business partnerships, and relations between nations.

Power imbalance, defined by the difference between two actors' dependencies on each other, is a measure of their relative power over each other. If two actors are equally dependent on each other, power in the relation is balanced. But if B is more dependent on A than A is on B, then power is imbalanced, in A's favor. The less dependent and more powerful actor, A, has a *power advantage* in the relation equal to the amount of the imbalance, and the more dependent and less powerful actor, B, is *power-disadvantaged*. An imbalance in power can derive from unequal value in the resources that A and B control for each other, from unequal alternatives, or from both.[18]

Consider, for example, a relation between a very senior member of an academic department (A) and a young hotshot in statistics (B). A values B's statistical expertise, and B values A's political support. Although each is dependent on the other, A has a power advantage in the relation: A has several sources of statistical advice in the department, but no other member of the department has the political clout that A can wield on B's behalf. In addition, of course, tenure is more valuable than statistical advice. Thus, A gains power both by controlling a more valuable resource, and by having greater access to alternative sources of the resource that B controls.

Because two actors' dependencies on each other can vary independently, the average power and power imbalance in their relation can also vary independently. For example, the power imbalance between parents and children, and between teachers and pupils, may be roughly similar, but parents and children normally have much greater power *over each*

---

[17] Lawler and Yoon (1996) have recently extended Emerson's concept of cohesion to reflect both average power and power imbalance; they propose that the cohesion of a relation increases with average power but decreases with power imbalance.

[18] Although power imbalance can derive from differences in value alone, it cannot develop in the *absence* of alternatives (Cook and Emerson 1978). As I will discuss, alternatives drive the use of reward power, through their effects on actors' preferences for exchange with different partners.

other – that is, their average power is greater – than do teachers and pupils. Together, these two dimensions define the amount and distribution of structural power in an exchange relation.

Power and power use

Power imbalance and average power are structural attributes of exchange relations and the networks in which they are imbedded. Social exchange theory distinguishes between these dimensions of potential (structural) *power* and actual behavioral *power use*, and posits a causal relation between the two.

Traditionally, the term "power use" has referred to the distribution or asymmetry of the exchange outcomes in a relation which are accrued over time (Cook and Emerson 1978; Emerson 1972b) – for example, the distribution of reciprocal favors, material benefits, or emotional support. An actor is said to be "using power" to the extent that she obtains greater rewards at lower cost than her exchange partner over the course of the relation.[19] I expand this concept in two ways.

First, I distinguish between the dynamic *process* of using power (i.e., *how* actors use their exchange resources to increase rewards or lower costs), and power use as a *consequence or outcome* of structural imbalance (i.e., the traditional meaning of the term as the distribution of exchange that power imbalance produces). The result is a tripartite conception of power as structure, process, and outcome.[20]

The *structure* of power in a relation determines the *potential* cost that each actor can impose on the other. This cost is equal to the other's dependence (Emerson 1972b); that is, the more dependent B is on A for rewards (because of either high value or low alternatives), the higher the cost that A can impose on B by not providing those rewards. When actors *use* power, they transform that potential cost into actual cost, through the *process* of withholding rewards from the partner. Thus, if B is dependent

---

[19] Emerson (1972b) originally defined power use by changes over time in the relative opportunity costs that A and B incur. This conception of power use is particularly appropriate for the reciprocal exchange relations I study. In reciprocal exchange, it is the potential to receive rewards *without* reciprocating that makes an asymmetrical exchange of rewards beneficial to the actor who rewards less often. Because that actor invests less time in the relation for a given level of returns, he or she has more opportunities to exchange with the alternative partner (i.e., the actor's opportunity costs are lower).

[20] Bacharach and Lawler (1981) use a similar tripartite conception of power.

on A for friendship, or advice, or political support, A uses his power over B by withholding those rewards from B.[21] Because power-advantaged actors can impose higher costs than their disadvantaged partners, they have a structural advantage. Over time, if A is more powerful than B, A can induce B to accept higher opportunity costs in return for A's rewards; that is, B will reward A even when A fails to reciprocate, thus forgoing rewards from B's alternative partners. This unequal distribution of exchange is the *outcome* of power use.

In our example of the imbalanced relation between the senior academic (A) and the young statistical hotshot (B), we would expect, over time, that B would pay a higher and higher price for A's political support, first giving statistical advice, then actually doing A's statistical analyses, and so forth – all at little cost to A, but at increasing opportunity cost to B.

Second, in keeping with social exchange theory's recognition that power can be balanced and its distinction between the average power and power imbalance in a relation, I include a second measure of power use: the *average* frequency or value of exchange in the relation. This outcome, which I call *exchange frequency*, refers to the total benefits obtained by both actors in the relation, whereas the first, which I call *exchange asymmetry*, refers to how those benefits are distributed within the relation and who fares better.

Over time, the structure of power and dependence produces predictable effects on the frequency and distribution of exchange as actors use power to maintain exchange or gain advantage. Several propositions summarize these predicted effects (Emerson 1972a, 1972b).

First, A's initiations of exchange with B increase with A's dependence on B. Across the set of potential partners for A, the probability of A's initiations of exchange vary as a direct function of A's dependence on each.

Second, the frequency of exchange in a relation increases with average power. Holding power imbalance constant, both actors have more to gain from exchange (and incur lower opportunity costs) the greater their mutual dependence. As Emerson (1972b:67) described it, two friends who are

---

[21] Reward withholding in reciprocal exchange is comparable with what Markovsky et al. (1988) call exclusion in negotiated exchange, as long as the withheld rewards are not obtained elsewhere. When actors are excluded from negotiated exchange transactions, they lose out on all prospect of obtaining benefits – whether equal or unequal – from an agreement. Exclusion is the mechanism that encourages disadvantaged actors to offer better terms in future negotiations.

highly dependent on each other are significantly controlled "by the relation."

Third, in an imbalanced relation in which A has a power advantage, A's power use will increase over time (until constrained by A's own dependence), as evidenced by either (a) increased rewards to A from B, or (b) decreased rewards to B from A (i.e., decreased costs for A). In short, the exchange ratio of the relation changes in favor of the more powerful, less dependent actor.

Numerous studies support these predictions. Across a variety of exchange settings, research shows that the average frequency of exchange in a relation increases with the average power of the relation (e.g., Bacharach and Lawler 1981; Lawler and Bacharach 1987; Michaels and Wiggins 1976), and that the asymmetry of reward exchange increases as power imbalance increases, in favor of the power-advantaged actor (e.g., Burgess and Nielsen 1974; Cook and Emerson 1978; Cook et al. 1983; Markovsky et al. 1988; Molm 1981, 1985). Power imbalance also affects the average frequency of exchange; holding average power constant, the frequency with which actors exchange tends to decrease as power imbalance increases (e.g., Lawler 1992; Molm 1990).

Forms of asymmetrical exchange. An exchange advantage does not necessarily imply that the more powerful actor receives better *absolute* outcomes than the partner. Rather, the more powerful actor will be able to enjoy more frequently, at lower cost, *the best outcomes available* to her in the relationship (Thibaut and Kelley 1959).

Whether a power advantage also produces better outcomes in an absolute sense depends on the extent to which the advantage is produced by differences in the *value* of exchange to the two actors, rather than differences in access to *alternatives*. When a power advantage is at least partially derived from the lower value that the more powerful (and less dependent) actor places on the other's exchange resources, then the more powerful actor may receive no greater absolute benefit from the relation than the less powerful actor. However, he will receive those benefits at lower cost, giving him more opportunities to obtain benefits from other relations.

Consider, for example, a friendship that is imbalanced because the two friends place different value on the time they spend together, even though their friendship networks are similar in size and availability of alternatives. Over time, the friendship is likely to assume a distinctly asymmetrical character: the more dependent friend will provide more and more favors, do more things that the partner enjoys, and so forth, to maintain the friendship and the value she derives from it. Thus, the less dependent partner gains more and more of the benefits that the other's friendship can provide – *but she places less value on them.* The subjective value that each receives from the friendship may actually be equal, but the less dependent partner obtains that value at lower cost. Maintaining the friendship requires less effort on her part, and thus she can devote more time to other activities from which she obtains greater value.

If, however, each friend enjoys each other's company and favors equally, and a power imbalance in the relation results from differences in alternatives rather than value (i.e., one friend has many others whose companionship she values, but the other friend does not), then the less dependent partner will, over time, acquire more absolute (as well as relative) value from the relation than the more dependent partner.

In the networks I study, power is determined by actors' access to partners who control more or less valuable resources. The number of alternatives that each actor has is held constant, as is the shape of the network. Actors' dependencies are determined by the relative value controlled by their alternative partners. Within relations, advantaged actors do not necessarily obtain greater absolute benefits than their disadvantaged partners, but because they receive those benefits at lower opportunity cost, they obtain more benefit within the network as a whole. Advantaged actors have access to more valuable alternatives, and more opportunities for exchanging with those alternatives.

Structure and agency in power use

The use of power can be *structurally induced* by power advantage, regardless of actors' intent to use power or to influence another's behavior, or it can be *strategic.* Emerson (1972b) allowed for both forms of power use, but argued that the distinction between them was unnecessary. Even in the absence of any conscious or intentional use of power, he proposed, an actor who possesses a structural advantage will, over time, obtain more rewards at lower costs. The effects of power imbalance are produced by the structural characteristics of exchange relations, not by the motives of exchange actors.

The mechanism that drives this process is the structure of the negatively connected network, which provides power-advantaged actors with access to more or better alternatives. When these actors pursue exchange with their alternatives, they inadvertently withhold rewards from their more dependent partners; that is, they "use power" over them. In the process, they drive up the cost of obtaining the rewards they control, while lowering their own costs of obtaining the partners' rewards. Thus, structurally induced power use results when asymmetries in dependencies produce unequal probabilities of exchange with alternative partners. Power-advantaged actors are more likely to pursue exchange with their more available or more valuable alternatives, and in the process they inadvertently make their disadvantaged partners pay higher costs for their rewards. In this way, power imbalance produces inequalities in the distribution of exchange benefits.

Actors can also use power strategically, by selectively giving and withholding rewards, contingent on the partner's prior behavior. This is the form of power use that Thibaut and Kelley (1959) assumed when they discussed the conversion of fate control (structural dependence) to behavior control (actual influence over another's behavior), and it is the form of power that those concerned with sanctioning free riders and defectors from cooperation have studied (e.g., Axelrod 1984, 1986; Yamagishi 1995). When actors use power strategically, they *create* contingencies that produce predictable consequences for their partners' behaviors, rather than simply responding to the consequences of their own behaviors. They make their rewarding actions contingent on some level of prior rewarding by the exchange partner, or they contingently punish the other's failure to provide sufficient rewards. Structure sets the boundaries within which actors can influence exchange through strategic action (Michaels and Wiggins 1976), but it does not determine strategic power use.

As I discussed earlier, one of the most important consequences of the interdependence of recurring exchanges is the opportunity it provides for actors to use strategies that affect their partners' behaviors. By selectively giving or withholding rewards for exchange partners, contingent on the other's prior behavior, actors can use their exchange resources to alter the frequency and distribution of exchange outcomes within the structural constraints of power. The power-advantaged actor can shift the asymmetry of exchange toward its structural maximum, and the power-disadvantaged actor can shift it toward its structural minimum.

The relative influence of structure and agency in the use of power is one of the central themes of this book. Emerson allowed for agency, but gave dominant emphasis to structure. I explore these issues further in Chapter 5 (which examines the effects of both structural power and exchange strategies on the distribution of exchange), in Chapter 6 (which revisits Emerson's argument that power use is structurally induced), and in Chapter 7 (which develops a theory of strategic power use).

Power-balancing mechanisms and structural change

My discussion of strategies has considered only efforts to change the distribution of exchange behavior and outcomes within existing structures. But actors can also attempt to change the structure of power itself, by varying actors' dependencies.[22]

Emerson (1962, 1972b) focused specifically on "power-balancing" mechanisms, which are strategies to change the structure of imbalanced relations in favor of the disadvantaged actor. Power imbalance can be reduced in one of four ways: by decreasing the value of exchange to the less powerful actor, increasing the value of exchange to the more powerful actor, increasing the alternatives available to the less powerful actor, or decreasing the alternatives available to the more powerful actor (possibly through coalition formation; see Cook and Gillmore 1984).[23]

With the exception of the first source of change, which could result from the psychological process of ceasing to want that which you cannot get, none of these changes is automatically induced by the occurrence of inequality, and most require resources or actions that may not be available to actors. For example, increasing the value of exchange to the more powerful actor means that the less powerful actor must acquire new resources; increasing the alternatives available to the less powerful actor means that he must obtain new exchange partners. Thus, Emerson's (1972b) statement that imbalanced relations are unstable and tend toward balance is rather

---

[22] Both Lawler (1992) and Leik (1992) note the distinction between strategies that operate within an existing structure and strategies that attempt to change the structure itself. Lawler refers to these as "power-use tactics" and "power-change tactics," respectively, and Leik uses the terms "strategic action" and "strategic agency."

[23] All four strategies reduce power imbalance, but they have different effects on the average power in the relation (Emerson 1972b; Lawler 1992). Increasing the dependence of the power-advantaged actor, either by increasing the value of exchange for that actor or decreasing her alternatives, *increases* average power. Decreasing the dependence of the power-disadvantaged actor, either by decreasing the value of exchange for that actor or increasing her alternatives, *decreases* average power. Which approach is used therefore affects the stability of the relation and its ability to overcome conflict.

questionable. While disadvantaged actors are motivated to change the structure, advantaged actors are equally motivated to resist change – and their current power advantage should give them the upper hand in the struggle for power. In contrast to Emerson, Lawler (1992) suggests that it is *balanced* relations that are unstable, because both actors are motivated to increase their structural advantage in the relation.

Many exchange structures are created and maintained by factors external to the relation itself. For example, networks based on friendship or intimate relations develop out of opportunity structures created by a combination of proximity and stratification, networks based on work relations develop out of economic conditions and the job markets they create, networks of voluntary associations are created by common interests often formed prior to the association, and so forth. These structures may change either as a result of changes in external circumstances, or through the efforts of actors who seek to improve their positions of power.

Although structural change is an important topic for study, it is not the focus of this research. My analysis assumes that actors exchange within fixed structures, created by factors external to the relation. Actors can use strategic action to improve their outcomes within the constraints of the existing structure, but they cannot alter the structure itself.

Dyadic and network theories of power

Emerson's (1962, 1972b) original theory of power and dependence was a theory of power in dyadic relations, as affected by their structural location in larger networks. The concept of alternatives captures the effect of imbedding dyadic relations in larger exchange networks, in which multiple actors offer resources in the same domain to those with whom they are connected. But his notion of the "availability" of alternatives describes only loosely the effect on dependencies of more distal relations – that is, the availability (or unavailability) of alternatives for alternatives, and so on. Subsequent work on exchange networks has undertaken the task of developing measures that assess the power of a structural position *within the network as a whole*, rather than within each of a series of relations (see Cook et al. 1983; Markovsky et al. 1988; and the June 1992 special issue of *Social Networks*). Most of this work varies the form of the network structure, while holding constant the potential value of exchange within component relations.

For my purposes, however, a network-level analysis of power would introduce complexities unrelated to the task at hand: the examination of how different bases of power affect the distribution of exchange. Understanding the differences between reward and coercive forms of power requires not only a structural analysis of dependencies, but a behavioral analysis of exchange processes and outcomes within exchange relations. Consequently, I restrict my attention to dyadic relations, imbedded in relatively simple networks whose structure determines the power and dependence within component relations.

Comparison with other theories of power

Exchange theory's conception of power-dependence relations engages several of the historical debates over power: whether power is an attribute of a person or a relation, whether power is potential or actual influence, whether power must be used with intent, and whether power requires conflict and overcoming resistance. For those familiar with these debates, it may be useful to consider the position of power-dependence theory vis-à-vis other theories on these issues.

Power as an attribute of an actor or a relation

Emerson's (1962) original formulation of power-dependence theory was in part a reaction to the reputational studies of community power in the fifties (e.g., Hunter 1953; Mills 1956). These studies treated power as a generalized characteristic of a person or group, measured by reputation in the community, and then rank-ordered individuals to form a "power structure."[24] Numerous critiques of this approach, notably by Emerson (1962) and Blau (1964) in sociology and by Dahl (1957) and Bachrach and Baratz (1963) in political science, succeeded in establishing the principle that power must be a characteristic of a relation, not an actor. As a result, there is now substantial agreement on this issue, at least in principle.

When measuring power, however, researchers often revert to approaches that treat power as an attribute of an actor. To a considerable

---

[24] Some resource-based conceptions of power also regard resources (such as wealth, knowledge, or military expenditures) as attributes of actors, without consideration of their value for other actors in particular power relations.

extent, this problem arises when power is measured as actual influence – something that an individual is seen to be exercising, to produce a response from another individual. Both Clegg (1989) and Lukes (1974) criticize Dahl for this approach, but the problem really lies with the next issue: whether power is defined as potential or actual influence.

Power as potential or actual influence

The vast majority of power theorists also agree that power exists as a potential (see, however, Mayhew, Gray, and Richardson 1969). Some qualify this position by arguing that only actual power use can be measured empirically (e.g., Dahl 1957; Etzioni 1968; Harsanyi 1962; Nagel 1975; Simon 1957), and others propose that power ceases to exist if it is not "successful," that is, if it does not produce the intended behavioral effects (e.g., Bierstedt 1950; Wrong 1979). If power can be determined only after the fact, by examining its effects on behavior or events, then defining power as a potential means little.

What theorists mean by potential power also differs markedly. To exchange theorists, the potential for power resides in the structural relations of dependence that give some actors greater control over resources that others value and greater access to others who control resources that they value. This view is shared by other theorists who define power in dependency terms, or as control over resources that affect other actors' outcomes (e.g., Bacharach and Lawler 1981; Blalock 1989; Chamberlain 1955; Coleman 1990; Lawler 1992). Not all resource-based theories adopt a structural approach, however.

Some theorists conceptualize potential power in more subjective terms, as a capacity or disposition *located in an actor*, which becomes relational only by virtue of the *beliefs* about that actor's power held by the target. Thus, Wrong (1979) argues that for power to exist as a potential, A must have the capacity to affect B's outcomes *and* B must believe that A has this capacity and would exercise it. The potential for power lies in anticipated reactions. Wrong interprets Weber's conception of power ("the probability that one actor in a social relationship will . . . carry out his own will despite resistance" [1947:152]) as similarly implying a judgment in the mind of the power target about the probability of the actor's power use.

By defining potential power and actual power use as separate variables, the relation *between* them becomes the central question in the analysis of power. Theorists who define power as a potential but then argue that it ceases to exist if it fails to affect behavior (e.g., Bachrach and Baratz 1963; Bierstedt 1950; Wrong 1979) cannot address this question. As Bach-arach and Lawler (1981) point out, this conception of power is essentially tautological. Distinguishing between potential power and actual power use removes the tautology and enables one to use the concept of power to predict the outcomes of power use.

Power as intentional or unintentional

The third debate, over intentionality, is part of a broader controversy about the relative emphasis on social structure or human agency in conceptions of power (see Barbalet 1987; Giddens 1976; Layder 1985; and Lukes 1974, 1977). Emerson's position, that power can derive from social struc-ture alone and have important consequences in the absence of intent by individual actors, is shared by Barbalet (1987), Layder (1985), and others. Numerous theorists disagree with this view, however, and instead argue that power must be used with intent (e.g., Bachrach and Baratz 1963; Russell 1938; Tedeschi, Schlenker, and Bonoma 1973; Weber 1947; Wrong 1979). Most of these writers also require that the effects produced must be the ones intended.

Requirements of intent sometimes lead to rather individualistic ap-proaches to the study of power. Bachrach and Baratz (1963), for example, argue that power must be defined separately from the standpoint of both the user and the target. Because the user's reasons for exercising power and the target's reasons for complying may vary independently, the same action may represent the use of power from the viewpoint of one but not the other. Similarly, theorists who require intent often conceptualize the exercise of power in terms of distinct, concrete actions by each individual: A must perform some act that expresses his wishes to B, and B must then comply – or not – with A's wishes. Some writers (e.g, Bachrach and Baratz 1963; Wrong 1979) also insist that A's directive to B must include the threat or promise of (negative or positive) sanctions if B fails to comply.

Power-dependence theory, of course, has no such requirements. In Emerson's view, social interaction is shaped by the opportunities and con-straints of structural dependencies, and driven by actors' motivations to obtain the things they value (see also Lawler 1992; Lukes 1974; O'Brien and Cook 1989). Together, these two forces produce predictable patterns of exchange, regardless of intent to use power. As we shall see in Chapter 6, extending this argument to coercive power is more problematic.

Power as conflictual or consensual

A fourth debate concerns the issue of whether power necessarily requires or implies conflict or overcoming resistance. Lukes (1974) distinguishes between two different views of power on this basis. The more traditional conception of power assumes that A affects B in a manner contrary to B's own interests. Thus, some conflict of interests is assumed, and power use produces a change in B's behavior that is contrary to what B would otherwise have done. Included within this tradition are most of the major power theorists (e.g., Bachrach and Baratz, Bierstedt, Dahl, Weber, and the community power theorists). In contrast to this conception of power as "power over" is an alternative perspective, particularly evident in the work of Parsons (1957, 1963a, 1963b) and Arendt (1970) (and, to some extent, Boulding 1989),[25] that conceives of power as "power to" – the ability to obtain objectives, rather than to control others. Power is viewed as the property of a collectivity, and it is supported and *legitimated* by that collectivity in order to advance group goals. Because it operates within a structure of shared norms that confers the right to request compliance on some agents of the collectivity, it is based on value consensus, not conflict.

Putting aside semantic differences about what deserves the label "power," this debate amounts to little more than the traditional distinction between power and authority. Power-dependence theory's analysis of power does not include authority or legitimated power, and on most grounds it falls quite clearly within the "power over" tradition. However, its position on conflict and overcoming resistance is distinguished in four ways from some other theories within that tradition.

First, because power can be balanced in a relation and still exist (in contrast to theories that restrict power to asymmetrical relations, including

---

[25] Boulding (1989) defines power as the ability to get what one wants. Although he distinguishes among three main kinds of power (destructive, productive, and integrative), he argues – like Parsons and Arendt – that productive power and integrative power are more widespread, more significant in human history, and more effective.

Blau 1964 and Dahl 1957), the definition of power does not require conflict. Second, for the same reason, power-dependence theory does not share
the zero-sum conception of power that is typically associated with the
"power over" tradition. Third, when power is imbalanced – which, realistically, is the almost universal state of affairs – conflict is inherent in
the unequal dependencies that create the imbalance. Because the more
dependent actor has a stronger interest in the exchange than the less dependent actor, their preferences for exchange will not coincide. Consequently, although actors may have conflicts on issues unrelated to their
dependency (e.g., two friends may disagree over which movie to see),
conflict will exist in the relation simply by virtue of their unequal dependencies (i.e., the more dependent friend will prefer more frequent interaction). Fourth, because power imbalance can produce unequal
exchange without intent and without awareness, the phrase "overcoming
resistance" must be interpreted with care. It does not necessarily imply
either the willful exercise of power or the willful resistance to that power;
it means only that the more powerful actor is able to impose greater costs
on the less powerful actor than the reverse, and as a result, the exchange
will shift in favor of the more powerful actor, and contrary to the interests
of the less powerful actor.

A fifth debate

Finally, there is a fifth debate in the literature that exchange theorists have
not engaged: the debate over whether power should be limited to coercive
power. Virtually all of the major power theorists include coercion in their
definitions of power, but some restrict power to coercion (e.g., Bachrach
and Baratz 1963; Bierstedt 1950; Lasswell and Kaplan 1950), whereas
others argue for a broader definition of power that includes coercion as
one of several forms or bases of power (e.g., Dahl 1957; Wrong 1979).
Because exchange theorists excluded punishment from the scope of social
exchange, power-dependence theory is restricted to reward-based power
and coercion is omitted from its analysis. In the next chapter I critically
evaluate this restriction and argue for its removal.

3. Punishment and coercion

This chapter challenges the restriction of social exchange theory to the mutual exchange of rewarding outcomes. I begin by examining how and why exchange theorists excluded punishment and coercive power from the scope of their theories. I argue that this scope condition is unnecessarily restrictive, and that it prevents the comparison of power based on both rewards and punishments. Next, I review theory and research from fields that have addressed punishment and coercive power, including macro theories of political power, social psychological theories of conflict and bargaining, and psychological studies of punishment. Finally, I extend the basic assumptions and concepts presented in Chapter 2 to incorporate punishment and coercion. I conclude by discussing the scope of the research program that occupies the remainder of the book.

The exclusion of punishment and coercion from social exchange theory

Although most social exchange theorists included both rewards and costs in their conceptual armament, they restricted costs to those incurred by actors from their own exchange behaviors. Costs that one actor imposes on another (punishment), and power based on the capacity to punish, were omitted from their theories.

Homans ([1961] 1974) and Blau (1964) explicitly excluded punishment and coercive power from the scope of social exchange, and Emerson (1962, 1972a, 1972b) did so implicitly.[1] Only Thibaut and Kelley (1959),

---

[1] Emerson's position on this issue is somewhat ambiguous. In a footnote to his 1962 paper on power and dependence relations, he explained that while it might appear that he is dealing with only one of French and Raven's (1959) bases of power, reward power, "closer attention to our highly generalized conception of dependence will show that it covers most if not all of the forms of power listed in that study" (1962:33, n. 9). Among those

whose theory was intended to encompass all patterns of interdependence in dyads (not only exchange relations), included punishment among the potential costs of interaction. Nevertheless, most of their discussion assumes mutually rewarding interactions, and their analysis of power does not include coercion.

As Heath (1976) has pointed out, there is no logical reason for excluding punishment and coercive exchanges from the theory's scope. An exchange "enables both participants to be better off than they would have been without it. . . . they need not necessarily be better off than they were before" (Heath 1976:19).[2] Heath goes on to suggest that whether participants are in fact better off than they were before is a good way of distinguishing exchanges of mutual rewards from coerced exchanges. For example, a husband or wife might prefer to spend more time at the office than at home, and might begin working longer and longer hours. But if family members react with anger and disapproval, the pattern is unlikely to persist: cutting back on work hours becomes preferable to enduring the unpleasant interactions. The worker is *not* better off than before the coercion began – remember, longer hours at work are preferred to shorter ones – but he or she is better off than persisting with long hours and frequent battles at home. More time at home is exchanged for a reduction in disapproval.

As this example illustrates, actors exchange benefits in both mutual reward exchanges and coercive exchanges. In purely coercive exchanges, however, the "benefit" for the target of coercion is a reduction or cessation of punishment. As I discussed in Chapter 2, such action is rewarding if the coercer first establishes the expectation that punishment will be imposed if the other fails to provide rewards, through either threats or a history of contingent punishment.

If the scope restriction cannot be justified on logical grounds, what accounts for it? While none of the exchange theorists is very explicit about the reasons for excluding punishment from the theory, its virtual absence

forms was coercive power. In 1972, however, Emerson defined cost solely as rewards forgone (1972a:56, Def. 11), and noted (in another footnote) that his chapter deals only with positive reinforcers. Thus, he restricted his analysis to the exchange of positively valued outcomes, but without specifying whether he regarded that restriction as a necessary scope condition of the theory.

[2] Kuhn (1963) makes a similar point, noting that the real power of an actor's capacity to either reward or punish lies in the positive value that compliance brings – that is, the rewards obtained or the punishments avoided.

from the two traditions on which the theory was based – microeconomics and behavioral psychology – is probably the primary factor. Economic exchanges involve only the exchange of positively valued goods.[3] And, at the time that the classical exchange theories were formulated (the late fifties and early sixties), behavioral psychology also focused almost exclusively on rewards. Early studies of punishment by Estes (1944), Skinner (1938), and Thorndike (1932) erroneously suggested that punishment was both ineffective and harmful; as a result, research on punishment was virtually abandoned. Behavioral theory became synonymous with reinforcement theory. New research on punishment did not resume until the mid-sixties, and many misperceptions about punishment remained long after contemporary research refuted them.

By the fifties, buttressed by Skinner's strong personal stance against punishment (described, most vividly, in *Walden Two* [1948]), the cultural ideology that Solomon (1964) later labeled "The Legend" was in full force. Psychologists, educators, and the general public shared the belief that punishment was cruel, ineffective as a means of controlling behavior, and produced harmful side effects and emotional reactions (Patterson 1982).

Homans and Blau were strongly influenced by these beliefs. Citing the findings of Thorndike, Estes, and Skinner, both argued that the use of punishment was ineffective in social relations and incompatible with mutual exchange. Blau (1964:224) noted that punishment "arouses emotional reactions that have undesirable consequences for behavior other than the one it is intended to affect" and that retaliation can become an end in itself, leading individuals to act contrary to their other interests. Homans ([1961] 1974:26) claimed that "The use of punishment is an inefficient means of getting another person to change his behavior: it may work but it seldom works well. . . . Punishment, moreover, is apt to produce hostile emotional behavior in the person punished."

Although Homans, like Heath, recognized that coercion can be analyzed as a form of exchange in which one actor receives rewards and the other accepts a smaller loss in order to avoid a greater one (Homans [1961,

---

[3] As Coleman (1990:38) notes, "In an exchange of economic goods, each actor, in offering an exchange, can only improve the lot of the other actor, which is why we usually think of such exchanges as both voluntary and mutually beneficial. But when events of other types are included, exchange can also be used to characterize phenomena that are ordinarily conceived of as coercion."

1974:78–81] uses the example of giving up one's money rather than one's life to a mugger), he argued that the end result is nevertheless punishing for the victim of the coercion. Consequently, the actor is unlikely to enter into such an exchange again if he can help it. When people do remain under the coercive control of others, Homans maintained, they do so only if they cannot escape.

If, indeed, coercion is observed only in "one-shot" transactions (such as Homans's example of the mugger and the victim), or in relations from which people cannot physically escape (e.g., prisons, concentration camps, military boot camp, slavery), then it does not belong in a theory that takes as its subject matter the continuing relations between mutually dependent actors. But considerable evidence refutes this notion. Virtually all social relations involve, from time to time, a mixture of reward and punishment, and the presence of some degree of coercion rarely provokes people into leaving relations. Most research suggests, instead, that it is the *ratio* of positive to negative experiences that determines satisfaction with relations (e.g., Patterson 1982).

In some relations, outcomes are primarily aversive for at least one of the actors. Yet the actor remains – not because she cannot physically escape, but because alternatives are even less desirable or because leaving the relation would increase rather than decrease punishment from a punitive partner. Women who remain in abusive relations are an example. Blalock (1987, 1989) has argued that exchange theory can and should analyze such relations, in which leaving is difficult or very costly.

The ubiquity of coercion in everyday life is one of the strongest arguments for including punishment and coercion within the scope of social exchange. The extent to which coercion is embedded in social intercourse has been obscured by the tendency of many writers, including Homans, to speak of exchange relations and coercive relations as if they were separate, mutually exclusive types, and to associate coercion with either legal punishment by the state or the threat of extreme harm by oppressors for captive victims (e.g., mugger and victim, master and slave, torturer and prisoner). As Blalock (1987) observes, analyzing reward-based exchange in isolation from the punishment that often accompanies it can give a distorted view of the consequences of reward power. For example, the exploitation that results from the market mechanisms of imbalanced reward exchange can provoke punitive reactions (e.g., sabotage or noncooperation) from the exploited (the power-disadvantaged actor), which may, in turn, be met by punitive reactions from the exploiter (the advantaged actor), sometimes cutting off any potential for the use of Emerson's balancing mechanisms in the relation.[4]

In summary, there are at least three major reasons for expanding social exchange theory to incorporate punishment and coercive power. First is the recognition that virtually all social exchange relations involve a mix of both positive and negative actions. The capacity to reward rarely exists in isolation from the capacity to punish. Second, restricting the scope of social exchange to reward-based exchange is not supported on logical grounds. The concepts of the theory are well equipped for analyzing relations that include both rewarding and punishing interactions. And third, as Blalock suggests, it is likely that reward and coercive power interact in interesting and theoretically important ways. Social exchange theory offers a broad and systematic framework for analyzing those effects.

Punishment and coercion have, of course, been studied from other theoretical perspectives, ranging from macro theories of political power to the micro analyses of behavioral psychologists. These perspectives provide an historical background of how various disciplines have analyzed coercion and offer useful points of comparison for this analysis.

Theoretical perspectives on coercive power

Social exchange theory's restriction of power to reward-based interactions departs from traditional analyses of power. Political power theorists err, if anything, in the opposite direction, with several defining power as purely coercive (e.g., Bachrach and Baratz 1963; Bierstedt 1950; Lasswell and Kaplan 1950; Weber 1947).

By far the more common approach, though, is to include coercion as one of several "bases" or sources of power. Some theorists (e.g., Lasswell and Kaplan 1950; Wrong 1979) further distinguish "bases" from

---

[4] Anderson and Willer (1981) also emphasize the interrelatedness of (reward) exchange relations and coercive relations, but in a rather different way: they propose that all exchanges of rewards occur within a larger coercive network (see also Gilham 1981). As I will discuss, they argue that most social relationships in modern societies are relations of reward exchange (because coercive power has been concentrated in the hands of the state), but their existence depends upon the larger coercive structure that maintains them. This analysis is intriguing. Because it addresses only economic exchange and the legal coercive power of the state, however, it ignores coercive relations that are intertwined with mutual reward exchange at the same structural level.

"forms" of power, by separately classifying power according to (1) the resources controlled by the power holder, and (2) the motives for compliance by the power subject. Exchange theory's relational conception of resources makes such a distinction unnecessary: because x is a resource for A *only* if it is valued by B, a resource is defined by both the power holder's control of it and the power subject's motives or interests.

The typologies of power bases in the literature are numerous and varied. Some are very particularized. For example, Dahl's (1961) power bases include social standing and the political resources of elected leaders, and Lasswell and Kaplan's (1950) eight bases include respect, skill, and enlightenment. The more influential classifications, however, are typically based on analytical rather than substantive differences, and they bear striking similarities to each other. Consider, for example, Etzioni's (1968) classification of utilitarian, coercive, and normative resources; Boulding's (1989) distinctions between productive, destructive, and integrative forms of power; Gamson's (1968) typology of inducement, constraint, and persuasion; Neuman's (1950) material benefits, violence, and persuasion; and French and Raven's (1959) more social psychological classification of reward, coercive, legitimate, expert, and referent bases of power. All of these typologies share three basic categories: *reward* (utilitarian, productive, inducement, material), *coercive* (destructive, constraint, violence), and *legitimate* (normative, integrative, persuasion) forms of power.[5] In short, reward and coercive power emerge as the most fundamental and generic bases of nonlegitimated power.

Definitions of coercion

Power theorists generally agree that reward power derives from the capacity to give or withhold rewards, or positive outcomes. But for many theorists, coercive power carries connotations that go beyond the basic requirement of the capacity to give or withhold punishment, or negative outcomes. These additional meanings include the severity of harm, restriction of freedom, and use of threat.

Most political theorists restrict coercive power to the potential use of

---

[5] French and Raven's expert and referent bases are both types of reward power, the first based on the information which A can provide for B, and the second on A's attractiveness to B.

severe deprivation, physical violence, threat of loss of life, and the like. The power of the state or the military is the most common model for this view of coercive power (regardless of legitimacy), and weapons are the most common tool for exercising power. Among those who appear to subscribe to this view are Bierstedt (1950), who defines power as "latent force"; and Lasswell and Kaplan (1950) and Bachrach and Baratz (1963), who both specify that the sanctions threatened must be "severe deprivations." On the other hand, some philosophers (e.g., Cook 1972) define coercion so broadly as to include *any* form of influence, including reward-based power.

Cutting across this issue is disagreement over a second question: whether coercion entails restriction of freedom. Because Bierstedt equates power with latent force, and its use with force itself, he argues that the use of power must render behavior involuntary. Similarly, Etzioni (1968) describes coercion as depriving subjects of the opportunity to choose. Kuhn disagrees only to the extent of suggesting that "coercion does not mean that one party has no choice, but that the bargaining advantage is so obviously one-sided as to leave little doubt of the outcome" (1963: 370). This position implies that coercive power is distinguished not only by the negative sign of the sanctions, but by an extremely imbalanced power relation.

Bachrach and Baratz (1963), in contrast, argue that power and force are distinct and that compliance with power must always involve choice. Part of this debate is more philosophical than theoretical (e.g., is compliance voluntary or forced when one of the "choices" is death?), but Bachrach and Baratz do exclude acts of physical force that eliminate choice (e.g., physically forcing someone into a prison cell), whereas this kind of act is the very essence of coercion for some theorists.

In contrast to most political theorists, social psychologists and bargaining theorists (e.g., Bacharach and Lawler 1981; French and Raven 1959; Tedeschi et al. 1973) typically define coercive power more broadly, as the capacity to give or withhold punishment. Punishment need not be severe (although it can be), and power need not be one-sided. This broader conception is the one I use in this analysis. While it encompasses many of the forms of coercive power discussed by political theorists, the scope conditions of my analysis necessarily exclude three types of coercion: legitimate coercive power or authority (e.g., the legal power of the state to punish criminals); single, isolated coercive acts (e.g., armed robbery);[6] and physical force that eliminates any choice.

A distinctive feature of many definitions of coercion, both macro and micro, is the requirement of threat (e.g., Bachrach and Baratz 1963; Boulding 1989; Willer and Markovsky 1993). Some theorists define coercive power only as *threatened* sanctions, arguing that if the threat must be carried out, power is not being "used," but rather has failed (e.g., Bachrach and Baratz 1963). Similarly, Willer and Markovsky (1993) argue that coercion will not be successful without threat. These arguments are based on one or both of two assumptions: (1) that coercion consists of a single event (i.e., a one-shot transaction), and (2) that the expectation of punishment (which is essential for coercion) must be created by threat. If coercion consists of a single transaction (e.g., a mugging), then A must threaten B to convey his intent to punish B (e.g., your money or your life!). If A instead waits and administers punishment when B fails to comply, it will be too late. But when actors engage in repeated transactions, A can punish B's failures to reward A, and the expectation of punishment can be created without threat, through contingent punishment (as in my example of the person whose long hours at work provoked coercion by family members).

The assumption of a one-shot transaction is also behind Kuhn's (1963) argument that the most distinctive aspects of coercive power are tactical and depend on the creation of beliefs – for example, the use of threat to convey the belief that A will administer sanctions if B does not comply. Thus, the "gun" that a robber carries may actually be a toy; it is the *belief* that it is a gun that matters. In a continuing relation, however, beliefs without substance are unlikely to persist; threats must eventually be backed up or they will lose their credibility (Boulding 1969).

Like Tedeschi et al. (1973) and Etzioni (1968), I regard threats and promises as modes of communication that may accompany power, rather than as an essential part of power. As Etzioni observes, the symbolic meaning they carry makes them more like persuasion than sanction-based power. Although they are common features of open, intentional influence,

---

[6] Wrong (1979) also excludes a single exercise of coercion, arguing that recurrent interaction is necessary for a power relation to exist – a position shared, of course, by exchange theorists.

power may be neither open nor intentional (Tedeschi et al. 1973). In addition, as I discuss in Chapter 9, the use of threats can produce effects unrelated to coercion per se. For these reasons, I exclude threats (and promises) from my analysis.

The use of coercive power

Despite the diverse views of the various power literatures on some issues, they share, with few exceptions, the normative position that coercion is an undesirable form of power that should be used only as a last resort. This position derives from several assumptions: (1) that the use of violence or physical force (assumed in many definitions of coercion) provokes reactions that have negative consequences for the social order; (2) that coercion is used by the powerful to subjugate the weak; and (3) that coercion is antithetical to certain forms of relationships or social organization that are characterized by a normative framework of cooperation, such as bargaining relations. All three premises are found in the writings of political theorists; bargaining theorists (e.g., Tedeschi and Bonoma 1972) primarily emphasize the third.

Some theorists (e.g., Bacharach and Lawler 1981; Blalock 1989) have taken issue with this position, arguing that the use of coercion is found in virtually all forms of social interaction, that it can be used for "good" purposes (e.g., by the disadvantaged against their exploiters) as well as bad, and that norms are emergent, fluid, and embedded in self-interest. Such views are relatively rare, however.

Not surprisingly, the negative connotations attached to coercion have led to a greater interest in how to *prevent* the use of coercive power than in studying the structural conditions that lead to its use. The prevention of the first use of coercive power is the focus of deterrence theories (e.g., Morgan 1977; Schelling 1960). Traditionally the province of political scientists, who applied it to policy debates over the arms race during the cold war, deterrence theory argues that higher levels of coercive power, when equally distributed, reduce (i.e., deter) the use of punishment. Critics of the theory question its long-term effects, however. Blalock (1989) notes that deterrence relies heavily on the assumption of credibility, and Boulding (1969) argues that maintaining credibility eventually requires the use of force. If so, then deterrence is unstable in the long run: coercive capability will eventually lead to conflict.

That is the prediction of an opposing theory, developed out of social psychological gaming research (e.g., Deutsch and Krauss 1962; Deutsch 1973), which suggests that higher levels of bilateral coercive power will produce an escalation of conflict (a "conflict spiral") rather than deter it. In direct contrast to deterrence theory, this approach argues that if coercive power is available, actors will use it. And, once initiated, conflict will tend to escalate.

Lawler's (1986) further development of these two theories traces their competing predictions to different intervening cognitive variables. Deterrence theory assumes that A's coercive power increases B's fear of A's retaliation if B were to use coercive power, and vice versa, and thus their mutual fear of retaliation inhibits their use of power. Conflict spiral theory instead proposes that A's own coercive power is a source of temptation to use that power, and once A does use it, B's fear of losing face leads B to retaliate.

The effects of coercive power

Theorists have tended to be of two voices on the effectiveness of coercive power, corresponding, Wrong (1979) suggests, to the conflict and consensus models of social theory (e.g., Dahrendorf 1959). On the one hand, the history of military conquest suggests that, at least in the short run, "coercive power is undoubtedly the most effective form of power in extensiveness, comprehensiveness and intensity" (Wrong 1979:42). Willer and his colleagues (Anderson and Willer 1981; Willer and Markovksy 1993) argue that the effectiveness of coercion accounts for the rapid development of market exchange in modern societies, by facilitating the centralization of coercive power in the hands of the state and forcing subjects of the state to develop reward exchange as a means of obtaining valued outcomes.[7]

On the other hand, numerous theorists make the opposite claim – that coercion is ineffective and destructive of social organization. Etzioni (1968) suggests that this is the mainstream position in both sociology and

---

[7] Willer uses this analysis to explain the ubiquity of reward exchange and the relative absence of coercion in modern societies. While that statement may accurately reflect the relative prevalence of these forms of relations in certain institutional settings (i.e., economic exchange and the political power of the state), it ignores the substantial amount of coercion existing in everyday life.

political science. And while some have proposed that coercion entails few costs (e.g., Kuhn 1963; Wrong 1979), those who are skeptical of the long-term effects of the mere threat or potential for punishment emphasize the many costs of actually using punishment (e.g., Boulding 1969; Tedeschi et al. 1973): the costs of surveillance and problems of visibility (noncompliers must be punished, and their noncompliance must be detected);[8] the use of time, effort, and resources; the arousal of hostility and antagonism in the targets of power use; and the consequent increase in resistance, retaliation, and instability. Furthermore, these effects tend to be involved in an accelerating system; that is, greater hostility and resistance increase the need for surveillance, which uses more time and resources, and so forth.

Summary

This brief review illustrates the widely disparate views that exist, across different disciplines and levels of analysis, on what coercive power is, when it is used, and what effects it will have. As it shows, for many theorists coercive power is not merely the negative counterpart of reward power. The added assumptions of severity and elimination of choice, which are peculiar to conceptions of coercion, make theoretical assertions about the relative use or effects of the two bases of power highly suspect. Furthermore, many discussions of power are based on unsystematic observations of particularistic events and actors. As a result, any proposed differences between reward or coercive forms of power may result not from the base of power per se, but from differences in the absolute or relative strength of power in the relations compared or other uncontrolled variables.

Unfortunately, theoretical and philosophical analyses of power vastly outnumber empirical studies of power that do control these dimensions. Few programs of research systematically study the use and effects of coercive power, and fewer still compare coercive power with reward power. In the next section I review three of the more extensive and systematic

[8] The issue of surveillance is primarily raised by political theorists, who envision the problems of a particular individual or societal agency attempting to control the behavior of many others with whom they are not in direct contact. In most social exchange relations, however, the contingent use of punishment raises no more problems of surveillance than the contingent use of rewards.

lines of research on punishment and coercion: social psychological "gaming" studies of conflict, programmatic research on dependence and punitive forms of power in bargaining relations, and psychological studies of punishment in laboratory and family settings.

Research on coercive power: three traditions

Threats and punishments in mixed-motive games

Research in this tradition studies the use of threats and punishment in mixed-motive, nonbargaining games. Two of the best-known research programs are Deutsch and Krauss's studies of the famous trucking game (Deutsch and Krauss 1962; Deutsch 1973), and the extensive research by Tedeschi and his associates on the use of threat and punishment in the prisoner's dilemma game (e.g., Tedeschi and Bonoma 1972; Tedeschi, Bonoma, and Brown 1971; Tedeschi et al. 1972; Tedeschi et al. 1973).

Deutsch and Krauss developed the argument that the capacity to punish gives rise to the use of that power, which, in turn, leads to the escalation of conflict through threat–counterthreat and punishment–counterpunishment spirals. They tested their ideas in the classic trucking game, an experimental setting that places two actors, representing different trucking companies (Acme and Bolt), in a situation of conflict. The goal of each actor is to move produce from a starting point to a destination, with payoffs contingent on the time it takes to reach the destination. Each actor can take a short route that must be shared by the two actors (i.e., both cannot use it at the same time), or one of two separate, longer routes that allow the two actors to avoid meeting each other. Deutsch and Krauss (1962) gave neither, one, or both actors a gate that could be used to block the opponent's access to the short route, thus creating conditions of no, unilateral, or bilateral punishment power. The use of this power imposed a cost on the other actor equal to the difference between the payoffs that could be obtained by taking the shorter and longer routes.

Their results showed that simply having the capacity to impose cost led to its use, and that in the bilateral condition, its use led to counteruse and substantial loss. The joint payoffs of both actors were much greater in the no-gate condition than in the bilateral power condition. In summarizing the results of this and related studies, Deutsch (1973) concluded that conflict is characterized by a tendency to expand and escalate, with the process often becoming independent of its initiating cause. He explains this tendency by a combination of competitive processes, misperceptions, and pressures for cognitive and social consistency.

In contrast, Tedeschi and associates base their predictions on decision theory and the analysis of subjective expected utility. This approach leads to a different hypothesis: that the use of threats and punishment will increase with the magnitude and probability of potential gains and decrease with the magnitude and probability of potential costs. Because potential costs increase with the other's punishment power, the implication is that bilateral punishment power should *reduce*, not increase, both actors' use of that power. As Bacharach and Lawler (1981) note, these ideas are similar to the deterrence theories of political scientists. However, the experimental paradigm that Tedeschi and his associates use examines only unilateral power and one-way influence (see Tedeschi et al. 1971). A single subject plays against a computer-simulated actor in a prisoner's dilemma game; either the subject or the simulated actor – but not both – has the power to threaten and punish the other. Experiments test the subject's use of threat and punishment, or the subject's compliance with the simulated actor's use of threat and punishment.

Their findings show, as predicted, that subjects' use of threats declines with the cost of actually using punishment, and that compliance with threats increases with both the magnitude of harm threatened and the credibility of the threat (see, e.g., Tedeschi et al. 1973). However, Tedeschi and his associates (1973) agree with Deutsch that if both actors have the power to punish, and if actual punishment (rather than mere threat) is used, then conflict is likely to intensify and escalate. They do not agree that these results hold for threats alone, but that would seem to be an empty argument: if threats are not backed up by actual punishment, their credibility will decline and they will cease to have any effect (or, as I suggest in Chapter 9, they may acquire different meanings that produce unintended effects).

Most of the research in this tradition examines variations in the capacity or use of threats and punishments, within a fixed reward structure. Consequently, the results do not address the question of how reward and punishment compare in their effects or how they interact with one another. Some research, including Tedeschi's, does compare the effects of threats and promises. In general, this research shows that bargainers tend to transmit promises with greater frequency than threats (e.g., Cheney, Harford, and Solomon 1972; Radlow and Weidner 1966), but threats are more likely than promises to produce immediate compliance (Rubin and Brown 1975).

As Bacharach and Lawler (1981) have discussed, this research primarily takes a tactical approach to power. The conception of structural power (or power capability) is not well developed, and manipulations of punishment power often confound absolute and relative dimensions of power (see, e.g., Hornstein 1965). The research program of Lawler and his associates addresses these problems and studies punishment power in a different context: explicit bargaining between two parties with conflicting interests.

Power processes in bargaining

Lawler's work with Bacharach and others on power in bargaining relations is one of the few efforts to investigate systematically both reward- and punishment-based power (Bacharach and Lawler 1981; Boyle and Lawler 1991; Lawler 1986, 1992; Lawler and Bacharach 1987; Lawler and Ford 1993; Lawler, Ford, and Blegen 1988). Theoretically, the approach distinguishes three aspects of power: structural (potential) power, the tactical use of that power (i.e., threats and concessions), and power outcomes (whether actors reach an agreement).[9] One of its strengths is its clear distinction between absolute and relative dimensions of structural power, which Lawler calls total power and relative power. While adopting Emerson's nonzero-sum conception of power, however, the approach departs from power-dependence theory in its greater emphasis on actors' interpretations and perceptions of power and their tactical use of power (i.e., the use of concessions and threats in bargaining).

Different branches of the program have investigated reward-based power, conceptualized in Emerson's power-dependence terms, and punishment-based power, based on Lawler's (1986) theory of bilateral deterrence. As Lawler (1992) notes, power-dependence and bilateral deterrence theories predict similar effects of some dimensions of the two bases of power: (1) when power in the relation is equal, high absolute power – on either base – should increase positive, conciliatory actions (i.e., rewards or concessions) and decrease negative, hostile actions (i.e., threats and

---

[9] I also use a tripartite conception of power (see Chapter 2), but my conceptions of power processes and power outcomes are rather different from Lawler's.

punishments); (2) unequal (imbalanced) power should produce more hostility and less conciliation (i.e., less frequent rewards and greater conflict) than equal power. Their research findings have generally supported these predictions. They also show that in relations of unequal power, the use of punitive tactics is not proportional to the relative power of the actors. Typically, actors with higher and lower levels of power do not differ significantly in their use of punishment.

Work in the punitive power branch of the theory has also tested bilateral deterrence against conflict spiral predictions, as explicated and developed by Lawler (1986), generally supporting the former over the latter (e.g., Lawler et al. 1988). Lawler suggests, however, that both theories may hold, under different conditions, with their relative support depending on the salience of the different intervening cognitions, fear of retaliation versus temptation (Lawler 1986), or the mutual reward dependence of the actors (Bacharach and Lawler 1981).

Although deterrence and conflict spiral theories make opposite predictions about the effect of coercive power on the use of punitive tactics (the central focus of Lawler's program), both theories imply that the actual use of punishment leads to an escalation of mutual conflict. Conflict spiral theory is explicitly based on the assumption that the use of coercive power will provoke retaliation, because of concerns with losing face, and deterrence theory is implicitly based on the same assumption. The logic of deterrence rests on the importance of preventing the initial use of punishment because of the expectation that, once used, punitive tactics will be retaliated and the resulting mutual antagonism will prevent the resolution of conflict. Research on explicit bargaining relations, like the nonbargaining gaming research, has generally supported these predictions. I discuss these findings in Chapter 9.

Most experiments in this research program study either the relation between reward-based power and concession tactics, *or* the relation between punishment-based power and punitive tactics. Findings from Lawler and Bacharach (1987), however, suggest the two can interact in potentially important ways. But because Lawler and his associates manipulate the two bases of power in different ways, it is difficult to compare their effects. They create variations in reward-based power by providing actors with information on the likelihood that they can get various agreements from a hypothetical alternative partner, if they fail to reach agreement with their experimental partner. They manipulate punishment-based power by varying the maximum percentage by which an actor can reduce the opponent's outcomes, across five opportunities to punish. In addition, all of the experiments examine the negotiation of a *single* agreement, over a number of bargaining rounds; consequently they do not address the use and effects of either base of power across repeated exchanges.[10] Thus, while Lawler's program is exceptional in its integration of the two bases of power, it leaves unanswered many of the questions that this analysis addresses.

Psychological studies of punishment and human behavior

The early psychological studies of punishment suggested conclusions similar to those of the conflict and bargaining experiments (Estes 1944; Skinner 1938; Thorndike 1932). Punishment appeared to be an ineffective means of changing behavior that produced negative emotional reactions. Subsequent research by psychologists, however, strongly refuted these early findings. Not only do contemporary psychologists agree that punishment is highly effective (see, e.g., Axelrod and Apsche 1983; Azrin and Holz 1966; Walters and Grusec 1977), but most believe that reinforcement (i.e., rewards) and punishment involve the same basic processes and produce parallel effects on behavior (e.g., Rachlin and Herrnstein 1969; Van Houten 1983). If anything, research suggests that punishment is *more* effective than reinforcement, producing faster and more enduring effects (e.g., Van Houten 1983). Although negative side effects can occur, positive side effects (e.g., improved social and emotional behavior, increased attentiveness) are at least as prevalent (Newsom, Favell, and Rincover 1983). Punishment does not seem to promote avoidance of the punisher, as Homans suggested, unless that person provides only punishment (and not reinforcement as well), and nonphysical punishment does not lead to aggressive behavior (Walters and Grusec 1977).

Most of this research, of course, is based on situations in which punishment power is unilateral. The targets of punishment, like those in Tedeschi's research, have little or no capacity to retaliate. Of greater relevance to exchange relations are observational studies by psychologists of coercive processes in families. Patterson's (1982) systematic, decade-long

---

[10] In contrast, Lawler's recent work with Yoon on commitment in exchange relations studies negotiations across multiple exchanges (Lawler and Yoon 1993, 1996).

research program is exemplary of this line of work (see also Burgess, Anderson, Schellenbach, and Conger 1981, and Gottman 1979). This research is also useful because its focus is the low-key aversive events that are commonly found in social interactions, but that are ignored by most analyses of coercion.

As other researchers have noted, family members have considerable coercive power over one another (e.g., Raush, Barry, Hertel, and Swain 1974). Apart from physical power, which is fairly asymmetrical (i.e., parents are physically stronger than children, and men are stronger, on the average, than women), all family members have access to numerous actions and verbal statements that are aversive to other family members. Patterson argues that coercion in families is very common, easily learned, highly effective, and that it generalizes to other settings. Most coercive acts are relatively low intensity (e.g., disapproval, whining), but in some families these "normal" patterns of coercive behavior build up, over time, into more intense, socially unacceptable levels of aggression.

Patterson estimates that by the age of 6 years, most normal children have learned how to use coercive tactics. Adults can quickly tire of interactions with children, and children learn that coercion is a way to restore adult attention. Consider, for example, this common sequence: the mother is talking on the telephone, the child whines for attention, the mother stops talking and gives the child attention, and the child stops whining. Both the child's use of coercion and the mother's compliance with coercion are reinforced. This effective tool gradually generalizes to interactions with others. Data collected in home and school consistently show very high rates of positive consequences provided by both adults and peers contingent upon coercive child behaviors (Patterson 1982).

The psychological research on punishment and coercion provides a somewhat different perspective than the social psychological work on gaming and bargaining experiments. While supporting the finding that the reciprocal use of punitive behaviors can escalate into higher levels of mutual aggression, this research nevertheless shows that coercive power can also be an effective means of influencing others who control desired outcomes. Moreover, the finding that children can successfully coerce adults – who ultimately control the greater coercive (and reward) power – suggests that coercion by low-power actors does not always provoke retaliation or resistance.

Conclusions and implications

These three research traditions address different aspects of coercive power
and study them under different conditions. The gaming research primarily
examines the effects of power tactics (the use of threats and punishments)
on compliance and conflict; Lawler's work mainly studies the relations
between structural power and power tactics (concessions, threats, and punishment), and the psychological research investigates the effects of punishment on behavior, with little or no analysis of structural power. All
three traditions depart, in various ways, from the conditions assumed for
this research – for example, by studying threats, negotiated exchange, or
unilateral power relations. Despite these limitations and the difficulties of
comparing the results, two conclusions are quite clear.

First, there is little agreement, theoretically or empirically, on how coercive power affects the use of punishment or how the use of punishment
affects the partner's behavior or the social relation. It is likely that the
answers to both questions depend on other qualifying conditions, and most
of the research has been conducted under conditions that are quite different
from the structure of repeated, nonnegotiated exchange relations.

Second, most research studies the effects of coercive power and reward
power separately and analyzes them from different theoretical perspectives. That is true even of Lawler's work, which studies both bases of
power, but with different theories (power dependence and bilateral deterrence), typically in different experiments, and using different manipulations. Consequently, questions of how the two bases of power compare
with one another and how they interact with one another are largely un-
addressed.

These conclusions suggest several guidelines that influenced the development of this project. First, analyzing both bases of power within a single
theoretical framework is essential for making significant progress toward
a comparative analysis of the two. Different theories produce conceptions
of power that are not comparable and manipulations of power that differ
both qualitatively and quantitatively. Exchange theory provides a common
base for developing parallel conceptions and manipulations of reward and
punishment power. Second, the task of constructing an exchange theory
of coercive power should begin with a clean theoretical slate, without
preconceived ideas about how coercive power might operate in exchange
relations or compare with reward-based power. The disparate views of

existing theories suggest that very different predictions can result from different starting premises; mine will be the assumptions of exchange theory. Third, research and theory development should focus primarily on exchange relations in which actors have *both* forms of power over each other. Not only is this the most common state of affairs in exchange relations, but it allows us to investigate questions that have been ignored in previous work.

Incorporating punishment and coercion in social exchange theory

Incorporating punishment and coercion within social exchange theory requires extending, and occasionally modifying, the assumptions and concepts introduced in Chapter 2. Here, I examine the implications of these changes for the basic elements of the theory – actors, resources, exchange processes, and exchange structure – and for its analysis of power and dependence.

Actors, resources, structure, and process

Actors and resources. Because both rewards and costs have traditionally been included in exchange theory, the scope condition governing actors' motivations (Table 2.1) readily accommodates an additional form of cost, the cost incurred from another's punishment. All three terms – rewards, punishments, and costs – were defined in Chapter 2. The conception of exchange resources, however, must be expanded to include the behavioral capacity to change another's outcomes in a *negative* direction. Actions that have this effect either increase negative value (e.g., disapproval) or decrease positive value (e.g., loss of status) for another.

Punitive acts, like rewarding acts, can incur various costs for the actor who performs them: opportunity costs, investment costs, and costs intrinsic to the behavior itself. These costs should not differ in any systematic way for rewards and punishments; that is, there is no reason to assume that performing rewarding actions is any more or less costly, on the average, than performing punishing actions. The same is not true of the fourth category of cost – the loss of a material resource – for the simple reason that punishment rarely involves a transfer of goods *from* the punisher *to* an exchange partner (although it frequently involves a transfer of goods in the opposite direction). Few material goods have negative value, although there are exceptions (a letter bomb is one). For this reason, transfers of material goods involve an additional cost that is not usually present with punishment. Such exchanges are excluded from this analysis (see Chapter 2).

Some research suggests that the second scope assumption, diminishing marginal utility (Table 2.1), may not hold for punishment. Coombs and Avrunin (1977), for example, propose that "good things satiate and bad things escalate," a principle that implies *opposite* effects for the marginal utility of positive and negative outcomes. On the other hand, Kahneman and Tversky's (1979) prospect theory (see Chapter 7), along with classical microeconomic theory, proposes that both positive and negative outcomes obey a principle of diminishing marginal utility. Dawes (1988) suggests that the actual experience of negative outcomes may follow an escalating principle, while choices based on anticipated outcomes follow a declining utility principle. Psychological research on the effects of punishment offers more support for the latter than the former, however, for both experienced and anticipated outcomes. Studies show, for example, that low-intensity punishment decreases in effectiveness over time (e.g., Azrin 1956; Holz and Azrin 1962). Similarly, if the intensity of punishment is gradually increased, it takes far more intense punishment to suppress unwanted behavior than if punishment is originally introduced at a higher intensity.

To the extent that both negative and positive outcomes follow a principle of declining marginal utility, the concept of exchange domains can be applied to punishment as well as rewards. Verbal reprimands and physical punishment, for example, might constitute different domains of value, in the sense that an increase in reprimands reduces the negative value (and effectiveness) of other punishers in the class of verbal rebukes, but not those in the class of physical punishment.

This issue, while important theoretically, has little effect on the experimental analysis of reward and punishment power in this book. My research compares rewards and punishments that represent gains or losses in a single resource domain. Punishment is operationalized as a decrease in positive value, not an increase in negative value. Consequently, gains should produce satiation, whereas losses produce deprivation. Furthermore, as I discuss in Chapter 4, the experimental control of value requires that both satiation and deprivation be minimized in research on power, as either process would change the value of outcomes and, consequently, change the value of power in exchange relations. I do so by using a resource – money – that is resistant to satiation because of its use as a general medium of exchange in society.

Rewards and punishments affect behavior in parallel, but opposite, directions: rewards increase and punishments decrease the frequency of behaviors on which they are contingent. Taking this difference into account, the assumptions about the behavior of individual actors in exchange relations (see Chapter 2) can be extended to punishment. *First*, actors should initiate exchanges with other actors who control resources within *either* a positively or a negatively valued exchange domain. Because actors are motivated to increase rewards and decrease costs, a unilateral positive action toward another can be used either to obtain reward or prevent punishment. *Second*, initiations that produce greater positive value (rewards) will increase in frequency relative to those that produce lesser positive value or negative value, and initiations that produce greater negative value (punishments) will decrease in frequency relative to those that produce lesser negative value or positive value. This rather wordy modification simply reflects the opposite effects of reward and punishment on behavior and the potential for either to occur. *Third*, either a decrease in the positive value or an increase in the negative value of a formed relation tends to produce behavioral change. *Fourth*, if the value obtained from a relation declines below the value that would be expected from terminating the relation, the relation will eventually end. This modification reflects the possibility that an actor will punish an exchange partner who leaves the relation; therefore, even if the value of a relation declines to zero or becomes negative, an actor will remain in the relation if leaving it is likely to be even more aversive.

The structure of exchange. The primary scope assumption about the structure of exchange is that actors are mutually dependent (Table 2.1). Although we commonly think of dependence in terms of positive outcomes, actors are also dependent on a partner who has the capacity to punish them. Generalizing the concept requires only that we define dependence more broadly, as the total range of outcomes – from positive to negative – that one actor controls for another. If A's behavior affects B's outcomes, in either a positive or a negative direction, then B is dependent on A for the quality of outcomes B experiences. When the outcomes are positive,

B is dependent on A for obtaining the things B finds desirable; when the outcomes are negative, B is dependent on A for avoiding the things B finds aversive. Cairns (1979) argues, for example, that children (both human and animal) who are abused by their mothers are highly dependent on them, and that their behavior reflects their dependence. They learn to attend closely to their mother's behavior, watching for cues of impending abuse, and to modify their own behavior in ways that avoid punishment.

Because the focus of this analysis is on the use of punishment to obtain rewards, through coercion, network connections are defined on the domain of rewards. For my purposes, two relations – for example, B–A and A–C – are negatively connected at A if and only if B and C are alternative sources of rewarding outcomes for A. If so, then B and C are competitors with each other for A's reward exchange, and coercive power provides an additional means through which they can obtain A's rewards. In this context, B and C's relative power to coerce A to reward them, and A's relative power to retaliate, become relevant.

For both rewards and punishments, dependence varies as a function of value and alternatives. A's dependence on B increases with the negative value that B can produce for A and decreases with the availability of alternative exchange partners who can also punish A. Alternative relations reduce the contingency of either reward or punishment on a particular partner's behavior, and thus reduce dependence on that partner. An actor who has alternative partners with the capacity to punish her is less dependent on any one of them for avoiding punishment, and consequently they will have less power over her.

To illustrate this somewhat counterintuitive point, consider again a simple three-actor network (B–A–C) that is negatively connected on reward exchange. In such a network, A's exchange of rewards with C reduces A's exchange of rewards with B, by definition. Assume that all actors can reward each other with equal value, and that B – but not C – can punish A. If B uses punishment to coerce rewards from A, then the probability that B punishes A should increase whenever A's reward exchange with C reduces A's reward exchange with B (i.e., B should punish A's failure to reward B). Therefore, to avoid punishment, A should exchange rewards with B rather than C, even though both actors can provide equal rewards to A.

Now consider what happens if both B and C have equal capacity to punish A. A's reward exchange with either B or C is equally likely to elicit the other's punishment, and thus A should be indifferent between them. A should exchange rewards no more often with B than with C. Thus, increasing the availability of punishment from alternative partners *decreases* A's dependence on B, and decreases B's power over A.

The process of exchange. I expand the concept of a transaction to include any contingent two-way exchange of outcomes. The reciprocity that is one of the defining characteristics of exchange applies to both rewards and punishments: just as benefits beget reciprocal benefits, so does harm beget reciprocal harm. Within the context of exchange relations that offer the potential for both rewards and punishments, the reciprocity of benefits may include the exchange of rewards for the withholding of punishment (if punishment is expected), and the reciprocity of harm may include the exchange of punishment for the withholding of rewards (if reward is expected). Reciprocity of any form need not be equal or immediate.

In reciprocal (nonnegotiated) exchange relations, actors individually perform actions that produce rewarding or punishing outcomes for their partners and respond sequentially to the outcomes produced by their partners. Their contingent use of rewards and punishments becomes part of a continuing relation that, over time, is likely to include components of three "ideal types" of transaction: mutual reward, mutual punishment, and coercion. *Mutual reward* consists of an exchange of rewarding outcomes. While mutual, the exchange may be variable in both frequency and reciprocity (e.g., in imbalanced relations, less dependent partners will reciprocate rewards less often). *Mutual punishment* consists of an exchange of punishing outcomes, again variable in frequency and reciprocity. Many theorists call mutual punishment *conflict* (e.g., Blalock 1989; Tedeschi et al. 1973; Willer 1981). Finally, unlike either mutual reward or mutual punishment, *coercion* is explicitly asymmetrical in nature, involving the potential flow of punishment from one actor and the potential flow of reward from another (Willer 1981).[11] A coerces B by punishing B when B fails to reward A, and withholding punishment when B's rewards to A are forthcoming. Only the latter half of this pattern – A's withholding of punishment in return for B's reward – constitutes an

---

[11] Willer (1981) distinguishes three ideal types of relation: exchange, conflict, and coercion. He restricts exchange to the mutual exchange of rewards, while I include both mutual reward and coercive exchanges.

exchange of benefits, but it is the first half that makes the absence of punishment rewarding to B. A variation on this pattern of "pure" coercion, and one in which I will be more interested, is when A coerces B by punishing B's failure to reward, but reciprocates B's rewards (*and* withholds punishment) when they are forthcoming. Such a pattern explicitly requires control over *both* rewards and punishments for another actor.

The relative mix of these different types of transactions should depend on the structure of power and dependence in the relation. That mix, in turn, determines the overall character of the relation: whether it is predominantly positive or negative, equal or unequal, frequent or infrequent. Unless relations become primarily aversive (and more rewarding alternatives exist), the use of punishment and coercion is not incompatible with exchange theory's scope assumption that "actors engage in recurring, interdependent exchanges with specific partners over time" (Table 2.1).

In bargaining relations, exchanges of rewards and punishments are less likely to be parallel.[12] As Bacharach and Lawler's (1981) work illustrates, those who study bargaining relations typically conceptualize the exercise of these two forms of power in different ways: actors negotiate an exchange of benefits, but they apply threats and punishments without negotiation – that is, reciprocally. Willer's (1987) experiments are an exception; his subjects do bargain over the terms of coercion. They negotiate the positive sanctions that the target of coercion transmits in exchange for the coercer's withholding of negative sanctions.

Power and power use

The structure of power. If the concept of dependence is extended to include dependence on another who controls negative as well as positive outcomes, then – by definition – power is also extended to include both reward-based and punishment-based power. A's *reward power* over B is equal to B's dependence on A for obtaining rewards, and A's *punishment power* over B is equal to B's dependence on A for avoiding punishment. For each of these bases of power, the average power and power imbalance in the relation can be distinguished, producing four central variables for

---

[12] For a comparison of the different processes involved in the exchange of rewards and punishments in the context of bargaining, see Bacharach and Lawler (1981:105–106).

the analysis of power: *average reward power*, *average punishment power*, *reward power imbalance*, and *punishment power imbalance*.

Throughout this analysis I will use the terms "punishment power" and "coercive power" fairly interchangeably, as I have already done in this chapter. However, the *act* of coercion refers specifically to the use of punishment power to obtain rewards from another; that is, it refers to punishment that is contingent on another's failure to reward. Punishment can also be used to retaliate against (or suppress) another's use of punishment. Because of the assumption that actors in exchange relations are motivated to obtain rewards, it is the coercive use of punishment power that is central to this analysis. But retaliatory punishment is necessarily involved, as well, both as a potential response to another's coercion, and as a means of suppressing such reactions to coercion. Structural punishment power affects an actor's capacity to do both: to coerce and to retaliate.

Analytically, the two bases of power are independent (although in natural settings, they can be correlated). Consequently, a relation can be balanced on one base of power and imbalanced on the other, or balanced on both, or imbalanced on both. If imbalanced on both, a fifth power variable – the *direction* of the power imbalances – becomes relevant; that is, the two bases of power can favor the same actor in the relation, or different actors. For example, an actor might be advantaged on both reward and punishment power (a husband whose wife is highly dependent on him for both economic support and restraint from physical abuse), or disadvantaged on reward power but advantaged on punishment power (a low-level employee who has information that could destroy the boss's career). Similarly, the average reward and punishment power in a relation can vary; that is, A and B can control resources with high positive value but low negative value for each other, or vice versa.

The use of power. Actors use power, of either base, by imposing costs on the partner. As Bacharach and Lawler (1981) have noted, the immediate costs are different for the two bases of power: actors use reward power by withholding benefits from the partner (see Chapter 2), and they use punishment power by inflicting harm, or actual losses, on the partner. For both bases of power, the costs that A can impose on B are equal to B's dependence on A (Emerson 1972b).[13] Consequently, actors who are power-advantaged on either base of power can impose greater costs than their more dependent partners, and they can better resist the costs that their partners impose.

While the immediate costs of reward withholding and coercion are different, the costs they impose in the long term are the same: if effective, both forms of power ultimately induce the disadvantaged partner to accept greater opportunity costs in exchange for either rewards or the cessation of punishment. The disadvantaged actor forgoes the potential benefits from alternative relations to provide rewards for the advantaged partner, while the advantaged partner either reciprocates the rewards but does so less frequently (reward power), or withholds punishment (coercive power). In our earlier example of the workaholic who was coerced by family members to spend more time at home, the workaholic accepted greater opportunity costs (forgoing the benefits that might have been obtained from longer hours at work) in exchange for the cessation of disapproval and criticism at home. It is the comparability of these processes that led Heath (1976) to argue that reward exchanges and coercive exchanges are essentially the same.

The outcome of power use. In the preceding chapter, I defined two relational outcomes of power use: the *asymmetry* or difference in the frequency or value of exchange in the relation (exchange asymmetry), and the *average* frequency or value of exchange in the relation (exchange frequency). With the addition of punishment, these two outcomes can be expanded to four: *reward asymmetry* (the asymmetry in the exchange of rewards), *punishment asymmetry* (the asymmetry in the exchange of punishments), *reward frequency* (the average frequency of rewarding in the relation), and *punishment frequency* (the average frequency of punishing in the relation).

Because a power advantage on either base provides the structural op-

---

[13] In using reward power, the potential cost that A can impose on B, by *not* rewarding B, is equal to the difference between the value of the rewards that A controls for B and the value of the rewards that B can obtain from alternatives to A. In using punishment power, the potential cost that A can impose on B, by punishing B, is equal to the difference between the value of the punishment that A can inflict on B and the value of the punishment that B's alternatives can potentially inflict on B. Thus, both costs equal B's dependence on A.

portunity to induce the partner to give more rewards and accept higher opportunity costs, however, both bases of power are predicted to affect the frequency and distribution of *reward* exchange. Punishment frequency and asymmetry, on the other hand, are indicators of the absolute and relative use of punishment power by both actors. Thus, the central theorems of power-dependence theory (see Chapter 2) can be extended, with little change, to include coercive power: (1) A's initiations of exchange with B increase with A's dependence on B for either obtaining rewards or avoiding punishment; (2) the frequency of reward exchange in a relation increases with either average reward power or average punishment power; and (3) in a relation imbalanced on either reward or punishment power, reward asymmetry will change in favor of the more powerful, less dependent actor.

These extensions of exchange theory's conceptions of power and power use allow the direct comparison of equivalent structures of reward power and punishment power. Potentially, either base of power can produce increased rewards and/or decreased costs for a power-advantaged actor. Whether the two bases do, in fact, affect exchange behavior in comparable ways is an empirical question and a central focus of the research.

A final issue. Although dimensions of reward power and punishment power can be defined separately and manipulated independently, the inherent relativity in what constitutes a reward or a punishment raises questions about whether these two bases of power are, in fact, *conceptually* distinct. If rewards and punishments are two sides of the same coin, then forms of power based on the capacity to give or withhold rewards or punishments for another are potentially interchangeable. If rewards are regularly given, they can be withheld as punishment. And if punishments are regularly given, they can be withheld as rewards. Both Blau (1964) and Wrong (1979) have noted this similarity. In Blau's (1964:117) words, "Regular rewards make recipients dependent on the supplier and subject to his power, since they engender expectations that make their discontinuation a punishment."

Analytically, there is no question that the two bases of power share a common, inseparable foundation (Bacharach and Lawler 1981). The interchangeability of the two is, in fact, essential for integrating coercion within exchange theory. Coercion can be conceptualized as an exchange of benefits only because the withholding of punishment is rewarding to an actor who has come to expect punishment.

Is the introduction of coercive power as a second power base in exchange theory merely illusory, then, or dependent on the additional assumptions of severity, restriction of freedom, and so forth that many theorists impose on coercion? Do relations based solely on reward power already possess the capacity to coerce, so that "extending" the theory to incorporate coercive power is both unnecessary and redundant?

Certainly, reward power can be used coercively. (One of the more famous examples is related in *The Lysistrata*, the Greek drama in which the women declare a sex strike until the men make peace.) But coercion is not the mechanism that underlies the predicted effects of reward power. In both balanced and imbalanced relations, power-dependence theory assumes that actors provide rewards to one another to obtain rewards, not to avoid punishment. In imbalanced relations, the advantaged actor's intermittent reciprocity of the disadvantaged actor's exchange is the regular, expected pattern of rewarding in that relation – it does not constitute punishment. Using reward power coercively, in either balanced or imbalanced relations, requires a reduction in whatever pattern of rewarding has been established. Such actions can and do occur, but they do not account for the effects of reward power, nor do they make the independent analysis of coercive power redundant.

The scope of the research

As we have seen, the basic assumptions and concepts of exchange theory can be logically extended to include punishment and coercive power. Whether the *theory* of power-dependence relations holds for coercive power as well as for reward power, however, is a question that must be answered empirically.

As this chapter has illustrated, systematic research that compares the two bases of power under equivalent conditions is rare. Consequently, we know very little about how reward and coercive power compare in their effects on behavior, how they interact with one another, and the conditions under which each is used. This program of research begins to tackle these questions. No single program, however, can examine all of the facets involved. Necessarily, the research is limited in scope, and that scope constrains both the questions asked and the conditions under which the answers apply.

In addition to the conditions that define the scope of social exchange theory (see Table 2.1), several other conditions define the theoretical boundaries of this research program. Some of these have been introduced already (e.g., the focus on reciprocal exchange); others have not.

First, actors are engaged in exchange relations for the primary purpose of exchanging benefits. Coercive power is studied in the context of relations in which all actors have some capacity to both reward and punish their exchange partners. Power is bilateral (i.e., two-way) and dual-base (i.e., involving the capacity to both reward and punish). Although a few experiments (primarily in Chapters 6 and 7) depart from these conditions, they do so only to answer theoretical questions about networks in which actors do have the capacity to both reward and punish one another.

Second, actors' resources in exchange relations are *behavioral capabilities* (rather than material possessions) that produce outcomes of *specific value* (positive or negative) for exchange partners. These might represent, for example, the capacity to give advice to a co-worker (with 1 hour of advice equal, perhaps, to "5 units" of reward value), or the capacity to reject a colleague's proposal (with rejection of the proposal worth, say, "8 units" of punishment value). The value of any single act is fixed; consequently, the total value given in exchange can be varied only by varying the frequency of behavior over time. Excluded from these behavioral capabilities are acts of physical force that eliminate choice.

Third, all benefits obtained through exchange are "consumed" – that is, they have no subsequent exchange value. (Or, more accurately, they have no exchange value within the network that is the focus of inquiry.)

Fourth, the only costs an actor incurs by his own exchange behaviors (either positive or negative) are the opportunity costs of rewards forgone from alternative choices. To simplify the analysis, other potential costs – investment costs, and intrinsic costs such as fatigue and effort – are scaled as zero. A fourth category of cost, the actual losses that are incurred when material goods are transferred from one actor to another, is eliminated by the restriction of resources to behavioral capabilities.

Fifth, exchange transactions are reciprocal, not negotiated. Actors do not explicitly bargain over the terms of exchange, nor do they have the ability to convey intentions to reward or punish through promises or threats. Instead, they initiate exchanges individually, without knowing whether, when, or to what degree the other will reciprocate. Their relations develop over time, as actors respond contingently to one another and gradually establish a stable frequency and ratio of exchange.

Sixth, the unit of analysis is the dyadic exchange relation. I study relations that are embedded in larger networks with negative connections, but my interest is in the power relations and exchange processes within the dyad, not the distribution of power in the network as a whole.

Seventh, variations in structural power are created by variations in the relative value of the resources controlled by alternative partners, holding constant the shape of the network and the number of alternative exchange partners to which each actor has access. Structural advantage or disadvantage arises from the relative availability of partners who control more or less valuable resources (i.e., for disadvantaged actors, the partners who control the more valuable resources are less dependent and therefore less likely to reciprocate exchange).

Eighth, actors cannot change the structure of the network, their position within it, or the value of the resources that they and others control.

Ninth, actors can choose between alternative exchange partners, but they cannot avoid a partner's attempts to influence or initiate exchange; that is, they cannot ''leave the field.'' Actors can continue to reward or punish others who no longer exchange with them.

Tenth, actors have full information about the values governing relative dependencies in their own exchange relations, but not in distal relations in the exchange network. Thus, they do not know the availability of their exchange partners' alternatives.

These are the theoretical conditions that govern the research. The next chapter describes how they are translated into a laboratory setting for the study of power and exchange.

4. An experimental setting for studying power in exchange relations

Experimental research, especially in laboratory settings, is relatively rare in the social sciences. Common criticisms of laboratory experiments (e.g., artificiality, lack of random sampling, irrelevance for real-world situations) suggest that their role in building and testing theories is not well understood. Consequently, in addition to describing the basic experimental setting used in this program, this chapter explains the theoretical logic that underlies experimentation in general, and this setting in particular. I begin with a brief discussion of the purpose of laboratory experiments and why artificiality is an advantage rather than a disadvantage for the task of this book: constructing and testing a theory of coercive power in social exchange. Then, I turn to a detailed description and explanation of the experimental setting I use for this task.

Laboratory experiments and theory construction: descriptive versus formal theory

Most criticisms of laboratory experiments are based on the assumption that the purpose of social science research is to obtain findings that can be generalized to natural settings and specific populations. Research on power, for example, should tell us something about power in families, in organizations, or in international relations. If so, then the more the research setting resembles families, organizations, or international relations, the more likely that our findings would apply to those settings. Thus, the obvious and enormous disparities between characteristics of those settings, and characteristics of an experimental setting in which undergraduate subjects sit in small isolated rooms, making choices on computers that produce small increments or decrements of money for other undergraduate subjects (which, as I discuss in a moment, is the kind of setting used for this research), make experiments seem trivial and irrelevant.

But generalizing to particular natural settings is not the aim of most experimental research. As a number of authors discuss (e.g., Cohen 1989; Martin and Sell 1979; Schlenker 1974; Zelditch 1969), many of the misunderstandings about experiments can be resolved by recognizing that different kinds of research methodologies serve different purposes. Both Zelditch (1969) and Martin and Sell (1979) distinguish between research designed to explicate relations in particular concrete settings (e.g., families or organizations in contemporary American society) and research designed to test abstract theories. The objectives I just described – explaining particular social events and processes, often tied to specific times and places – are the objectives of *descriptive theoretical research* (Martin and Sell 1979). If I were interested in explaining the distribution of power among husbands and wives in contemporary American society, for example, or the distribution of power among Eastern European countries after the end of the cold war, I would be conducting descriptive theoretical research. Often, in descriptive theoretical research, the investigator is interested in generalizing the findings to a particular population, such as American married couples.

But the purpose of this research is not to tell us anything *directly* about power in particular settings, but to build and test a theory of power at a level abstract enough to apply to power structures and power processes in any setting that meets certain theoretical conditions. This is what Martin and Sell (1979) call *formal theoretical research*.[1] To test abstract theories, particularized settings are not an advantage. Instead, the setting should be as abstract as the theory – it should create only those aspects of the phenomena studied that are theoretically relevant, under controlled conditions that meet the scope conditions of the theory. The results of research obtained under these conditions cannot be generalized directly to natural settings, but they can be used to support or reject predictions derived from the theory. Once tested and supported, the theoretical principles themselves can be generalized or applied to settings that meet the conditions assumed by the theory.

---

[1] "Formal" in this context implies theory that is abstract and logically rigorous, but not necessarily mathematical.

For the purpose of theory testing and building, the artificiality of laboratory experiments is an advantage. Because the experimenter has control over virtually every aspect of the setting and conditions under which subjects are studied, he or she can create experimental conditions that meet the assumptions of the theory and operational variables that meet the theoretical specifications of the conceptual variables, even if these include conditions and combinations of variables that rarely occur naturally. Events that would seldom recur under the same conditions in natural settings can be replicated, again and again, to produce multiple tests of their effects. Most important, the experimenter can disentangle the effects of variables that would typically be confounded in natural settings, not merely by using statistical controls, but by physically making variables independent of one another. This is accomplished in three ways: (1) by random assignment of subjects to experimental conditions, which isolates the effects of the environment (in this case, the effects of structures of power) from the effects of characteristics of the people interacting in the environment; (2) by creating orthogonal manipulations of multiple theoretical variables (e.g., dimensions of reward power and punishment power); and (3) by holding constant other variables that are not theoretically relevant but that might affect results (e.g., some kinds of information about the exchange process).

In short, if the research goal is to test and construct abstract theory, a setting that simulates the natural world is far from desirable. What is called for, instead, is a setting very unlike the natural world, one that creates certain theoretically relevant conditions and eliminates all other variation that might confuse our understanding of those conditions.

Implications for the study of power

Let us consider, more specifically, the advantages of laboratory experimentation for this research. There are several major difficulties in studying the effects of power structures of different bases on behavior in natural settings, whether by survey or observational methods. First, it is very difficult to separate the effects of the *power structure* from the effects of characteristics of the *actors* (individuals or groups) who occupy particular positions in the structure. In natural settings, actors are not randomly assigned to positions of power; on the contrary, those who occupy more powerful positions usually differ, in many ways, from those who occupy less powerful positions. Structural position and actor characteristics become irrevocably confounded.

This confounding of structural power and individual characteristics was a central theme of Kanter's (1977) classic study of men and women in a large corporation. Because of it, she argued that we often mistakenly attribute structural effects to personal characteristics of individuals, such as gender. For example, because women in organizations are concentrated disproportionately in low-power positions, we confuse the effects of low power with the effects of gender. Laboratory experiments avoid this kind of confounding by randomly assigning individuals to power structures and to positions within those structures. Random assignment makes individual characteristics *independent* of the characteristics of the structures, by randomly distributing, across all experimental conditions, the probability of occurrence of any and all individual characteristics.

Second, it is difficult to measure or compare levels of power that are based on different resources (such as approval, expert advice, political support, or status) with any precision. Many exchange resources cannot easily be quantified, and their value varies across different actors and changes over time. Problems of measuring resource value are inherent in applications of exchange theory in natural settings, of course, but the problems are far greater for testing theory than for applying tested theory. Applications of theory can often tolerate a degree of imprecision and an ordinal level of comparisons that would be unacceptable for basic tests of theory.

Related to this problem is the difficulty of comparing different bases of power: power based on control over rewarding or punishing events. In natural settings (and, as we saw in the preceding chapter, even in some experimental settings), this can easily become a case of comparing apples and oranges. Because actors often control forms of reward and punishment that are quite different from one another (e.g., an employer might reward with a promotion but punish with verbal criticism), it can be difficult to equate their values. To avoid the comparison of qualitatively different forms of reward and punishment in these experiments, I compare gains and losses of a single outcome, money. This restricts my ability to generalize to other forms of punishment, but it has the distinct advantage of allowing me to create objectively equivalent levels of power on the two bases.[2]

---

[2] Research suggests, however, that the form of punishment I study – called ''response

The standard experimental setting

All of the experiments use a standardized laboratory setting that facilitates theory development. Because the setting, experimental procedures, and operationalization of the variables are uniform across experiments, results can be cumulated with greater reliability. This chapter describes the basic setting; some modifications, required for individual experiments, are discussed in later chapters.

In developing a standardized setting for studying power and social exchange, several considerations are important. The setting must meet the general scope conditions of the theory (see Table 2.1) and the more specialized conditions of exchange assumed for the project (see Chapter 3). It must provide repeated opportunities for direct, reciprocal exchange among the same actors, give actors control over resources that affect outcomes of value for other actors, and structure exchange relations that create varying degrees of mutual dependency among actors for these outcomes. The manipulation of power and the measurement of power use within this setting must be consistent with exchange theory's conceptual definitions of those concepts, and, ideally, the measurement of both should be at the ratio level. Most important, it must be possible to create fully equivalent structures of reward power and punishment power, differing only on the base of power, and to create parallel variations in average power and power imbalance on those bases. Finally, variables that are unrelated to the theory and extraneous to the investigation must either be controlled or randomly distributed across the experimental conditions.

To meet these conditions, I created a laboratory setting in which undergraduate student subjects earn money through reciprocal exchange with partners to whom they are connected in a four-actor exchange network. Subjects are mutually dependent on one another for their monetary earnings in the experiment, and they exchange points – worth money – via computer, while seated in isolated rooms. I manipulate dimensions of power by varying the amounts of money (represented by points) that actors in the network can add to (reward power) or subtract from (punishment power) their partners' earnings on each of a series of exchange opportu-

cost" by psychologists (e.g., Weiner 1962) – follows the same principles as other punishment techniques (e.g., Pazulinec, Meyerrose, and Sajwaj 1983).

nities. Subjects engage in reciprocal, nonnegotiated exchanges (i.e., they individually make choices on their computers that affect other actors' earnings), with the same partners, for 100 to 250 opportunities. The frequencies of their rewarding and punishing actions toward each other across these opportunities provide the data for computing measures of power use.

With this general framework in mind, let us turn to a more detailed discussion of how, and why, each of the major elements of exchange theory – the actors, exchange resources, exchange structure, and exchange processes – are operationalized in this setting.

Operationalizing actors, resources, structure, and process

The actors: experimental subjects

The actors in all of the experiments are individual persons: undergraduate students who are recruited to serve as experimental subjects. The use of undergraduate students as subjects is a frequent target of criticisms of laboratory experiments. Critics argue that the lack of a representative sample inhibits generalization to a broader population and renders any findings trivial, a "social psychology of the undergraduate student" (e.g., Borgatta and Bohrnstedt 1974).

The lack of random sampling in experiments, regardless of the use of undergraduate subjects, does indeed preclude the generalization of results to any given population. But, as I have just discussed, generalization to a particular population or setting is not the aim of theoretically driven experimental research. For theory testing, representativeness of subjects is not an advantage. What is important is that subjects meet any conditions of the theory that pertain to individuals. If, for example, the theory applies only to individuals who have red hair and are left-handed, then the theory must be tested on individuals who meet those criteria – not on a representative sample, which would invariably include some individuals who did not meet the theoretical criteria.

Social exchange theory requires that actors meet just one condition: that they act in ways that tend to produce more of what they positively value and less of what they negatively value (see Table 2.1). This condition implies that subjects must value the domain of exchange outcomes used in the experiment. Thus, rather than randomly sampling subjects from a population, I recruited subjects on the basis of their desire to earn money, the exchange outcome in the experiments. Recruitment announcements (which were delivered in classes, dormitories, and through campus mail) offered no scientific or educational benefits for participation; in particular, course credit was never awarded. Instead, the announcements emphasized that the *only* condition for participation in the experiment was a desire to earn money. The isolation and control of the subject rooms eliminated other, potentially competing rewards (and punishments), and the experimental instructions again emphasized that subjects should try to earn as much money as possible.

Because exchange theory does not assume that characteristics such as age, education, or social class affect subjects' behavior – except through their effects on what subjects value – it makes no *theoretical* difference whether undergraduate students or other people are used as subjects. Using a population that is very heterogeneous on characteristics such as education or age, however, would pose practical problems. It would be difficult, for example, to use the same experimental instructions with subjects of very different educational levels. Young children would preclude the use of money as an exchange domain. Full-time workers would present scheduling problems and likely require the use of larger amounts of money. Undergraduate students meet the theoretical criteria required of subjects and at the same time pose fewer practical problems than many alternatives.

While random *sampling* is not necessary and would, in fact, fail to meet theoretical requirements, random *assignment* is essential. In survey research, random sampling is used not only for purposes of generalization, but to prevent systematic error – that is, to insure that errors are randomly distributed throughout the sample. In experimental research, random assignment of subjects to experimental conditions (or of experimental conditions to subjects) fulfills the same function: it randomly distributes error across conditions. Stated in a different way, random assignment removes any systematic association of individual characteristics with experimental conditions, by transforming systematic variability into random variability. Thus, it allows us to assume, within the limits of statistical probability, that individual subjects in different experimental conditions do not, on the average, differ from one another.

Subjects were scheduled to participate in experimental sessions by availability. They were randomly assigned to positions in a four-actor exchange network, and networks were randomly assigned to conditions in the experiment. All experiments were conducted with 10 networks per condition (with equal numbers of all-male and all-female networks);[3] thus, all tests of significance are based on the same number of cases within conditions.

The exchange resource: control over money

Consistent with virtually all experimental research on social exchange, I use money as the valued outcome of exchange. Rather than receiving a set amount of money for participation in the experiment, subjects earn money through exchange. This practice often gives the mistaken impression that social exchange researchers are primarily interested in economic exchange, or that our results can only be generalized to economic exchange. Both assumptions are incorrect.

The experimental setting is designed to create the theoretical conditions of social – not economic – exchange. The resource in the experiments is not money per se, but the capacity to perform behaviors that produce monetary gains or losses for another. Each actor in the network had the capacity to add to (reward power) or subtract from (punishment power) the total earnings cumulated by each of their exchange partners, on each of a series of exchange opportunities. Unlike economic exchanges, money was not transferred from one actor to another. Adding to another's earnings did not reduce a subject's own earnings, and subtracting from another's earnings did not increase a subject's own earnings. The only cost of initiating an exchange was the "opportunity cost" of not exchanging with an alternative partner. These costs depend on the partner's behavior, of course, and in reciprocal exchanges their value is uncertain.

The amount of money an actor could add or subtract on any single opportunity, for any particular partner, was fixed and determined by the actor's structural position in the network. For example, an actor in position A of the network might have the following four choices from which to select on each exchange opportunity: add 2 points to partner B or 6 points

---

[3] Gender is not a variable of theoretical interest for this project, and previous studies of power-dependence relations have reported few effects of gender on exchange and power use (e.g., Cook and Emerson 1978). Because power and gender are closely related in many natural settings, however, concerns with gender effects tend to arise in experimental settings, as well. Classifying subjects by gender allowed us to examine the possibility of gender effects and to address questions about the relation between gender and power use. Very few effects of gender were found in any of the experiments. For a summary of some of these findings, see Molm and Hedley (1992).

to partner C, or subtract 5 points from B or 3 points from C. Each point was equal to a designated number of cents.

The values of exchange actions were fixed for two reasons. First, much of social exchange, unlike economic exchange, involves the exchange of outcomes of nondivisible value – for example, voting for a colleague's proposal, or inviting a friend to dinner. Specific actions have consequences of specific value. Outcomes of nondivisible value are particularly characteristic of reciprocal exchanges, the subject of this research. (Actors are more likely to negotiate the exchange of outcomes with divisible value.) At the same time, however, it is also true that actors often have a choice among several behaviors that would produce different amounts of positive (or negative) value in a particular domain; for example, you might vote but not lobby for your colleague's proposal, or you might invite a friend for drinks but not dinner. To simplify the analysis, my experimental setting restricts actors to only two behaviors in relation to each partner, one that produces positive value and one that produces negative value. With increasing knowledge about the effects of power, the complexity of the setting can be increased.

In short, although money is a divisible outcome, it is not divisible in the context of the exchanges studied in these experiments. Actors could vary the value they produced for a partner only by varying the frequency with which they performed actions of fixed value. Many exchanges take this form – in fact, any exchange in which value is increased by devoting additional time to the relation (e.g., time spent contributing to household tasks, or giving advice to a colleague).

I use money to operationalize the positive or negative value of exchange outcomes because of its advantages for experimental control. First, because money is a general medium of exchange in society, subjects are more likely to value it than any other outcome. Using money as the exchange outcome and recruiting subjects on the basis of their desire to earn money therefore assures, within reasonable limits, that subjects will meet the motivational assumption of social exchange theory. It is not necessary that all subjects value money to the same degree, or that a gain of $5 or a loss of $1 means the same thing to all subjects: random assignment assures that differences in the value attached to specific monetary amounts are randomly distributed across conditions. It *is* necessary, however, to assume that subjects value money, in the sense that they will try to obtain more and lose less of it in the experiment.

Second, the value of money can be quantified, using a ratio level of measurement. This means that power, which varies with exchange value, can also be measured on a ratio scale. Whereas few outcomes in social exchange relations can be quantified in this way, this property of money is extremely valuable for testing theory. In particular, it means that we can create levels of reward power and punishment power that are quantitatively as well as qualitatively equivalent (at least objectively; subjective differences are addressed in Chapter 7), because they are based on the capacity to produce equivalent gains and losses of the same valued outcome, money.

Third, money is resistant to the effects of satiation or diminishing marginal utility within the ranges typically offered in experimental sessions. On the surface, this property seems to violate one of the assumptions of social exchange theory: that all outcomes of value obey a principle of satiation or diminishing marginal utility. In reality, of course, it does not; money is subject to satiation effects just like any other outcome. One dollar means less to a millionaire than to a poor person. But for experimental purposes, using an outcome that produces satiation very slowly has an important advantage: we can assume the value of the outcome is stable during the course of the experiment. Without that assumption, it would be impossible to manipulate power. Satiation reduces the value of an outcome; if value changes in unknown ways, so does power. In natural settings, of course, value and power do change; in experimental settings, any changes in value must be under the control of the experimenter.

Because exchange theory assumes that the domain of value does not affect theoretical predictions, results obtained from experiments using money can be generalized to other outcomes. This assumption does not imply that all people value the same outcomes, or that people who value different outcomes necessarily behave in similar ways. But it does imply that *if* we could measure the value of other outcomes with the same precision with which we can measure the value of money, and *if* two actors valued outcomes that were qualitatively different but quantitatively equal in value, and *if* all other conditions of exchange were equal, then the two actors should behave in similar ways to obtain the outcomes they value. Thus, people who value homeless shelters and money may be different in many ways, but the theory assumes that they are alike in the sense that they will try to produce more of whatever they value (homeless shelters or money) and will respond similarly to structural variations in the opportunity to do so.

One question that might reasonably be raised is whether the amount of money at stake in the experiments is sufficient to motivate subjects. The recruitment announcements guaranteed subjects a minimum of $6 for participation and the opportunity to earn up to $20. Because subjects could lose as well as gain money, they began with an initial number of points in all experiments. Both the number of points with which subjects began and the monetary value of each point cumulated were set so that the average amount earned by subjects in the experiments was about $15.[4] This level of earnings – $15 for a 2-hour session – was well above the going rate for students in work/study jobs on campus at the time. Both the recruitment announcement and the experimental instructions clearly stated that the amount subjects earned – over and above the guaranteed $6 – depended on their behavioral interaction in the experiment.

Because of budgetary constraints and ethical considerations, it is nevertheless impossible to create in experiments the *range* of variation in value that might be found in natural settings. To the extent that we must settle for less variation and weaker extremes of positive and negative value, the effects of our experimental variables will necessarily be weaker. The criterion for sufficient variation, then, is whether variations in value produce statistically significant differences in behavior. As the experiments will show, they clearly do.

The exchange structure: exchange networks and the manipulation of power

The networks. In all experiments, subjects participated in negatively connected exchange networks composed of four actors (see Figure 4.1 for examples). Each actor could potentially exchange with two of the three other actors in the network; thus, each actor had access to two alternative exchange partners in the network.

Negative connections were created by making the choice of partners mutually exclusive, so that exchange with one partner precluded exchange with the other partner for that opportunity (Cook and Emerson 1978).

---

[4] The number of points with which subjects began depended on the particular experiment and condition; with few exceptions, however, it was substantially smaller than the amount of money that subjects could earn through exchange. The monetary value of each point varied from 1 to 3 cents, with value depending primarily on the number of exchange opportunities in the experiment (i.e., in experiments with fewer opportunities, subjects earned more on each opportunity).

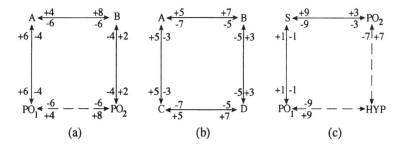

Figure 4.1. Three examples of experimental exchange networks
Note: The letters, A, B, C, D, and S (for subject) indicate positions occupied by real actors. The POs in (a) and (c) are computer-simulated actors ("programmed others"), and HYP in (c) is a hypothetical actor. The dotted lines between the POs in (a) and between the POs and HYP in (c) indicate that those relationships were implied rather than real.

Thus, the more frequently an actor exchanged with one partner, the less frequently she exchanged with the other (the definition of a negative connection). This procedure produced the competition between disadvantaged actors that drives the unequal distribution of exchange benefits in imbalanced relations.[5]

Real or simulated partners. Experimental instructions informed subjects that they were participating in a group of four persons, that each person would be able to interact with two of the other three persons, and that each person could act toward only one partner on each exchange opportunity. In reality, however, some of the actors in many of the experiments were computer-simulated actors, programmed to behave in specific ways. I used three different combinations of real and simulated actors, for different experimental purposes.

The early experiments in the program (Chapter 5) studied networks comprised of two real subjects (A and B) and two computer-simulated

---

[5] Markovsky et al. (1988) have called this procedure the "one-exchange rule" and have incorrectly argued that it is a methodological condition unrelated to the theoretical requirements of power-dependence theory. They and other exchange theorists, following their lead, have varied the number of exchanges per opportunity in which actors can engage (see, e.g., the June 1992 issue of *Social Networks*). But if A can exchange with both B and C on a single opportunity, then A's relations with B and C are no longer negatively connected (indeed, they are not connected at all – the A–B exchange has no effect on the A–C exchange). The competition between B and C for A's resources, which drives the effect of structural power in imbalanced networks, is removed.

actors (see Figure 4.1a; ignore, for the moment, the numbers on the arrows, which are discussed later). The relation between the two subjects was the focus; the simulated actors functioned as alternative partners who responded with controlled strategies. In later experiments (Chapters 6 and 7), I studied networks of four real actors, primarily to eliminate any possible effects of the simulated actors' programmed strategies on subjects' behavior (see Figure 4.1b). These networks typically created two structurally equivalent relations (A–B and C–D) which were the focus of the analysis. And in still other experiments (Chapters 8 and 9), one real subject participated with two computer-simulated actors and a hypothetical fourth actor (see Figure 4.1c). These experiments were designed to study the effects of an exchange partner's (manipulated) strategies on the subject's response to those strategies.

In all of the experiments, subjects believed they were interacting with real people. This deception was easily maintained because of the computer-mediated interaction and the lack of any face-to-face contact. In addition, for reasons of efficiency, we typically scheduled four subjects for each experimental session regardless of whether the four interacted with each other or with simulated actors. Even though subjects did not see one another, this practice added credibility to the deception (subjects had to wait for one another, they could hear doors opening and closing as other subjects were escorted to their rooms, etc.). Although subjects occasionally expressed suspicions that one or more of their partners were computer-simulated, they were no more suspicious of their computer-simulated partners than of their real partners.

The manipulation of power. Theoretically, power in negatively connected networks is a function of two variables: the *value* of exchange and access to *alternative* sources of the valued resource. Experimentally, this means that power can be operationalized by varying value, alternatives, or both. Much of the experimental work on network-level power holds constant the potential value of exchange relations and manipulates the availability of alternatives, by varying the form and shape of the network (e.g., Cook et al. 1983; Markovsky et al. 1988). Researchers often use graph theoretic methods to compute operational definitions of power, based on network paths or related algorithms (see the June 1992 issue of *Social Networks* for a series of articles testing different measures of network-level power). Because my interest is in power at the level of the relation, rather than the network per se, I instead hold constant the shape of the network and the number of alternative partners for each actor and manipulate power by varying the relative value of exchange with alternative partners. I used the basic form of a four-actor closed network (shown in the examples in Figure 4.1) not because of any theoretical interest in this particular network form, but because, for most purposes, my tests of the theory required an exchange relation between two actors, each of whom had an alternative partner. Creating a potential relation *between* these two alternative partners – thus closing the network – introduced some variability in their availability; that is, the alternative partners were not dependent solely on the actors of interest. As I will discuss, subjects did not know just how available their partners were (they did not know the relative dependence of their alternatives' alternative). In the majority of the experiments, the alternatives were simulated actors and their "real" availability was determined by their programmed responses.

Within an exchange relation (e.g., the A–B relation), *I operationally define B's dependence on A, and A's power over B, as equal to the value that B can receive from A's behavior, divided by the total value that B can receive from both of B's potential partners in the network.* (The converse is true, of course, for B's power over A.) Note that value per se does not determine power, but rather the value of exchange *in relation to* the value of alternatives.

This definition has the statistical advantages of ratio-level measurement. Actors' dependencies on their two partners always sum to 1.0, and their dependence on any single partner varies from 0 (that partner controls no outcomes of value for the actor) to 1.0 (the actor's potential outcomes are solely under the control of that partner). Similarly, power imbalance and average power also range from 0 to 1.0.

I manipulated the four dimensions of structural power introduced in Chapter 3 – average reward power, average punishment power, reward power imbalance, and punishment power imbalance – by varying the number of points actors could add to each other's earnings (reward power) or subtract from each other's earnings (punishment power) on each exchange opportunity. On any single opportunity, each actor in the network could potentially gain a total of 10 points from both partners, and each actor could potentially lose a total of 10 points from both partners. Thus, a subject's net outcome on any single exchange opportunity could range from +10 points (if both partners added to her points) to −10 points (if both partners subtracted from her points). An actor's power over an exchange partner on either base (and the partner's dependence on the actor) consisted of the proportion of this total that the actor controlled. If, for example, A could gain 8 points from B and 2 points from C on a single opportunity, then B's reward power over A was .8 [8/(8+2)], and C's reward power over A was .2 [2/(8+2)]. Similarly, if A could lose 6 points from B and 4 points from C, then B's punishment power over A was .6 [6/(6+4)], and C's punishment power over A was .4 [4/(6+4)]. The imbalance on reward or punishment power in any dyadic exchange relation in the network equaled the difference between the individual power measures of the two actors on that base, and average power equaled the average of their power on that base.

When both bases of power were imbalanced, a fifth structural variable – the direction of the power imbalances – could be manipulated. The power imbalances were *reinforcing* when the same actor was power-advantaged on both reward and punishment power, and *opposing* when one actor was advantaged on reward power and the other on punishment power.

An illustration. The three hypothetical networks in Figure 4.1 illustrate the operational definition of power and the graphic display of networks that I use in this book. On each double arrow representing the exchange relation between two actors, the number closest to an actor is the number of points that actor can gain (+) or lose (−) from the other's rewarding or punishing action. Potential gains are shown on the outer perimeter of the network, and potential losses on the inner perimeter. Note that the numbers of points each actor can gain (or lose) from both partners always sum to 10.

Figure 4.1a displays a network with two real actors (A and B) and two computer-simulated actors, or "POs" ("programmed others"). The dotted arrow between the POs indicates that their exchange relation is implied rather than real. In this network, reward power in the A–B relation is imbalanced while punishment power is balanced. A's reward power over B is .8 (A can produce 8 points for B on each opportunity, while PO_2 can produce only 2 points for B), but B's reward power over A is only .4 (B can produce 4 points for A on each opportunity, while PO_1 can produce 6 points for A). Consequently, reward power imbalance in the A–B relation is .4 (.8 − .4), and A is the advantaged actor. In contrast, punishment power in the relation is balanced: each actor controls 6 of the other actor's potential 10-point loss; thus, each actor's punishment power over the other is .6. Note that *average* power in the A–B relation is the same (.6) on both bases of power, even though power imbalance differs. In the two actors' relations with their alternative partners (the POs), both bases of power are balanced. The average power of these relations differs, however. In the A–PO$_1$ relation, average reward power is .6 and average punishment power is .4. In the B–PO$_2$ relation, average reward power is .2 and average punishment power is .4.

In Figure 4.1b, four real actors interact in a network in which the relations between A and B, and C and D, are imbalanced on both bases of power. In this network, A and C are in structurally equivalent positions, as are B and D. Reward power is imbalanced in favor of A and C, and punishment power in favor of B and D. These power imbalances are *equal* and *opposing*. The reward power of A and C over B and D is .7, compared with B and D's reward power of .5 over A and C – a power imbalance of .2, in favor of A and C, the advantaged actors. Punishment power imbalance is also .2, but on this base of power, B and D are advantaged. The other two relations in the network – A–C and B–D – are balanced on both bases of power, but differ in average power: average reward power is .5 in the A–C relation but .3 in the B–D relation, while average punishment power is .3 in the A–C relation and .5 in the B–D relation.

Finally, Figure 4.1c displays a network in which one real subject (S) interacts with two computer-simulated partners (POs); the fourth actor in the network is hypothetical (HYP). This network illustrates a relation between S and PO$_2$ that is imbalanced on both bases of power, with the balances *equal* and *reinforcing*. S is disadvantaged in his relation with PO$_2$ on both reward power and punishment power. S's power over PO$_2$ on both bases is only .3, while PO$_2$'s power over S is .9 – a sizable power imbalance of .6 on both bases, in PO$_2$'s favor. S's relation with PO$_1$ is balanced, and average power on both bases is very low – only .1.

These examples illustrate the three combinations of real and simulated actors used in the experiments, but they display only a small sample of the possible combinations of the structural power variables. As they show, power imbalance and average power are orthogonal dimensions; each can vary independently of the other within a relation. In addition, each base of power can vary independently of the other.

The exchange process: reciprocal exchange across repeated opportunities

The process of exchange must meet the scope assumptions that exchanges are reciprocal and nonnegotiated, and that actors engage in relatively enduring relations with the same actors. To satisfy the first condition, subjects individually performed rewarding or punishing actions, directed at specific partners, without negotiation and without knowledge of either partner's intentions. On each exchange opportunity, all actors in the network simultaneously chose (1) which partner they would act toward on that opportunity and (2) an action toward that partner (to add or subtract a fixed number of points). These two choices gave the subject a total of four behavioral options on each opportunity: reward partner i, punish partner i, reward partner j, or punish partner j.

Because each side of an exchange was individually performed, subjects potentially could gain (or lose) money from one, both, or neither of their partners on each opportunity. The partner might reciprocate the exchange on the same opportunity, the next opportunity, a later opportunity, or not at all. The result of this process is not a series of discrete, two-sided exchange transactions, but an ongoing sequence of individually performed, sequentially contingent actions that produce an exchange relation of variable content, frequency, and asymmetry. In reciprocal exchange, actors can receive rewards *without* reciprocating. It is this potential that makes an asymmetrical exchange of rewards beneficial to the actor who rewards less often. Because that actor invests less time in the relation for a given level of returns, she has more opportunities to exchange with the alternative partner (i.e., her opportunity costs are lower).

To meet the assumption that exchange relations are relatively enduring, subjects exchanged with the same two partners over a very large number of exchange opportunities, typically 200–250.[6] This number of opportunities allowed exchange relations to develop gradually, based on the behavioral assumption that actors learn from the consequences of trying

---

[6] In contrast, most other social exchange experiments, especially those on negotiated exchange, typically entail no more than 15 to 60 exchange opportunities.

different patterns of exchange with alternative partners. In essence, the experiment compressed, within a 2-hour period, the number of exchanges that might occur over weeks, months, or years in natural settings. The large number of opportunities also helped to compensate for the weaker exchange values in the experiments; that is, the rate of learning is likely to be slower when the stakes are less. During the first 50 opportunities or so, subjects typically explored exchange with both partners and tried out different patterns and frequencies of exchange. Over time, exchange relations gradually stabilized. The number of opportunities in the experiments was set, after pretesting, to be long enough to allow time for stabilization, but short enough to prevent boredom from influencing behavior.

Long-term exchange relations between the same actors facilitate the study of dynamic exchange processes: the contingencies that develop over time between one actor's behavior and another actor's behavior. Although actors could not negotiate agreements, they could influence one another's behavior by making their rewarding or punishing actions contingent on desirable or undesirable actions of their partners. I study these contingencies of action, or *exchange strategies*, in relation to both structure and behavior. In some experiments they are measured as dependent variables; in others they are manipulated – with the aid of computer-simulated actors – as independent variables.

Controlling extraneous sources of variation

Other aspects of the experimental setting were designed not to satisfy theoretical requirements, but to control or eliminate extraneous sources of variation that might confuse our understanding of the theoretical variables.

The use of computer-mediated interaction

One of the hallmarks of laboratory experiments is the physical isolation of subjects from the influence of extraneous stimuli. In the study of social exchange, these stimuli include characteristics of the exchange partner; consequently, subjects are often isolated not only from outside "noise" but from each other.

In all experiments subjects were seated individually in small subject rooms, each equipped with a desk and a computer, and they interacted with each other only through a computer network. They did not meet each other before or after the experiment, nor did they have any communication with each other beyond the computer-mediated interaction. All they knew about their exchange partners was that they were students like themselves who had volunteered for the experiment to make money. They did not know their gender, race, year in school, or any other characteristics. The computer-mediated interaction allowed subjects to make choices that affected each other's earnings, to receive feedback on other actors' choices, and to keep track of their own earnings from the exchange. In addition, it made it possible to use computer-simulated partners in some experiments.

Computers standardized the interaction, by providing subjects with specific kinds of information, a limited number of behavioral choices, and a set sequence of events. This standardization is valuable for theory construction. But the primary reason for computerized interaction is to eliminate the many sources of extraneous variation that face-to-face contact would introduce. Isolating subjects from one another assures that their behavior is affected solely by characteristics of the exchange relations, and not by characteristics of the individual actors (e.g., their gender, appearance, demeanor, voice) or uncontrolled verbal communication between actors.

The removal of personal characteristics, verbal communication, and the like from the setting in no way implies that these variables are unimportant, or that they do not affect how actors use and respond to power. On the contrary, they are eliminated precisely because of their potential effects on behavior. While these effects might be of great interest for testing another theory, they make it more difficult to discern the effects of structural power.

Isolating subjects from one another also served another purpose: it eliminated other potential social rewards or punishments that might otherwise compete with the effects of money. Because subjects never met, saw, or talked with their exchange partners – and knew that they would not meet them afterward – competing social pressures (concerns with approval, liking, responses to characteristics of the other subjects, and so forth) were minimized. For the same reason, I used procedures that should minimize experimenter effects such as evaluation apprehension and social desirability. The experimenters were carefully trained and supervised students (both graduate and undergraduate), not authority figures, who were clearly designated as my research assistants. Their contact with subjects was minimal. Again, removing the potential for these social consequences in no way implies that they are unimportant; rather, they are removed because any uncontrolled rewards or punishments might confound, or make it difficult to detect, the effects of the monetary consequences that *are* manipulated.

Exchange information

The experiments provide subjects with information about the experimental task itself and about three aspects of the exchange: the exchange structure, exchange process, and exchange outcomes. While information might conceivably affect the process or outcomes of exchange, it is not a theoretical variable in social exchange theories or in this study. Consequently, the amount of information that subjects have is held constant throughout the series of experiments.

Because we know little about how information affects the process and outcomes of social exchange, it is difficult to know how decisions about its control might affect the results. Providing subjects with full information about the exchange structure, for example, might either encourage or constrain power use. The most conservative position on this issue is to assume that the effects of these experiments hold only under comparable information conditions; I suspect, though, that at least some kinds of information are fairly unimportant for the effects of exchange structure on exchange process and outcomes.

Information about the experiment. Recruitment announcements described the experiment as a study of social interaction. They informed prospective subjects that they would participate in the experiment with three other students, that they would interact with each other through computers, and that they would never meet or talk to the other participants. Most important, they would earn money in the experiment – at least $6 and as much as $20, with the exact amount depending on the choices that they and the other participants made in the experiment and on the experimental condition to which they were randomly assigned.

The experimental instructions displayed on subjects' computer screens provided full and detailed instructions on the experimental task (see Appendix II). Subjects learned what kinds of choices they would have to make in the experiment, how to make them on the computer, and what kinds of information they would receive. They learned that their earnings depended on their partners' choices, and their partners' earnings on their choices.

All of this information was conveyed as neutrally as possible. There was no "cover story" for the experiment; it was described simply as a study of social interaction. The only deception involved the use of computer-simulated actors in some of the experiments. The experimental instructions omitted any terms that might be cognitively or affectively loaded, or that might act as "demand characteristics" (Orne 1962), including terms such as "exchange," "power," "reward," "punish," and even "partner." Instead, the instructions described subjects as participants who interacted with other participants, made choices, and added or subtracted points. The instructions assured them that there were no right or wrong choices in the experiment, that their only objective should be to make as much money as possible, and that how they did that was up to them.

Information about the exchange structure. Emerson (1972b) proposed that structural power produces predictable exchange outcomes regardless of actors' information about the power structure or their relative positions in it. To test this assumption, Cook and Emerson (1978) developed an exchange setting in which actors were unaware of their relative dependencies on each other and knew only their own exchange outcomes. By eliminating information about the exchange structure, they showed that the effects of structure can occur even when subjects are unaware that they have power.

My setting, in contrast, deliberately allows for both structurally induced and strategic power use and provides subjects with information about the values of exchange controlled by both actors in each of their immediate exchange relations. Throughout the exchange period, subjects' computer screens displayed the fixed amounts of money that they and their two partners could gain or lose from each other on each exchange opportunity (see Figure 4.2). This information, called the "earnings schedule," allowed subjects to infer the relative dependencies of self and other in their own exchange relations. I do not assume they necessarily did so, however, or that they fully understood their relative power from the information in the schedule. Furthermore, subjects were

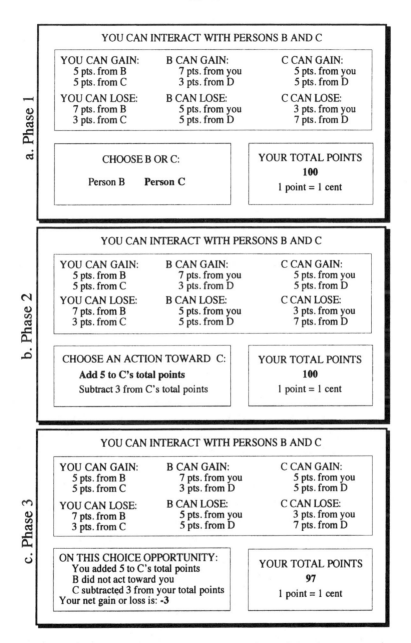

Figure 4.2. Subject A's computer screens for the three phases of an exchange opportunity (values based on the network in Figure 4.1b)

not told how much money the fourth actor in the network – their alternatives' alternative – could lose or gain. Thus, they did not know how dependent this actor was on either of their two partners and, consequently, they did not know how "available" that actor was as an alternative for either of their exchange partners. Actors would rarely have information about such distal dependencies, but omitting it also prevented subjects from judging too closely the behaviors of computer-simulated partners (i.e., subjects knew neither the dependencies nor the behavior of the fourth actor toward the subjects' two partners).

Information about the exchange process. Subjects' information about the exchange process is consistent with the level of information that actors engaged in reciprocal exchanges would typically have. After subjects chose a target partner and an action on an exchange opportunity – without negotiation and without knowledge of either partner's intentions – they learned what actions others had taken and how those actions affected their own outcomes.

The subject's computer screen signaled the start of an exchange opportunity by asking the subject to choose a partner (Figure 4.2a) and then an action toward that partner (Figure 4.2b). After all actors made these choices, the computer reminded subjects of their own choices and informed them of their partners' choices – that is, whether each partner added n points to or subtracted n points from the subject's earnings, or did not act toward the subject (Figure 4.2c). Not acting toward one partner implied acting toward the other, but subjects were not told what actions (positive or negative) their partners took toward others. Each subject's total points changed to reflect any gains or losses on that opportunity (compare b and c of Figure 4.2), and then a new request to choose a partner initiated the next exchange opportunity (i.e., Figure 4.2a). (Note, in Figure 4.2, that the earnings schedule and total points [cumulative earnings] are displayed at all times, and that only the value of the total points and the information in the "choice box" change.)

This process was repeated as many times as there were exchange opportunities in the experiment. Subjects knew there would be a large number of opportunities in the experiment, but not how many.

Information about exchange outcomes. The experiment provided subjects with both per trial and cumulative information about their own outcomes from the exchange, but with no information about their partners' outcomes. Subjects knew the consequences of their own actions for their partners, of course, but they did not know the net amount that their partners received from both of their partners on an exchange opportunity, nor did they know their partners' cumulative outcomes.

This information was omitted primarily to prevent comparisons between the outcomes of self and others. Exchange theory assumes that actors are concerned only with their own outcomes, and not with the *relation* between their own outcomes and their partners' outcomes. Concerns such as equity and equality challenge that assumption. Although omitting information on partner's outcomes should reduce equity effects, this experimental setting – unlike some (e.g., Cook and Emerson 1978) – does not eliminate them altogether. Because subjects do have information of the potential values in the exchange structure and of the actual values exchanged on each opportunity, they can still be influenced by perceptions of the fairness of the structure and the process of exchange. In Chapter 8, I report the results of two experiments that specifically examine those perceptions in relation to exchange structure and behavior.[7]

Postexperimental information. The experiment concluded with a brief explanation, presented on subjects' computer screens, of the purpose of the experiment and any deception used. The experimenter then met with subjects individually to (1) pay them the money they had earned, (2) answer any remaining questions about the experiment, (3) make sure that subjects were not upset about the deception (if any), and (4) request that subjects not talk about the experiment.[8]

---

[7] Information on partners' outcomes could also increase competitive motives – that is, the desire to maximize the *difference* between own and others' earnings. Subjects rarely reported competitive motives on the postexperimental questionnaire, however. They were more likely to report that they tried to "equalize the money earned by you and the others." Even this response, however, was strongly related to the subjects' power positions: disadvantaged actors were more likely than advantaged actors to report concerns with equalizing earnings. For disadvantaged actors, equalizing earnings was comparable with maximizing earnings; equality of earnings was the best outcome these actors could hope for.

[8] Procedures suggested by Wuebben, Straits, and Schulman (1974: ch. 5) and Aronson, Brewer, and Carlsmith (1985) were used to help assure that subjects did not talk about the experiment to other potential subjects. The primary concern was that subjects not reveal the use of computer-simulated partners in the experiments that used them; our checks on the effectiveness of these procedures indicate they did not.

Measures of the dependent variables

The experiments investigate how different exchange structures, varying on the power to reward and the power to punish, affect actors' behaviors toward one another and their evaluations of each other. In all but the single-subject experiments in Chapters 8 and 9, the unit of analysis is the exchange relation, and the behavioral interaction between the actors in the relation is the focus of analysis. Patterns of behavioral interaction provide the data for measures of both exchange *process* (or power strategies) and exchange *outcome*.

Measures of exchange process

Measures of exchange process examine the dynamic contingencies between the two actors' behaviors toward one another – that is, how A's behavior at time t_1 affects B's behavior at time t_2, and vice versa. These contingencies are computed by examining the relation between actors' behaviors at lagged intervals across the entire period of exchange. I provide more detailed information about these measures in Chapter 5, which reports analyses of actors' strategies. In later chapters (8 and 9) that study the effects of an exchange partner's strategy as an *independent* variable on a subject's response to that strategy, I manipulate these contingencies by varying the conditional probabilities with which computer-simulated actors respond to the behaviors of real subjects.

Measures of exchange outcome

Measures of exchange outcome examine the overall frequencies of actors' behaviors toward one another, computed for the entire exchange period or for blocks of opportunities within it (called "trial blocks"). For each base of power, I examine the average frequency of exchange on that base (i.e., the average frequency with which the two actors rewarded each other or punished each other) and the asymmetry of their exchange frequencies (i.e., who rewarded or punished more, and by how much). The asymmetry of reward exchange is my measure of what Emerson (1972b) called *power use*. Because actors in these experiments exchange outcomes of fixed value, I measure power use by the differences in actors' frequencies of exchange rather than by the differences in the value they obtain through exchange. As I explained in Chapter 2, when dependencies are manipulated by varying the relative value of exchange, the more powerful actor is expected to receive the benefits he or she most values from the other more frequently, but the absolute value of these benefits will not necessarily be greater (Thibaut and Kelley 1959). Thus, a higher value of power use, in A's favor, indicates that A received the benefits of B's exchange at lower (opportunity) cost. The less A "pays" for B's exchange, the more opportunities A has to engage in exchange with A's other partner.[9]

The frequency measures are divided by the number of exchange opportunities, thus standardizing the measures so that they vary from 0 to 1. For example, if there are 200 exchange opportunities in an experiment, and A rewards B on 60 of those opportunities, then the frequency of A's rewards to B is .3 (60/200). The relational measures of actors' behaviors are then computed by calculating the *average* of these standardized measures for the two actors (exchange frequency) or the *difference* between the measures for the two actors (exchange asymmetry). Four measures of exchange outcome result: the average reward exchange in the relation (*reward frequency*), the asymmetry of reward exchange in the relation (*reward asymmetry*), the average punishment exchange (*punishment frequency*), and the asymmetry of punishment exchange (*punishment asymmetry*).

Throughout this book, I follow the convention of calculating reward asymmetry by subtracting the reward exchange of the *less* dependent actor from the reward exchange of the *more* dependent actor, and punishment asymmetry by subtracting the punishment exchange of the *more* dependent actor from the punishment exchange of the *less* dependent actor. Thus, a positive value on either measure indicates a distribution of exchange in favor of the power-advantaged actor, who is expected to receive rewards more frequently and punishments less frequently than the disadvantaged actor. If, for example, A is advantaged and B is disadvantaged in the A–B relation, then both reward asymmetry and punishment asymmetry are

[9] In contrast, experiments that manipulate power in exchange networks by varying the availability of alternatives while holding constant the value of exchange (e.g., Cook et al. 1983; Markovsky et al. 1988) typically measure power use by the differences in the amounts of money that actors earn. When power is manipulated by differences in access to alternatives, a power advantage will produce greater absolute value (i.e., more money) for the actor.

calculated so that positive values favor A. When reward and punishment power imbalances are opposing, both measures are calculated so that positive values favor the actor with the reward power advantage.

In experiments in which a single real subject interacts with computer-simulated partners, the unit of analysis is the individual subject and the dependent variables are measures of the subject's behavioral or evaluative reactions to the strategies of the programmed partner(s). The behavioral measures are again standardized. Only measures of individual behaviors – the frequency with which the subject rewarded or punished the partner – are examined in these experiments.

Evaluations of exchange partners

Measures of subjects' evaluations of their partners are derived from their answers to postexperimental questionnaires. At the end of each experiment, subjects evaluated their partners' behaviors toward them on a series of semantic differential scales shown on their computer screens. These scales were designed to measure dimensions of affect and perceptions of justice. Subjects also evaluated the perceived fairness of the earnings schedule (i.e., the exchange structure as presented to the subjects). I created multiitem scales from these responses with the aid of factor analyses and reliability tests. These scales and the measurement techniques are discussed in greater detail in the chapters that examine them: justice in Chapter 8, and affect in Chapter 9. Subjects were also asked to write, in an open-ended format, descriptions of any strategies that they used to make money, using a notepad supplied for that purpose.

Theory building with a standardized setting

The laboratory setting I have just described satisfies the scope conditions of social exchange theory (Table 2.1): it makes actors mutually dependent on one another for some outcome (or outcomes) that they value, and provides repeated opportunities for them to exchange these outcomes contingently with one another over time. It also meets the additional conditions outlined in the preceding chapter – conditions assumed for this project, but not for all exchange relations: (1) all actors have some capacity both to reward and to punish their exchange partners, (2) resources are behavioral capabilities that produce outcomes of fixed value, (3) benefits obtained through exchange have no subsequent exchange value, (4) the only costs of performing exchange actions are opportunity costs, (5) exchanges are reciprocal rather than negotiated, (6) the unit of analysis is the dyadic relation, imbedded in a larger network with negative connections, (7) variations in power are created by variations in relative value, (8) actors cannot change the structure of the network or the value of resources, (9) actors cannot avoid a partner's rewarding or punishing actions, and (10) actors have full information about the values governing mutual dependencies in their immediate exchange relations.

A standardized setting that meets a set of theoretical conditions is one of the tools that makes laboratory experimentation such a powerful method for developing and testing theory. Because all experiments are conducted under the same set of conditions, using similar procedures, and because variables are manipulated in comparable ways, information can be cumulated across many experiments conducted over a long period of time. With this setting, it is possible to conduct systematic, cumulative research that tests, modifies, and builds theory.

The next five chapters illustrate this process, by describing how a cumulative series of experiments, conducted in the standardized setting, was used to develop and test a theory of coercive power in social exchange. Chapter 5 describes the early experiments, which tested whether Emerson's theory of power-dependence relations could be extended, without modification, to incorporate coercive power. These experiments showed that under the scope conditions of the theoretical program, power-dependence theory's predictions do not hold for coercive power. The effects of coercive power are consistently far weaker than those of equivalent structures of reward power. Nevertheless, these experiments offered important theoretical clues that contributed, inductively, to the next stage of theory development. In particular, they suggested that the key to understanding the weak effects of coercive power lay in understanding why it was used so rarely, by analyzing its effects on the *power user*.

Building upon these initial findings, the next four chapters take up the task of modifying and extending exchange theory to incorporate coercive power. Chapter 6 argues that the use of coercive power, unlike the use of reward power, is not structurally determined by power imbalance. Chapter 7 proposes that in lieu of structurally induced power use, coercion must be used strategically, and develops a theory that explains why the strategic use of coercion is often constrained in social exchange relations. Chapter

8 shows that justice norms further repress the use of coercion. Chapter 9 argues that the weak effects of coercion result solely from its low use, and predicts that when coercion is used consistently, its effects will be equivalent to those of reward power. The predictions of each of these chapters are tested in new experiments, using the standardized setting. In this way, the research program uses experimentation as a tool for both deductive theory testing and inductive theory building, taking advantage of a single setting that meets a common set of scope conditions.

5. The early research: experimental tests and theoretical puzzles

The 10-year research project consisted of two distinct phases: an initial phase that compared equivalent structures of reward and punishment power and tested exploratory hypotheses about differences in structural effects, and a second phase that constructed and tested a theory of coercive power in social exchange.

This chapter describes the research and results of the first phase; the next four chapters are devoted to the second. This rather unequal division of labor reflects the greater importance of the second phase of theory construction. Theories are rarely built in a vacuum, however, and deductive theorizing is most productive when it builds upon an initial knowledge base. As Chapter 3 illustrated, that base was small and inconsistent at the beginning of the project. The five experiments in the first phase expanded and strengthened it, and shaped the direction of the subsequent work.

The chapter begins with a discussion of each of the five experiments: their objectives, design, results, and implications. The analyses in this portion of the chapter focus on how the manipulations of structural power affect the frequency and distribution of exchange in the relation. Then, in the second part of the chapter, I use the combined data set from all five experiments to examine the dynamic process of exchange and actors' exchange strategies.

Concentrating the work of the first phase in a single chapter makes for rather dense reading. For those readers who are more interested in the results and implications of the experiments than in the details of their design and analysis, it is quite possible to follow the main story line through the introductory and implications sections of the chapter while skimming the descriptions of method and analysis.

Experiment 1: equal structures, unequal effects

The first experiment addressed the most basic question for the research: can exchange theory's analysis of power-dependence relations be extended, without modification, to incorporate coercive power? That is, do equivalent structures of power, differing only on the base of power and dependence, have equivalent effects on the frequency and distribution of exchange?

As we saw in Chapter 3, the conceptual extension of power-dependence principles to coercive power is straightforward. A's control over outcomes that B values – either positively or negatively – makes B dependent on A, and affects the level of potential cost that A can impose on B. Actors who are less dependent on their partners for either rewards or punishments can impose greater cost on their partners than their partners can impose on them. Their structural advantage in the relation provides the means to obtain a behavioral advantage in the exchange.

Thus, A's initiations of exchange with B are predicted to vary as a direct function of A's dependence on B. Actors who are more dependent on another, either for gaining rewards or avoiding punishments, should reward the other more frequently. The greater the average power (dependence) in the relation, the more frequently A and B should reward each other. If either reward power or punishment power is imbalanced, the more dependent actor should reward her partner more frequently than the partner reciprocates.

Based on this logic, the first experiment tested what I will call the *hypothesis of structural equivalence*: the prediction that equivalent structures of imbalanced reward power and punishment power produce equivalent power use. Because testing the null hypothesis of equivalent effects is always problematic, however, the experiment instead compared relations of balanced and imbalanced power for each base of power, and examined whether power imbalance has comparable effects for the two bases.

The hypothesis of structural equivalence implies that it should be possible to combine both bases of power into a single measure of overall power: the sum of an actor's reward *and* punishment power over another. That is, if reward power and punishment power have equal effects, then a relation in which power is *balanced* overall can be created either by balancing both bases of power in the relation, or by creating equal but opposing imbalances on the two bases. Similarly, power in a relation can be *imbalanced*, overall, as a result of an imbalance in reward power, punishment power, or both. The design of Experiment 1 uses this reasoning to test the hypothesis.

Design

All five experiments in this phase of the research studied exchange networks composed of two real subjects (A and B) and two computer-simulated actors (POs, or "programmed others"). Each real subject could exchange with the other real subject or with one of the simulated actors. The relation between the two real subjects, A and B, was the primary focus. When power in this relation was imbalanced, A was always the advantaged (and B the disadvantaged) actor. If *both* bases of power were imbalanced, in opposing directions (so that the power imbalances favored different actors), A was always advantaged on reward power and B on punishment power.[1]

In Experiment 1, five different exchange structures varied the balance or imbalance of reward and punishment power in the A–B relation within conditions of overall power balance and imbalance (see Figure 5.1). In two of the conditions, power is balanced overall; in the remaining three, power is imbalanced at a level of .4, in favor of A. In previous experiments on reciprocal exchange in purely reward-based networks, this level of power imbalance produced significantly greater power use than a balanced relation (Molm 1981, 1985).

The two conditions of balanced power (Figure 5.1a,b) consisted of one condition (5.1a) in which both reward and punishment power were balanced, and one condition (5.1b) in which a reward power imbalance of .4, favoring A, opposed a punishment power imbalance of .4, favoring B. If reward and punishment power have equivalent effects, power use should be equal and near zero in both conditions (i.e., the distribution of exchange should be equal). When the two bases of power are imbalanced but in opposing directions, B's punishment power advantage should

---

[1] The first experiment studied 12 networks in each condition; all subsequent experiments are based on an N of 10 networks per condition. In all five experiments, subjects exchanged for 250 opportunities.

Balanced power

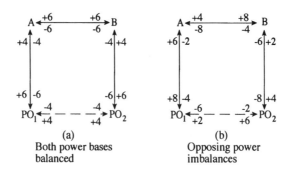

(a)
Both power bases
balanced

(b)
Opposing power
imbalances

Imbalanced power

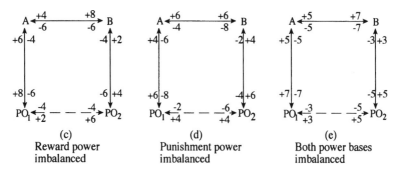

(c)
Reward power
imbalanced

(d)
Punishment power
imbalanced

(e)
Both power bases
imbalanced

Figure 5.1. The exchange networks in Experiment 1

counter A's reward power advantage, thus balancing the overall power in the relation.

The three imbalanced structures (Figure 5.1c–e) all gave A an equal power advantage over B, but varied the source of the advantage. In one structure (5.1c), reward power was imbalanced at .4 in A's favor while punishment power was balanced; in a second structure (5.1d), punishment power was imbalanced at .4 in A's favor while reward power was balanced; and in the third structure (5.1e), the power imbalance of .4 was divided equally between the two bases of power – that is, a reward power imbalance of .2 and a punishment power imbalance of .2 gave A a combined power advantage of .4 over B. Again, if reward power imbalance and punishment power imbalance have equivalent effects, power use in all three imbalanced structures should be equal and greater than in the balanced conditions. A's power advantage – on either base – should shift the distribution of reward exchange in A's favor, with B giving rewards to A more often than A reciprocates.

In all five structures, average reward power and average punishment power in the A–B relation were held constant at .6. Average reward power must be at least .5 in order for reward exchange, whether symmetrical or asymmetrical, to be mutually beneficial (Michaels and Wiggins 1976). Thus, this experiment tested the effects of reward and punishment power under conditions in which some ratio of reward exchange in the A–B relation was structurally supported.

The simulated actors. Both the programmed strategies of the simulated actors and their structural relations to the real subjects were held constant in all five structures. Thus, analytically, the simulated actors could be treated as experimental controls. Both structurally and behaviorally, they were designed to be available, reliable, and reciprocating partners. While the value of their exchange necessarily varied, their "availability" as alternative partners did not.

In all conditions, the power relation between each real subject and that subject's PO was imbalanced at .2, on both bases, in favor of the real actors, A and B. The average power of the two relations between the two real subjects and their simulated partners was held constant at .5 across conditions, a level that was high enough to make them reasonable alternatives, but lower than the average power of the relation between the two real subjects.

The simulated actors responded contingently to the behavior of their paired subjects on the previous exchange opportunity. Their programmed behavior followed a modified tit-for-tat strategy: they never initiated punishment, occasionally initiated rewarding, and mainly reciprocated the subject's prior behavior, but at probabilities less than 1.0 (.8 or .9), to prevent suspicion.[2] All probabilities were ran-

---

[2] On each opportunity each actor could reward, punish, or not act toward a given partner; thus, nine conditional probabilities – specifying the probabilities with which the PO responded with each of these three actions, given each of the three immediately prior actions by the subject – describe the strategies of the POs. These probabilities are as follows, with R = reward, N = nonexchange (not acting toward the other), P = punishment, and p(i|j)

domized over blocks of 10 actions of the specified type by the subject.[3]

Although the choice of these particular probabilities was necessarily somewhat arbitrary, they are consistent with the structural relation between the subjects and their simulated partners and with the objective of creating reliable alternatives. As the analysis of exchange processes later in the chapter will show, the strategies of the simulated actors are not unlike those of real subjects.

Results

The hypothesis of structural equivalence predicts effects of structural power on the traditional measure of power use: the asymmetry of reward exchange in the A–B relation. In addition to this central variable, Table 5.1 reports the mean values for three other measures of exchange outcomes in the A–B relation: reward frequency (the average frequency of rewarding in the relation), punishment frequency (the average frequency of punishment in the relation), and punishment asymmetry (the asymmetry of punishment in the relation). To facilitate comparisons across experiments, I compare the effects of power on these same four variables throughout this chapter.[4]

= the probability of PO's behavior i at time t, given the prior occurrence of the subject's behavior j at time t − 1:

$p(R|R) = .9$ $p(R|N) = .1$ $p(R|P) = 0$
$p(N|R) = .1$ $p(N|N) = .9$ $p(N|P) = .2$
$p(P|R) = 0$ $p(P|N) = 0$ $p(P|P) = .8$

Note that the three probabilities in each column sum to 1.0. For example, in the first column, the probabilities with which the PO responds to the subject's prior rewarding with rewarding, nonexchange, or punishment sum to 1.0.

[3] For example, if the PO were programmed to reciprocate the subject's rewards .9 of the time and to respond by not acting toward the subject the remaining .1 of the time, the order with which the PO responded to the subject's rewards with one of these two behaviors was randomized across every 10 rewarding actions by the subject. Those 10 rewarding actions need not be consecutive, of course, and typically would not be. This procedure produces a better distribution of the behaviors than randomizing over all opportunities, particularly with very high or very low probabilities such as the ones used here.

[4] Remember that all measures are standardized, by dividing the frequency of behavior by the number of exchange opportunities (250). Thus, measures of exchange frequency range from 0 to 1, and measures of exchange asymmetry range from −1 to +1. Because A is always the advantaged actor when power is imbalanced, reward asymmetry is calculated by subtracting the frequency of A's rewards to B from B's rewards to A (i.e., reward asymmetry = [B's rewards − A's rewards]), and punishment asymmetry by subtracting B's punishment from A's punishment (punishment asymmetry = [A's punishment − B's punishment]). Thus,

Table 5.1. *Mean exchange outcomes by structural power condition, Experiment 1*

Structural power[a]	Reward exchange		Punishment exchange	
	Frequency	Asymmetry	Frequency	Asymmetry
Balanced power				
Both power bases balanced	.60	.01	.04	.01
Opposing power imbalances	.48	.17	.03	.00
Imbalanced power				
Reward power imbalanced	.43	.21	.02	-.01
Punishment power imbalanced	.65	.01	.04	.00
Both power bases imbalanced	.58	.07	.02	.01

[a] In all conditions, overall power imbalance = .4, average reward power = .6, and average punishment power = .6.

Testing the hypothesis. The hypothesis of structural equivalence predicts (1) no differences in mean power use among structures *within* conditions of overall power balance and power imbalance, and (2) significantly greater power use for the three structures with imbalanced power than for the two structures with balanced power. Planned comparisons tested these predictions with the appropriate t-tests.

Not only do the results fail to support the hypothesis of structural equivalence, but they show exactly the opposite. All conditions *within* each of the categories of overall balance and imbalance do differ significantly from each other on reward asymmetry (i.e., pairwise t-tests show that the two balanced conditions differ significantly from each other, and among the three imbalanced conditions, each differs significantly from each of the other two conditions), but mean power use (reward asymmetry) for the two balanced structures does not differ significantly from mean power use for the three imbalanced structures.

The reason for these unexpected findings becomes apparent if we ignore the categories of overall power balance and imbalance, and instead compare conditions of power balance and imbalance *within each base of power.* To illustrate, Table 5.2 rearranges the data in Table 5.1. The top

a positive value on either indicates a distribution of rewards or punishments that favors the power-advantaged actor.

Table 5.2. *Mean exchange outcomes in Table 5.1, rearranged by base of power*

Structural power	Reward exchange		Punishment exchange	
	Frequency	Asymmetry	Frequency	Asymmetry
Condition means by				
reward power imbalance				
Power imbalance = 0 (5.1a,b)	.63	.01	.04	.00
Power imbalance = .2 (5.1e)	.58	.07	.02	.01
Power imbalance = .4 (5.1c,d)	.46	.19	.02	.00
Condition means by				
punishment power imbalance				
Power imbalance = 0 (5.1a,d)	.52	.11	.03	.00
Power imbalance = .2 (5.1e)	.58	.07	.03	.00
Power imbalance = .4 (5.1b,c)	.56	.09	.02	.01

half of the table shows the mean values of the exchange outcomes for each level of reward power imbalance in the network (0, .2, .4), ignoring punishment power imbalance. And the bottom half shows the mean values by punishment power imbalance, while ignoring reward power imbalance. Rearranged in this fashion, the central finding of the experiment becomes clear: *reward asymmetry increases with reward power imbalance, but punishment power imbalance has no effect on the asymmetry of reward exchange.*

The top half of the table, organized by reward power imbalance, shows very clear and consistent effects of reward power imbalance on *both* the frequency and asymmetry of reward exchange. Reward asymmetry (i.e., power use) *increases* systematically with power imbalance: from .01 when power is balanced, to .07 when power imbalance is .2, to .19 when power imbalance is .4 ($F_{2,47} = 30.10$, p < .001). These values are comparable with those found in previous experiments for similar imbalances in reward power, in structures in which actors had no power to punish each other (Molm 1981, 1985). At the same time, reward frequency *decreases* systematically as power imbalance (and conflict in the relation) increases ($F_{2,47} = 15.38$, p < .001).[5] And, as power-dependence theory predicts,

[5] Note that when both bases of power are balanced, A and B distribute their rewards in rough proportion to their relative dependencies; that is, they reward each other 60% of the

reward asymmetry increases significantly over time when reward power is imbalanced ($F_{3,87} = 7.56$, $p < .001$).[6]

In contrast, the bottom half of the table, organized by punishment power imbalance, shows no significant effects of punishment power on either reward frequency ($F_{2,47} = .60$) or reward asymmetry ($F_{2,47} = .07$).

Together, these results indicate that the hypothesis of structural equivalence must be rejected. Not only do equivalent structural variations in the imbalance of reward power and punishment power fail to produce equivalent effects on reward exchange, but *punishment power has no effects whatsoever* on either power use – as measured by the asymmetry of reward exchange – or the frequency of mutual exchange.

The use of punishment. Analyzing actors' use of punishment helps to explain why punishment power is so ineffective. The means in Tables 5.1 and 5.2 show very low frequencies of punishment by both actors. Punishment directed toward the simulated partners was equally low. Moreover, punishment frequency was unrelated to structural power; neither reward nor punishment power imbalance had any effect on it. It was also unrelated to power position: punishment asymmetry is near zero in all five condi-

---

time, and the POs 36% of the time (see Table 5.1). While this distribution appears to support Herrnstein's (1970) matching law, it does not maximize A's and B's rewards. In this particular structure, A and B could earn the most money by exchanging exclusively with each other. Rather than reflecting matching (which is predicted only for variable-interval schedules of reinforcement), it is instead likely that three factors contribute to the tendency for A and B to reward their alternative partners (the POs) as often as they do: (1) the POs were programmed to initiate exchange with A and B occasionally when A and B were ignoring them, a strategy that may have elicited more rewarding from A and B; (2) the POs were more dependent in their relations with A and B, which may have suggested (incorrectly, given their programming) that some exchange with them would be profitable for A and B; and (3) the POs had the potential to punish A and B (even though they used punishment only to retaliate and never to coerce). In Experiment 6 (Chapter 6), the same structure of balanced reward power produces a reward frequency of .88 when all three factors are changed (i.e., the simulated actors are replaced with real actors, all relations in the network are balanced, and punishment power is eliminated).

[6] I obtained this result by dividing the exchange period into four trial blocks, with 65 exchange opportunities in each of the first two blocks and 60 in each of the second two blocks, and conducting a repeated-measures analysis of variance with trial block as a within-subjects variable. (The 250 exchange opportunities of the experiment are not divisible into four equal trial blocks. Because a 5-minute break occurred after 130 trials, it was reasonable to divide the prebreak period into two blocks of 65 trials each, and the postbreak period into two blocks of 60 trials each.)

tions, indicating that actors who were disadvantaged on punishment power punished as often as their advantaged partners.

The one variable that did affect the use of punishment is time. A repeated-measures analysis showed that punishment declined significantly over the course of the exchange ($F_{3,165} = 10.91$, $p < .001$). Most of the decrease occurred between the first and second trial blocks. Although no trends over time were predicted, the conditions that should provoke the use of punishment would lead us to expect the opposite; that is, that punishment would *increase* over time, after a period of insufficient reward exchange from the partner or a decline in the partner's reward exchange.

Implications

Despite the structural comparability of reward and punishment power, these results strongly refute predictions of the comparability of their effects on behavior. Punishment power imbalance affected neither the frequency nor the asymmetry of reward exchange, nor did it modify the typical effects of reward power. Punishment was rarely used, its use was unrelated to the structure of power or the actor's position of power in the relation, and it declined over time. ,

While punishment power failed to benefit actors who were structurally advantaged on that base, it also exhibited few of the detrimental consequences that some of the theories reviewed in Chapter 3 predict. No cycles of escalating conflict were observed, and actors did not avoid exchange partners who had greater potential to punish them. Instead, actors continued to exchange rewards with each other at frequencies roughly proportional to their average dependence on each other (i.e., .6), except when the conflict generated by reward power imbalance reduced the frequency of their exchange. And, even though that conflict reduced reward exchange, it did not increase punishment.

In short, these results fail to support either a direct extension of exchange theory's analysis of power-dependence relations to coercive power, or alternative predictions of other theories. The surprisingly low use of punishment raises as many questions as it answers. Clearly, a structural advantage on punishment power does not, by itself, induce more rewards from the disadvantaged partner. Nor does it necessarily lead to the use of the power advantage, as measured by the frequency of punishment. Why actors did not use punishment more, and what effects it might have if it were used with greater frequency, remain to be seen.

Experiments 2, 3, 4, and 5: new findings and persistent differences

I conducted four additional experiments with three main aims: (1) to determine whether the findings of the first experiment would hold under different structural conditions, (2) to extend the test of structural equivalence to the effects of average power, and (3) to examine the effects of varying structural conditions that should encourage or constrain the use of punishment power.

Because Emerson (1972b) assumed that power imbalance was sufficient to produce power use, power-dependence theory offers few insights into other structural conditions that might affect the use of power. As we saw in Chapter 3, however, this question has been central to theories of deterrence and conflict spiral. Experiments 3–5 examine some of the predictions of these theories, which apply primarily to the effects of *average* power. Experiment 2 extends Experiment 1's analysis of the effects of power imbalance.

Each of these experiments manipulated two or more of five structural power variables: average reward power; average punishment power; reward power imbalance; punishment power imbalance; and, when both reward and punishment power were imbalanced, the direction of the power imbalances – that is, whether the two imbalances reinforced or opposed each other. These manipulations, and the values at which the nonmanipulated variables were held constant, are summarized in Table 5.3 for all four experiments. Table 5.3 also reports the mean values of the four exchange outcomes (reward frequency, reward asymmetry, punishment frequency, and punishment asymmetry) for each experimental condition, and Table 5.4 reports the summary results of analyses of variance on these means. Repeated-measures analyses of variance, examining means across four trial blocks, supplemented these analyses and are reported in the text.

Table 5.3. *Mean values of structural power and exchange outcomes, Experiments 2–5*

| Experiment/ condition | Structural power[a] | | | | | Exchange outcomes | | | |
| | Reward | | Punishment | | | Reward | | Punishment | |
	Avg	Imbal	Avg	Imbal	Dir[b]	Freq	Asym	Freq	Asym
a. *Experiment 2[c]*									
Condition 1	.6	**0**	.6	**.4**	–	.67	.00	.03	.00
Condition 2	.6	**0**	.6	**.8**	–	.57	.04	.04	.01
Condition 3	.6	**.4**	.6	**.4**	**R**	.42	.20	.03	-.03
Condition 4	.6	**.4**	.6	**.8**	**R**	.37	.19	.05	-.03
Condition 5	.6	**.4**	.6	**.4**	**O**	.48	.17	.02	.01
Condition 6	.6	**.4**	.6	**.8**	**O**	.52	.15	.06	-.01
b. *Experiment 3*									
Condition 1	.6	**0**	**.3**	**0**	–	.70	-.01	.01	.00
Condition 2	.6	**0**	**.9**	**0**	–	.64	.02	.02	-.01
Condition 3	.6	**.2**	**.3**	**.2**	**R**	.49	.11	.01	.00
Condition 4	.6	**.2**	**.9**	**.2**	**R**	.56	.14	.02	.00
c. *Experiment 4*									
Condition 1	**.35**	.5	**.35**	.5	**R**	.16	.11	.02	.00
Condition 2	**.35**	.5	**.35**	.5	**O**	.16	.05	.02	-.02
Condition 3	**.35**	.5	**.65**	.5	**R**	.20	.10	.04	.00
Condition 4	**.35**	.5	**.65**	.5	**O**	.22	.09	.06	.00
Condition 5	**.65**	.5	**.35**	.5	**R**	.39	.27	.05	-.03
Condition 6	**.65**	.5	**.35**	.5	**O**	.45	.14	.07	-.05
Condition 7	**.65**	.5	**.65**	.5	**R**	.38	.21	.02	-.01
Condition 8	**.65**	.5	**.65**	.5	**O**	.44	.22	.03	-.03
d. *Experiment 5*									
Condtiion 1	.55	**.3**	**.35**	.5	**R**	.27	.14	.01	.00
Condition 2	.55	**.3**	**.35**	.5	**O**	.36	.14	.07	-.04
Condition 3	.55	**.3**	**.65**	.5	**R**	.33	.18	.05	-.02
Condition 4	.55	**.3**	**.65**	.5	**O**	.43	.11	.04	-.02
Condition 5	.55	**.7**	**.35**	.5	**R**	.24	.22	.04	-.03
Condition 6	.55	**.7**	**.35**	.5	**O**	.38	.18	.06	-.05
Condition 7	.55	**.7**	**.65**	.5	**R**	.37	.22	.05	-.02
Condition 8	.55	**.7**	**.65**	.5	**O**	.42	.28	.03	-.03

[a]Manipulated variables are shown in bold type.
[b]Dir = direction of power imbalances when both reward power and punishment power are imbalanced; R = reinforcing (both imbalances favor actor A), O = opposing (reward power imbalance favors actor A and punishment power imbalance favors actor B).
[c]Conditions 1 and 5 are from Experiment 1.

Table 5.4. *F-ratios from analyses of variance, Experiments 2–5*

	df	Reward exchange		Punishment exchange	
		Frequency	Asymmetry	Frequency	Asymmetry
a. *Experiment 2*					
PPI	1	1.16	0.00	4.41*	0.11
RPI	2	17.09***	15.43***	0.08	1.87
PPI x RPI	2	0.22	0.33	0.45	0.21
Residual	54				
b. *Experiment 3*					
APP	1	0.01	1.40	1.94	0.14
PI	1	13.09***	24.83***	0.42	1.10
APP x PI	1	2.37	0.00	0.15	0.94
Residual	36				
c. *Experiment 4*					
ARP	1	78.01***	26.71***	0.87	2.38
APP	1	0.48	0.38	0.21	0.97
DIR	1	1.32	3.93*	0.69	0.84
ARP x APP	1	1.45	0.01	8.01**	0.08
ARP x DIR	1	1.14	0.20	0.00	0.04
APP x DIR	1	0.09	3.26	0.16	0.28
ARP x APP x DIR	1	0.01	0.83	1.03	0.15
Residual	72				
d. *Experiment 5*					
RPI	1	0.08	11.02***	0.03	0.68
APP	1	6.49*	1.31	0.01	0.03
DIR	1	11.00***	0.42	1.91	0.63
RPI x APP	1	0.19	1.10	0.76	0.08
RPI x DIR	1	0.00	0.83	1.59	0.18
APP x DIR	1	0.65	0.13	7.59**	1.37
RPI x APP x DIR	1	0.78	2.95	0.32	0.01
Residual	72				

Note: PPI = punishment power imbalance, RPI = reward power imbalance, PI = power imbalance (both bases), APP = average punishment power, ARP = average reward power, DIR = power direction.
*p < .05   **p < .01   ***p < .001

Experiment 2: variations in punishment power imbalance

Two findings from Experiment 1 – the equal use of punishment by actors in different positions of power, and the tendency for punishment to decline after initial use – suggest that the partner's retaliation may have inhibited the use of more persistent and effective levels of punishment. As Lawler and Bacharach (1987) also found, actors typically reciprocated a partner's punishment even when punishment power was imbalanced. Although a partner who is weaker on punishment power cannot reciprocate with equal force, the equal probability of the partner's reciprocity may nevertheless have deterred the use of punishment under the moderate levels of power imbalance in that experiment.

If actors reciprocate punishment more frequently than they reciprocate reward withholding, then higher levels of punishment power imbalance may be required to produce the same effects on reward exchange as lower levels of reward power imbalance. Greater imbalance on punishment power should decrease the probability that actors weaker on punishment power will retaliate, and increase the use of punishment by the punishment-advantaged actor. If so, the effects of punishment power imbalance on the frequency and distribution of rewards in the relation should increase.

Design. The experimental design compared two levels of punishment power imbalance (.4 and .8) under three different structural conditions that varied its relation to reward power: balanced reward power, imbalanced reward power that reinforced punishment power imbalance, and imbalanced reward power that opposed punishment power imbalance (Table 5.3a). When reward power was imbalanced, it favored actor A; punishment power imbalance favored either A (reinforcing imbalances) or B (opposing imbalances).

Because two of the six structures required for this design were studied in Experiment 1 (those in which a punishment power imbalance of .4 was combined with either reward power balance or an opposing reward power imbalance of .4), only the additional four conditions were run to reduce costs. In all structures, average reward power and average punishment power were held constant at .6. The structural relations of the simulated actors to their real partners, and the probabilities of their programmed behavior, were identical to the values used in Experiment 1 (i.e., power imbalances of .2, and modified tit-for-tat strategies).

Results. Analyses of variance on the means for punishment frequency and punishment asymmetry in Table 5.4a provide partial support for the predicted effects of punishment power imbalance. The frequency of punishment does increase when punishment power imbalance is increased to .8, as predicted, although its absolute level is still quite low – the highest condition mean is only .06 (see Table 5.3a) – and punishment still declines over time ($F_{3,162} = 10.09$, $p < .001$). The effect of punishment imbalance on punishment frequency occurs under all three conditions of reward power.

The asymmetry of punishment does not increase, however, because *both* actors increase their punishment as imbalance increases. This finding supports Lawler's (1986) theory of bilateral deterrence, which predicts more frequent use of punishment by both actors as punishment power imbalance increases (see Chapter 3).[7] Thus, although a stronger power advantage reduces the cost of retaliation, it does not reduce its probability. As in Experiment 1, neither of the manipulated power variables affects punishment asymmetry.

Is the small increase in punishment by both actors, and the greater cost of punishment to the disadvantaged actor, enough to boost the effect of punishment power on reward exchange? Analyses of variance on reward frequency and reward asymmetry suggest not, showing no effect (main or interactive) of punishment power imbalance on either variable (Table 5.4a). As in Experiment 1, only reward power imbalance affects reward exchange. The nature of this effect is rather different from Experiment 1, however: actors were most likely to exchange rewards when reward power was balanced, as we would expect, but they were also more likely to exchange rewards when power imbalances on the two bases were opposing rather than reinforcing. In other words, punishment power imbalance increased mutual reward exchange when that outcome benefited the actor who was advantaged on punishment power.

Repeated-measures analyses of variance also indicate that under this condition of opposing power imbalances, a high (.8) punishment power imbalance has significant effects on reward exchange over time that do not show up in the analyses of overall frequencies. In this single condition, reward asymmetry *decreased* and reward frequency *increased* over time. In contrast, in each of the other three conditions in which both bases of

---

[7] Lawler (1986) argues that disadvantaged actors will also increase their use of punishment because they expect to be attacked. They use punishment to demonstrate that they cannot be intimidated or to communicate to their exchange partner that an attack will involve some retaliation costs. Lawler and Bacharach's (1987) research supports this analysis.

power were imbalanced, reward asymmetry *increased* and reward frequency did not change.

Implications. This experiment shows that, although actors are more likely to use punishment power when it is highly imbalanced, punishment power imbalance still fails to approximate the effects of reward power imbalance on reward exchange. The results do indicate that an opposing punishment power imbalance increases reward exchange in the relation, and they offer some indication that a punishment power advantage may, over time, increase the relative benefits of exchange for the power-advantaged actor if (1) punishment power is highly imbalanced, and (2) it opposes reward power imbalance.

In other respects, the findings mirror those of Experiment 1: the frequency of punishment is very low, its use declines over time, and actors punish each other with equal frequency, regardless of their relative power.

Experiment 3: variations in average punishment power

Experiment 3 tested whether the weak effects found for punishment power imbalance in Experiments 1 and 2 also extend to average punishment power. Those experiments held constant the average power in the relation, on both bases. Experiment 3 manipulated average punishment power and compared its effects on exchange under conditions of both balanced and imbalanced power.

Whereas power imbalance is expected to affect reward asymmetry, average power should affect reward frequency. Higher magnitudes of punishment power enable actors to impose greater losses on their partners, at no greater opportunity cost to themselves. This increases the average dependence of actors on each other (both are highly dependent on one another for *avoiding* aversive outcomes) and, by power-dependence principles, it should increase the average frequency of rewards in the relation, as actors reward each other more frequently to prevent the other's punishment.

Some theories, however, propose that the costs *to the punisher* of using punishment power also increase with the magnitude of harm inflicted, and thus inhibit its use. The discussion in Chapter 3 suggested that most of the negative reactions associated with the use of coercive power – retaliation, withdrawal from the relation, and so forth – are more likely to occur as the severity of punishment increases. It is this expectation of retaliation and fear of its associated costs that is the basis for deterrence theorists' predictions that the use of punishment will *decrease* as the mutual capacity for punishment increases (Lawler 1986). On the other hand, conflict spiral theorists, focusing instead on the greater potential gains of using punishment that delivers "more bang for the buck," predict that punishment frequency will *increase* as average punishment power increases. Because both theories (unlike power-dependence theory) predict a negative relation between the actual use of punishment and reward exchange, these predictions also imply that reward frequency should increase (bilateral deterrence) or decrease (conflict spiral) with average punishment power.

Design. Experiment 3 tested these alternative predictions with a 2 × 2 factorial design that crossed two levels of average punishment power (.3 and .9) with two levels of overall power imbalance (both reward and punishment power balanced, and both reward and punishment power imbalanced at .2 in favor of actor A). In all four conditions (see Table 5.3b), average reward power was held constant at .6. The structural relations of the simulated actors to their real partners, and the probabilities of their programmed behavior, were identical to the values used in Experiments 1 and 2 (i.e., structural power imbalances of .2 and modified tit-for-tat strategies).

Results. Analyses of variance on the mean values in Table 5.3b found no support for any of the predictions. As Table 5.4b shows, average punishment power affected none of the exchange outcomes. Power imbalance produced the usual effect of *reward* power imbalance; that is, reward frequency decreased and reward asymmetry increased when power was imbalanced. Punishment frequency and asymmetry were unaffected by either average punishment power or power imbalance. As in Experiments 1 and 2, actors rarely used punishment, and its frequency declined over time.

Results of a repeated-measures analysis of variance suggest that average punishment power does affect reward frequency over time, but only when power is imbalanced (the three-way interaction of average punishment power, power imbalance, and trial block on reward frequency is significant, $F_{3,108} = 3.35$, $p < .05$). In the imbalanced power conditions, reward frequency increased over time when average punishment power was high, but not when it was low. This effect is in the direction predicted by power-dependence theory, but – like the other effects observed – it is weak.

Implications. The results of this experiment show that the weak effects of punishment power imbalance also extend to average punishment power. Neither the relative nor the absolute magnitude of punishment power has any effect on the *overall* frequency or asymmetry of reward exchange. But under some conditions, very high levels of both tend to produce changes over time in the frequency and asymmetry of reward exchange, in the directions predicted by power-dependence theory.

The next two experiments explored whether the weak effects of punishment power observed in the first three experiments would hold under different conditions of reward dependence. They asked, in essence, whether the two bases of power interact in ways that were obscured in the first three experiments. In Experiments 4 and 5, dimensions of reward power that were held constant in the previous experiments – average reward power and the degree of reward power imbalance – were systematically varied.

Both experiments tested hypotheses proposing interactions between average punishment power and actors' reward dependence in their effects on punishment frequency. These hypotheses were suggested by Lawler's (1986) "conditionalization assumption," which proposes that the conflicting predictions of bilateral deterrence and conflict spiral theories may each hold under certain conditions. Lawler argues that conditions which enhance the relative salience of fear of retaliation should increase deterrence effects, whereas those that heighten the salience of the temptation to use punishment should increase conflict spiral effects. In short, the effects of average punishment power depend on other variables. Although Lawler's analysis stresses intervening cognitions, these cognitions are analogous to the potential costs (fear of retaliation) and potential gains (temptation) of using punishment power. In exchange relations, these costs and gains are influenced not only by punishment power imbalance, but by actors' reward dependence on each other.

Both experiments continued to study the effects of punishment power imbalance, as well. But rather than manipulating the amount of imbalance, they examined how reward power imbalance affects the use and effects of punishment power imbalance, by comparing structures in which an actor who was advantaged on punishment power imbalance was either advantaged or disadvantaged on reward power imbalance.

Experiments 4 and 5: interactions of punishment power with reward power

Because Experiments 4 and 5 are structurally very similar, it is convenient to discuss them together. Both experiments manipulated two of the same variables – average punishment power and the direction of power imbalances – but examined their effects under different conditions of reward power. Experiment 4 manipulated average reward power; Experiment 5 manipulated the degree of reward power imbalance.

Both average reward power and reward power imbalance affect the potential costs and benefits of using punishment power. Lawler's conditionalization principle suggests that deterrence effects should be more likely when potential costs are more salient, and conflict spiral effects when potential benefits are more salient.

As average reward power increases, both actors have more at stake in maintaining the relation. Therefore, the potential costs of using punishment increase relative to the gains (i.e., actors stand to lose more if punishment makes the partner withdraw from the relation). Consequently, when average reward power is high, the relation between average punishment power and punishment frequency should be negative (a deterrent effect). When average reward power is low, and the stakes are similarly low, the relation between average punishment power and punishment frequency should be positive (a conflict spiral effect).[8]

Increasing reward power imbalance, while holding average reward power constant, should have the opposite effect. Because it increases conflict in the relation, power imbalance typically reduces reward exchange.

---

[8] This analysis is contrary to Bacharach and Lawler's (1981) finding of a positive relation between punitive capability and the use of punishment when reward dependence is high, and a negative relation when reward dependence is low. They interpreted this finding as support for an orientation emphasizing the maximization of gain rather than the minimization of loss. Their study investigated the interaction between average reward and punishment power when power was balanced, however, and in a bargaining situation in which reward alternatives to the relation were hypothetical (i.e., reward power could not actually be exercised). Under these conditions, minimization of loss would be expected to be of lesser importance. When power is imbalanced, the actor with the greatest incentive to use punishment – the one who lacks reward power but has greater punishment power – should emphasize minimizing loss.

Consequently, the potential gains of using punishment power to coerce rewards increase, and the potential costs decrease. Thus, the relation between average punishment power and punishment frequency should be positive when reward power imbalance is high (a conflict spiral effect), and negative when reward power imbalance is low (a deterrence effect).

Design. In both experiments, a 2 × 2 × 2 factorial design manipulated three dimensions of structural power in the A–B relation: average punishment power (.35 or .65), the direction of power imbalances (reinforcing or opposing), and either average reward power or reward power imbalance. Experiment 4 manipulated average reward power (.35 or .65) while holding reward power imbalance constant at .5; Experiment 5 manipulated reward power imbalance (.3 or .7) while holding average reward power constant at .55. Both experiments held punishment power imbalance constant at .5 (see Table 5.3c,d).

In all conditions of both experiments, the relation between each real subject and the simulated partner was balanced on both reward power and punishment power, and the simulated actors responded with programmed strategies identical to those used in the previous experiments.

Results. The analysis of variance results for both experiments are summarized in Table 5.4c,d. Let us first examine the results for the analyses of punishment frequency and asymmetry.

In each experiment, an interaction between average punishment power and one of the other variables affects the frequency of punishment. In Experiment 4, the effect of average punishment power on punishment frequency depends on average reward power, as predicted; in Experiment 5, it depends on the direction of power imbalances – not on reward power imbalance, as predicted. Actors are more likely to use low rather than high magnitudes of punishment power (a deterrent effect) when average reward power is high, or when power imbalances are opposing. And they are more likely to use high rather than low magnitudes of punishment power (a conflict spiral effect) when average reward power is low, or when power imbalances are reinforcing.

To call any of these effects a "conflict spiral" is a bit of a misnomer, however. As in previous experiments, punishment frequency declined over time and its magnitude was low, even in conditions with the highest use of punishment.

Although the interaction between average punishment power and power direction was not predicted, it nevertheless supports the logic on which the predicted interactions were based: actors are more likely to use low rather than high magnitudes of punishment power (i.e., "less risky" power) when the structural basis for mutual reward exchange is stronger and the costs of retaliation are potentially greater. In Experiment 4, high average reward power provides that structural base; in Experiment 5, opposing power imbalances provide it. When balances are opposing, the interests of both actors in maintaining the relation are more equal: each is dependent on the other for either rewards or punishments and each can inflict more than trivial damage on the other. When power imbalances are reinforcing, or average reward power is low, either the advantaged actor or both actors risk little by using strong punishment power.

As in the previous experiments, none of the manipulations affected the asymmetry of punishment. For the first time, however, punishment asymmetry departed significantly from zero (see Table 5.3c,d). As the negative values for this variable indicate, the actor who was disadvantaged on reward power – B – punished more frequently than A, the advantaged actor, in both experiments. This relation held regardless of B's punishment power.[9]

These two experiments produced somewhat higher frequencies of punishment than the previous experiments, at least in some conditions. Did increased use of punishment power affect the impact of dimensions of punishment power (average punishment power, and whether punishment power imbalance reinforced or opposed reward power imbalance) on reward exchange? To some extent, it did, although the interactions that affect punishment frequency do not affect reward exchange. Both experiments show an effect of power direction on reward exchange, and Experiment 5 shows an effect of average punishment power. The direction of all three effects is consistent with power-dependence predictions. In Experiment 5, reward frequency was higher when average punishment power was higher and when power imbalances were opposing rather than reinforcing. In Experiment 4, reward asymmetry was lower when B had an opposing punishment power advantage than when both power imbal-

---

[9] I obtained this result by conducting a repeated-measures analysis of variance on punishment frequency for the individual actors, treating the actor (A or B) as a within-group factor. The effect of actor was significant in both experiments (in Experiment 4, $F_{1,72}$ for actor = 5.06, p < .05; in Experiment 5, $F_{1,72}$ for actor = 13.57, p < .001).

ances favored A, although reward asymmetry still favored A in both conditions (see Table 5.3c).

The results for reward frequency help to explain why the direction of power imbalances, and not reward power imbalance per se, interacted with average punishment power in its effects on punishment frequency. While reward power imbalance failed to have the expected negative effect on reward frequency, the direction of power imbalances did: reward frequency was lower when imbalances were reinforcing. This finding suggests that reinforcing imbalances on the two power bases created more conflict than highly imbalanced reward power.

Implications. These experiments produced the strongest effects so far of dimensions of punishment power on reward exchange. All of the effects are consistent with power-dependence theory, but their occurrence across experiments is rather inconsistent. Both experiments manipulated average punishment power, but only Experiment 5 found an effect of average punishment power on reward frequency. Both experiments manipulated the direction of power imbalances, but this variable affected reward asymmetry in Experiment 4 and reward frequency in Experiment 5. All three findings support the tentative effects of average punishment power on reward frequency in Experiment 3, and of power direction on *both* reward frequency and asymmetry in Experiment 2.

The results support Lawler's conditionalization principle and, more generally, support the principle that the use of punishment is influenced by the potential gains and losses for the punisher. They also imply a considerable degree of interdependence between the two bases of power – or, at least, an influence of reward power on the use and effects of punishment power. Not only do the effects of average punishment power depend on the structure of reward power, but actors who were disadvantaged on reward power punished more frequently *regardless* of punishment power, and the direction of power imbalances on both bases had a stronger effect on reward exchange than punishment power imbalance alone did, in Experiment 2.

Summary of the structural analyses

Four main conclusions emerge from these five experiments.

First, across a wide range of variations in dimensions of both reward power and punishment power, the effects of punishment power fail to

THE EARLY RESEARCH   125

equal or even approximate the effects of comparable dimensions of reward power. Most analyses show no effects of punishment power on either the frequency or the asymmetry of reward exchange. The few effects that do appear are substantially weaker than the comparable effects of reward power. Although an opposing punishment power imbalance sometimes reduces reward asymmetry, for example, it never eliminates it or reverses its direction in favor of the actor who is advantaged on punishment power.

Second, despite the persistent weakness of punishment power, the cumulative pattern of findings suggests that the effect of punishment power on reward exchange – when one occurs – is positive. Reward exchange either increases with average punishment power or is unaffected by it. Imbalanced punishment power either benefits the punishment-advantaged actor or has no effect on reward exchange. The experiments provide no support for the negative effects of punishment power on reward exchange that Homans, and other theorists discussed in Chapter 3, proposed.

Third, the findings also fail to support the predictions of some theories that the use of punishment leads to escalating cycles of conflict. In all of the experiments, punishment declined rather than increased over time. One of the most surprising and consistent findings of the experiments is the extremely low use of punishment. Even those structural variables that significantly increased the use of punishment did so within a small range (e.g., increasing punishment from .02 to .06).

Fourth, as with reward exchange, variations in the use of punishment nevertheless fit a pattern that is consistent with the central assumptions of social exchange theory: punishment was used more frequently under structural conditions that increased the potential gains of using punishment power and decreased the potential losses. Thus, punishment increased with punishment power imbalance and with reward power disadvantage, and actors used riskier – but more potent – magnitudes of punishment when mutual dependence was lower or relational conflict was greater. The one exception to this pattern is the consistent tendency for actors in unequal positions of punishment power to use punishment equally often.

Throughout this analysis, I have implicitly assumed that the low use of punishment power is one cause of its weak effects; that is, if actors would only use this base of power more often, it would be more effective. But as we saw in Chapter 3, that assumption is controversial. Numerous theories take the opposite position, that while the *potential* power to punish is sometimes beneficial, the actual *use* of punishment never is.

In reality, of course, the mere frequency of punishment tells us little about its potential effectiveness. Psychological studies of punishment suggest that effective punishment must be consistent, contingent, and directed toward behaviors that the actor wants to reduce. Although frequency may be related to effectiveness, in the sense that consistency probably requires some less-than-minimal frequency of punishment, it tells us nothing about the contingency of punishment or the behaviors on which it is contingent. That information requires a sequential analysis of the dynamic process of exchange – an analysis that examines how actors respond to each other's behaviors over the course of a continuing exchange relation.

The analysis of process: exchange strategies

In exchange relations, punishment can be used contingently or noncontingently. Random or noncontingent punishment is likely to do little but provoke animosity. Contingent punishment – punishment that is contingent on specific actions of an exchange partner – can be used for two different purposes: retaliation or coercion. *Retaliatory punishment* is punishment that is contingent on a partner's prior punishment; *coercive punishment* is punishment that is contingent on a partner's failure to reward. Both forms of punishment represent strategies for decreasing a partner's undesirable behaviors – punishment or failure to reward – but only coercive punishment is also intended to increase the partner's reward exchange.

The low levels of punishment asymmetry in all of the experiments suggest that punishment was frequently retaliated; that assumption, however, is based on comparisons of actors' overall frequencies of punishment, not on an analysis of sequential response probabilities. Equal frequencies might be produced by retaliation, or by equal frequencies of coercive (or even noncontingent) punishment.

Examining how actors use punishment requires analyzing the conditional relations between sequential behaviors of the two actors in a relation. To the extent that A's punishment increases with B's prior punishment, A's use of punishment is retaliatory. And, conversely, to the extent that A's punishment increases with B's prior nonexchange (i.e., neither rewarding nor punishing A), A's use of punishment is coercive.[10]

[10] The third possibility – that A's punishment increases with B's rewarding – is both

I used a combined set of data from all five experiments to answer four questions about actors' strategies of punishment. First, how did actors use punishment? Was retaliatory or coercive punishment more common, overall? Second, what structural conditions encouraged or constrained the use of retaliatory and coercive punishment? Third, what effects did the relative frequency of retaliatory and coercive punishment have on exchange outcomes, net of structural power? Fourth, how do the causes and consequences of retaliatory and coercive punishment compare with the causes and consequences of comparable reward strategies – that is, reciprocal rewarding or reward withholding?

Method

The data set consisted of 290 cases (29 experimental conditions, with 10 networks per condition).[11] In each of these cases, the exchange relation between A and B produced 250 sequentially ordered behaviors for each actor. Each of these behaviors fit one of three categories: A (or B) rewarded, punished, or did not act toward the partner.

To determine how much each actor's use of punishment was influenced by the other actor's immediately prior punishment (retaliatory punishment) or immediately prior nonexchange (coercive punishment), I conducted four logistic regression analyses for *each* dyadic exchange relation.[12] Each actor's use of punishment at time $t + 1$ was regressed on either the other actor's nonexchange or the other actor's punishment at time t, while controlling for the actor's own behavior at time t.[13] The estimated logistic coefficient for the lagged dependence of one actor's behavior on the other's provides an index of the contingency of that actor's behavior on the

---

theoretically implausible and empirically false; B's prior rewarding decreased the probability of A's punishment.

[11] As noted earlier, Experiment 1 studied 12 networks per condition. So that the conditions in all experiments would be represented by equal N's, only the first 10 networks run in each condition of that experiment were included in this data set.

[12] In preliminary analyses I examined relations between two actors' behaviors for up to five lags. The effect of one actor's behavior on another's was rarely significant for more than one lag, however; therefore, the analyses I report here examine only how one actor's behavior is affected by the other actor's immediately prior behavior.

[13] I transformed the behavioral variables into dichotomous variables for each analysis. Of the three categories of behavior (rewarding, punishing, and not acting or nonexchange), the category of interest was coded "1" and the remaining categories were coded "0."

other's behavior (Allison and Liker 1982).[14] A positive coefficient indicates that one actor's prior punishment or nonexchange *increased* the likelihood of the other actor's punishment; a negative coefficient indicates a decrease in likelihood.

These regressions produced two measures of the contingency of punishment for each actor in the A–B relation: the contingency of that actor's punishment on the other's prior nonexchange (coercive punishment) and the contingency of that actor's punishment on the other's prior punishment (retaliatory punishment).[15] I then created two dyadic measures from each set of measures for the individual actors, producing four measures of contingent punishment in the relation: the average and asymmetry of retaliatory punishment, and the average and asymmetry of coercive punishment. The average measures were computed by averaging the individual measures for A and B; the asymmetry measures by subtracting the contingency of A's behavior on B's behavior from that of B's behavior on A's behavior. Thus, a positive measure of asymmetry indicates that A – the advantaged actor in all reward-imbalanced relations – influenced B's behavior more than the reverse, whereas a negative measure indicates a stronger effect of B's behavior on A's subsequent response.

So that these punishment strategies could be compared with contingent reward strategies, I created comparable measures for the use of rewards: the contingency of rewarding on the other actor's prior rewarding (reciprocal rewards), and the contingency of nonexchange on the other actor's prior rewarding (reward withholding). High values on measures of either reciprocal rewarding or reciprocal (retaliatory) punishing indicate a tendency toward reciprocity in exchange, or "tit-for-tat" strategies. Both reward withholding and coercive punishment, on the other hand, are power strategies; they represent the use of reward or punishment power to increase the actor's exchange advantage, by lowering costs or increasing rewards.

---

[14] This coefficient, which is the natural logarithm of the odds ratio, has a range of minus infinity to plus infinity. It is zero when the two actors' behaviors are statistically independent. Allison and Liker (1982) recommend using the coefficient of a logistic analysis as an index of contingency primarily because it is insensitive to the distribution of marginal totals. Thus, the variation across dyads and across behavioral categories in the number of observations does not affect the measure of contingencies between behaviors.

[15] Because subjects rarely used punishment, the coefficient estimates in some of the analyses were based on too few observations to be reliable. To give greater weight in the analysis to the more reliable estimates, I divided the logistic coefficients by their standard errors. The resulting measures are equivalent to the t-ratios for the coefficients.

Table 5.5. *Mean values for exchange strategies, Experiments 1–5*

| Strategies[a] | Relational measures | |
	Average[b]	Asymmetry[c]
Reward strategies		
Reciprocal rewarding (R|R)	3.06	1.13
Reward withholding (N|R)	-2.43	-1.02
Punishment strategies		
Retaliatory punishment (P|P)	1.12	-0.12
Coercive punishment (P|N)	0.21	-0.03

[a](i\|j) = the contingency of one actor's behavior i at time t + 1 on the occurrence of the second actor's behavior j at time t, where i and j = R (reward), N (nonexchange), and P (punishment).
[b][(A's i\|j) + (B's i\|j)]/2.
[c](B's i\|j) – (A's i\|j).

These strategy measures then served as dependent or independent variables in subsequent analyses of the effects of structure on strategy, and strategy on exchange outcomes.

Results

Use of contingent punishment. Table 5.5 shows the mean values of the relational measures for the four exchange strategies: reciprocal rewarding (R\|R), reward withholding (N\|R), retaliatory punishment (P\|P), and coercive punishment (P\|N).

As the average strategy values indicate, actors were much more likely to respond reciprocally to either rewards or punishments than to engage in either of the nonreciprocal power strategies (reward withholding or coercive punishment). Although the means for both the retaliatory and coercive punishment strategies are positive, indicating that both punishment and nonexchange tended to increase rather than decrease the likelihood of a partner's punishment, retaliatory punishment was clearly more probable. The asymmetries of both retaliatory and coercive punishment are very low; A (the power-advantaged actor) was slightly more likely to punish in retaliation; both actors were equally likely to coerce. (Remember, though, that because A is more likely to provide the occasion for coercion – by not rewarding B – B's *frequency* of coercion will be higher than A's.)

The asymmetry values for the reward strategies show that B was more likely than A to reciprocate rewards, and A was more likely to withhold rewards, patterns that are consistent with the respective power positions of both actors (i.e., A was the advantaged actor in all reward-imbalanced structures, which comprise 24 of the 29 conditions). The strong negative value for reward withholding indicates that actors were unlikely, on the average, to respond to a partner's rewards with nonexchange. This finding is not surprising; certainly, an actor who is disadvantaged on reward power is unlikely to respond with nonexchange, and even an advantaged actor would be expected to reciprocate rewards part of the time.

Effects of structure on strategies. To estimate the effects of structural power on the strategies in Table 5.5, I used ordinary least-squares regression. Analyses regressed each of the eight strategy measures on the actual ratio values of the structural power variables. Because punishment power imbalance sometimes favored A (when reward power was balanced or power imbalances were reinforcing) and sometimes favored B (when power imbalances were opposing), I created two separate variables: punishment power imbalance favoring A and punishment power imbalance favoring B. Each variable was zero when punishment power did not favor the designated actor, and took the value of punishment power imbalance in the relation when it did.

The results of the regressions for the *reward* strategies show a single structural determinant: reward power imbalance (Table 5.6). As reward power imbalance increases, average reward reciprocity decreases, average reward withholding increases, and the asymmetry of reciprocity – the likelihood that B will reciprocate rewards more often than A – increases. The asymmetry of reward withholding is not affected (remember, however, that it favors A overall).

The results for the *punishment* strategies are markedly different. First, none of the structural power variables has any effect on retaliatory punishment. Second, *both* reward power and punishment power affect the use of coercive punishment, and the effects of reward power are stronger than the effects of punishment power.

The likelihood of using coercive punishment increases primarily with an actor's reward dependence. When average reward dependence in-

Table 5.6. *Unstandardized coefficients for regressions of exchange strategies on structural power, Experiments 1–5 (N = 290)*

| Structural power | Reward strategies | | | | Punishment strategies | | | |
| | Reciprocal | | Withholding | | Retaliatory | | Coercive | |
	Avg	Asym	Avg	Asym	Avg	Asym	Avg	Asym
ARP	1.17	1.29	0.08	0.03	0.21	0.18	2.48***	1.73
APP	0.07	0.86	-0.63	-2.10	0.58	0.01	-0.01	-0.46
RPI	-2.25***	3.44***	2.55***	-1.32	-0.61	-0.19	-0.44	1.54**
PPI-A	-0.02	0.26	0.54	-1.09	0.30	0.00	0.63*	-1.13*
PPI-B	0.53	-0.67	0.09	0.08	0.58	1.10	0.89**	-0.65
F-ratio	5.00***	3.01**	7.73***	1.56	0.86	1.42	5.68***	2.44*

Note: ARP = average reward power, APP = average punishment power, RPI = reward power imbalance, PPI-A = punishment power imbalance favoring A, PPI-B = punishment power imbalance favoring B. Multiplicative interaction terms are omitted because none is significant.
*p < .05   **p < .01   ***p < .001

creases, both actors are more likely to use coercive punishment (as indicated by the significant effect of average reward power on the average coercion in the relation), and as reward power imbalance increases, the more dependent partner, B, is more likely to use coercion than the less dependent partner, A (as indicated by the significant effect of reward power imbalance on the asymmetry of coercion in the relation). Reward dependence increases the extent to which an actor benefits from the other's rewards and is hurt by the other's failure to reward; consequently, it provides a strong incentive to use coercion. Punishment power also influences coercion, but to a lesser degree. Both actors are more likely to use coercion when they are advantaged on punishment power and less likely to be hurt by retaliatory punishment. However, B's punishment power advantage also increases A's tendency to use coercion, and consequently punishment power imbalance has a significant effect on the asymmetry of coercion only when it favors A (the negative value indicates that A is more likely to use coercion than B when A is advantaged on punishment power).

With the exception of that one finding, the implications of these results are clear: actors are more likely to use coercive punishment when they have more to gain from the other's increased reward exchange (reward dependence is high) and less to lose from the other's retaliatory punishment (punishment power is imbalanced in their favor), predictions that are consistent with the assumptions of power-dependence theory.

The absence of any effect of structural power on retaliatory punishment supports several theories that argue that retaliation is affected more by cognitive or emotional considerations (such as saving face or appearing tough) than by structure (see, e.g., Bacharach and Lawler 1981; Rubin and Brown 1975). Retaliation is more common than coercion, but actors tend to retaliate regardless of their absolute or relative power. These findings help to explain the weak effects of structural power on punishment frequency: the more typical use of punishment, retaliation, is unaffected by structural power. The effects of structure that we observed were primarily effects on coercive punishment.

In the earlier analyses of punishment frequency, average punishment power interacted with dimensions of reward power. Average reward power and opposing power imbalances increased punishment frequency when average punishment power was low. Those interactions are not significant for punishment strategies. Nevertheless, the main effects of average reward power and opposing power imbalances on coercive strategies suggest that the earlier interactions were primarily effects on coercion, too.

Effects of strategies on reward exchange. Finally, to examine how these strategies affect reward exchange, I conducted separate regression analyses on the two measures of reward exchange, reward frequency and reward asymmetry. These regressions estimated the effects of the four exchange strategies and punishment frequency after entering the five structural power variables in the equation. To reduce the number of variables in each equation, the regressions of reward frequency included only the average measures of strategy (plus punishment frequency), and the regressions of reward asymmetry included only the asymmetry measures of strategy.[16]

The results, summarized in Table 5.7, are very clear: net of structure, both retaliatory punishment and coercive punishment affect both reward frequency and reward asymmetry, whereas reward strategies have no ef-

---

[16] I also conducted analyses that included both average and asymmetry measures. The results indicated that only average strategy and frequency measures affected average reward exchange, and only asymmetry measures affected reward asymmetry.

Table 5.7. *Unstandardized coefficients for regressions of reward exchange on exchange strategies and punishment frequency, Experiments 1–5 (N = 290)*

Predictors[a]	Reward frequency	Reward asymmetry
Exchange strategies		
Reciprocal rewarding (R|R)	0.00	-0.00
Reward withholding (N|R)	-0.01	-0.01
Retaliatory punishment (P|P)	0.02*	-0.02***
Coercive punishment (N|P)	0.06***	-0.01*
Punishment frequency	-1.00***	0.15
F change	9.21***	8.61***

Note: Coefficients estimated after controlling for structural power variables (average reward power, average punishment power, reward power imbalance, punishment power imbalance favoring A, punishment power imbalance favoring B).

[a]Reward frequency is regressed on the average strategy and punishment frequency measures; reward asymmetry is regressed on the strategy asymmetry and punishment asymmetry measures.

*p < .05   **p < .01   ***p < .001

fect. Reward frequency increases with the use of both retaliatory and coercive punishment, and reward asymmetry increases in favor of the actor who uses these punishment strategies more frequently. The positive effect of retaliatory punishment is interesting; rather than leading to escalating aggression, it appears that retaliatory punishment is an important element of strategies designed to decrease other actors' nonexchange *and* punishment, and to increase their reward exchange.

Whereas the contingency of punishment increases reward frequency, the frequency of punishment has a negative effect: the more frequently exchange partners punish each other, the less likely they are to reward each other. This finding requires some clarification, however, because punishment frequency is *positively* correlated with punishment strategies (r = .30 for coercive punishment, and .41 for retaliatory punishment, p < .01). Strong and consistent contingencies of punishment obviously require actors to use punishment with some frequency. What this finding indicates is that punishment has a positive effect on reward exchange only if it is used contingently, to punish undesirable behaviors. With contingency controlled, the effect of punishment frequency is negative. (Punishment asymmetry has no effect on reward asymmetry – hardly surprising in view of its low variance.)

Implications

Several important findings emerge from the analyses of exchange process. First, the use of contingent influence strategies is clearly more important for punishment power than for reward power. Reward strategies appear to act primarily as intervening variables between reward power imbalance and power use; with reward power imbalance controlled, their effects disappear. But punishment strategies have significant and positive effects on reward exchange even after controlling for structural power.

Second, while reward strategies are influenced only by reward power, the analogous link between punishment power and punishment strategies is weak at best. Coercive punishment is influenced as much by reward dependence as by punishment power, and retaliatory punishment – the more common use of punishment – is not influenced by structure at all.

Together, these findings suggest two important conclusions: (1) *how actors use punishment power is more important than how much power they have*, and (2) *we cannot predict the former from the latter*. It is not surprising, then, that punishment power has so little effect on reward exchange, or even on the use of punishment, in these experiments. Nor is it surprising that increased use of punishment does not always increase reward frequency: it is the contingency of punishment, not its frequency per se, that influences reward exchange.

Conclusions

The combined findings of the analyses of exchange outcome and exchange process suggest that reward power and punishment power do not operate on behavior in similar ways, despite their comparable structures. Understanding why, and analyzing the implications for exchange theory, is the task that occupies the remainder of the book.

Six of the central findings of the research in this chapter are critical to the theory that I develop in the next four chapters. First, the most basic finding – that structures of reward power and punishment power have effects on reward exchange that are similar in direction but vastly different in magnitude – provides the puzzle to be solved. The second finding, the very low use of punishment across varying structural conditions, forms the proximate or immediate cause of the weak effects of punishment power: I argue that power of any base must be used more often to be effective. The third and fourth findings – that both the frequency and the contingency of punishment are influenced as much by reward dependence as by punishment power, and that these effects are related to the potential costs and benefits of punishment for the user – become key insights for explaining why punishment power is used so rarely. And the fifth finding, that contingent punishment can be an effective tool for increasing reward exchange and shifting the asymmetry of reward exchange in an actor's favor, is the basis for the final argument: that far from being ineffective, coercive power – when it is used – works extremely well.

6. The structural determination of power use

This chapter begins to build and test a theory that explains why reward power and punishment power have such different effects on social exchange. Its focus is one of the most consistent and surprising findings of the previous experiments: the infrequent use of coercion by actors in all structural positions. I assume that the low use of coercion is the *immediate* cause of the weak effects of punishment power; to explain those effects, we must first explain why actors use coercion so rarely. Chapters 6 through 8 address that question. In this chapter, I consider when and how power use is induced by the structure of power alone; in Chapters 7 and 8, I examine factors that affect strategic power use.

The assumption that structural power is effective only if it is used is consistent with exchange theory; the suggestion that power use is problematic is not. Emerson assumed that if actors possessed a structural power advantage, they would use it. The incentive to use power was inherent in power itself. This chapter shows that this principle holds only for reward power and explains why.

I argue that the coercive use of punishment power, unlike the use of reward power, is not induced by a structural power advantage. This is the *primary* reason that it is used less frequently. I show that when this difference between reward and punishment power is eliminated, by creating experimental conditions in which a structural advantage on either base of power *does* induce the use of that power, the hypothesis of structural equivalency is supported: the two bases of power have equivalent effects on the distribution of exchange.

Using power: reward and punishment power compared

As we saw in Chapter 3, the use of either base of power imposes costs on the exchange partner. When actors use reward power, they deprive the partner of potential rewards; when they use punishment power, they administer actual losses. While the immediate costs imposed by the two forms of power are different, the mechanisms through which they affect behavior are similar: if successful, the use of either base of power by an advantaged actor induces the disadvantaged partner to accept higher opportunity costs (i.e., to give more frequently to the partner, thus forgoing potential rewards from other relations), in exchange for either rewards or the cessation of punishment.

Despite the similarity in the ways that reward and punishment power affect the *target* of power use, they represent different mechanisms for increasing the exchange advantage of the *power user*. The use of reward power *decreases the opportunity costs* of exchange for the actor using it; the coercive use of punishment power *increases the actor's rewards*. This contrast results from two factors – the use of punishment to coerce, and the distinction between reward withholding as an act of omission and punishment as an act of commission – and it affects the relation between structural power and the incentive to use power.

When A uses reward power in a relation of reciprocal exchange with B, the primary and immediate advantage for A is reduced opportunity costs. By reciprocating B's rewarding only intermittently, A obtains the advantages of B's exchange at lower cost. In operant terms, A has B on an intermittent reward schedule; in economic terms, A pays less for the benefits obtained from B. A's use of reward power may also increase the rewards A receives (if withholding rewards from B makes B give more frequently to A) *but A will benefit from using power even if B's rewarding remains the same.* If A can lower his costs while maintaining B's rewards, A's net benefits will increase.

The primary advantage of the coercive use of punishment power, in contrast, is an increase in rewards for the coercer. A coerces B to give rewards to A that B would otherwise not provide. In return for these potential gains, the coercer incurs opportunity costs (and, as I discuss in the next chapter, the potential for retaliatory costs as well). Punishment is not an act of omission, like reward withholding; it requires time, resources, or both.[1] Time spent rebuking an employee or sabotaging a factory is time

---

[1] This statement is not true, of course, if punishment takes the form of a reduction in expected rewards (i.e., if regularly given rewards are withheld as punishment). My analysis here applies to the coercive use of punishment power, not to the coercive use of reward

that might otherwise have been spent in productive pursuits; resources spent on armies and wars are resources that might have been spent on economic development and social services. Thus, the relative emphasis on increasing rewards or decreasing costs is exactly the opposite of reward power: coercion compels the exchange partner to provide more benefits; if that coercion also reduces costs (by deterring the other's punishment), that is an added benefit. But more typically, the coercer pays a price for the rewards obtained.

Although the distinction between reducing costs and increasing gains may seem trivial (both achieve the objective of boosting net benefits – rewards minus costs – for the actor), its implications for predicting when actors will *use* power are important. The benefits that these two forms of power use provide are likely to be valued by actors who occupy different positions of reward power.

Because the primary advantage of using reward power (by withholding rewards) is a reduction in opportunity costs, it is actors whose reward dependence on the partner is *low* and who are *advantaged* on reward power who will benefit most from using it. For a power-advantaged actor, an increase in rewards from the partner (which are either valued less, or available elsewhere) is less valuable than a decrease in opportunity costs, which allows the advantaged actor to pursue exchange with other partners. Consider, for instance, Homans's ([1961] 1974) classic example of the exchange of advice and approval between a senior, experienced worker and a new junior employee. The costs of giving advice are high for the experienced worker; his time is more valuable, and he can get approval elsewhere. Hence, he primarily benefits from the exchange if his costs are low – that is, if he can secure the junior worker's approval and deference for only occasional advice.

Coercive power, on the other hand, is more likely to be used by an actor whose opportunity costs are low (i.e., the actor's alternatives are less valuable), against a partner who controls rewards of high value but fails to provide them. These conditions describe the position of an actor whose reward dependence is *high* and who is *disadvantaged* on reward power, like the junior worker in our example. Thus, if the junior worker fails to

---

power (see Chapter 3 for a discussion of this issue). I assume that either adding negative outcomes or removing positive outcomes requires action and incurs opportunity costs.

secure the senior's advice by offering approval, he might resort to coercive tactics (perhaps by making a pest of himself with daily visits), until the senior worker takes time to help him.[2]

What this analysis implies is that the advantage of using *either* reward power or coercive power depends on the structure of *reward* power, not the structure of coercive power. As power-dependence theory predicts, reward power should be used by actors who are *advantaged* on reward power. And actors who should benefit the most from the use of coercion are those who are *disadvantaged* on reward power – that is, actors who lack the reward power to secure the exchange of those on whom they are highly dependent.

We saw some support for this assertion in Chapter 5; reward power had more impact than punishment power on the use of coercive strategies. Both average reward dependence and reward power disadvantage increased the use of coercion. In addition, numerous studies, both experimental and nonexperimental, show that actors who are weak on reward power are more likely to use coercive tactics (e.g., Kanter 1977; Patterson 1982; Raush et al. 1974). Whereas legitimated, institutionalized forms of punishment are typically used by powerful actors such as the state, noninstitutionalized forms of coercion are more common among actors who lack other means of influencing those on whom they are most dependent for rewards. Children whine to attract attention, low-level managers become bossy and critical, and rebel factions adopt terrorist techniques.

In short, while a structural advantage on reward power provides the incentive to use that power, a structural advantage on punishment power does not. The incentive to coerce derives, instead, from dependence on another for rewards. This important difference between reward and punishment power will influence my analysis of power use for the next several chapters. Here, I consider its implications for one of power-dependence theory's most fundamental tenets.

---

[2] Oliver (1980) makes a similar point, but for different reasons, in her analysis of rewards and punishments as selective incentives for collective action. As she notes, "positive and negative incentives are radically different in the view of the person who *uses* them, even though they are the same to the persons *receiving* them" (1980:1361). Oliver's distinction stems from the fact that positive incentives are given to the k who cooperate, while negative incentives are given to the n-k who do not cooperate. Thus, the cost of providing a standard private good is an increasing function of k for a reward, but a decreasing function of k for a punishment.

"To have power is to use it":
Emerson's structural determinism

Emerson argued that as long as actors meet the assumption of behaving in ways that increase rewards and decrease costs, the incentive to use power is inherent in the structural potential for power. In his words, "to have a power advantage is to use it" (1972b:67). No intent to use power or to influence another's behavior is necessary; the same structural conditions that provide actors with the *capacity* to use power also provide the *incentive* to use power, whether knowingly or not. It is for this reason that Emerson did not distinguish between *using power* as a dynamic process, and *power use* as an outcome of structural imbalance (i.e., the asymmetrical distribution of exchange that results). He argued, in effect, that power use is an unintended by-product of actors seeking their own self-interest in structurally imbalanced relations; therefore, a separate concept of actors voluntarily "using" power to influence others was unnecessary.[3]

Demonstrating that power use need not be volitional was one of the first objectives of Emerson and Cook's research program (e.g., Cook and Emerson 1978; Cook et al. 1983). Their experiments on negotiated exchange showed that imbalanced structures produce the predicted effects on power use even when subjects are unaware of the power structure and are informed only of their own benefits. Subjects in more powerful positions obtain more benefits from exchange agreements than subjects in less powerful positions.

This effect of structural power rests on the assumption that actors follow the basic behavioral principles introduced in Chapter 2, by (1) initiating reward exchange with other actors who control resources they value, (2) increasing exchange patterns that are more rewarding and decreasing those that are less rewarding, and (3) changing behavior when rewards decline.[4]

---

[3] This idea is similar, of course, to Adam Smith's principle that an individual, seeking only his own gain, is "led by an invisible hand to promote an end which was no part of his intention." ([1776] 1937:423). But when this process occurs in a power-imbalanced network, it produces inequality in costs and benefits rather than the social optimum that presumably results from a perfectly competitive market.

[4] A modified version of these principles applies to negotiated exchanges. As Cook et al. state: "In our experimental setting, by 'rational' we mean that each actor in the network explores alternative sources of benefit in the network (a) through extending offers to others and (b) by comparing offers and counteroffers from others. Each actor maximizes benefit by (a) accepting the better of any two offers, (b) lowering offers when offers go unaccepted, and (c) holding out for better offers when it is possible to do so" (1983:286, n. 12).

These principles assume only that actors respond, consciously or not, to the consequences of their own behaviors. Actors need not be aware of their power over others, or make any conscious effort to influence others.

When actors in structurally imbalanced relations follow these principles, their interaction will produce the distribution of exchange predicted by power-dependence theory – an asymmetry in exchange that favors the less dependent actors. This "power use" will occur without the aid of purposive influence strategies, and often without any awareness that cost is being imposed on the partner.

To illustrate, consider the exchange network in Figure 6.1a, in which all actors have only reward power over each other. Actors A and C are power-advantaged in their respective relations with B and D (they are less dependent on them for rewards within the network), but equal in power to each other. Power-dependence theory predicts that the structural imbalance in the A–B and C–D relations will produce asymmetrical exchange, with B rewarding A (and D rewarding C) more frequently than A (or C) reciprocates. In the A–C and B–D relations, exchange should be equal, but more frequent in the A–C relation than in the B–D relation because average power is greater in the A–C relation.

In the absence of information about the power structure, actors should initially explore exchanges with all available partners. Because some exchanges will be more rewarding than others, actors will begin to differentiate among partners: A and C will increase the frequency of exchange with each other and decrease exchange with B and D. B and D, however, will increase the frequency with which they reward A and C, their more valued exchange partners, and decrease the frequency with which they exchange with each other. This pattern will produce the expected asymmetry in A and C's favor. It will be maintained if A and C reciprocate B and D's rewarding often enough to make this pattern more valuable to B and D than exchange with each other. If they do not, B and D will decrease the frequency of their rewards to A and C. If that occurs, however, the decline in A and C's rewards will prompt a change in their behavior and some action toward B and D. In time, the distribution of exchange in the network will stabilize, and it will stabilize on a pattern that supports the predictions of power-dependence theory. Exchange in the A–B and C–D relations will be more profitable for both actors than turning exclusively to their alternative partners, but it will be asymmetrical: B and D will reward A and C more frequently than A and C reciprocate.

Networks with a single power base
(power imbalance favors A and C)

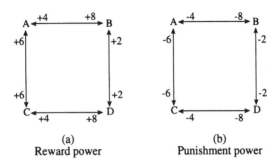

(a)
Reward power

(b)
Punishment power

Networks with both reward and punishment power
(punishment power imbalance favors A and C)

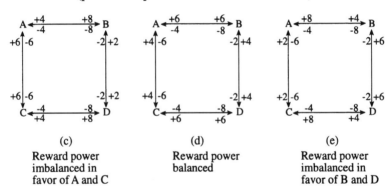

(c)
Reward power
imbalanced in
favor of A and C

(d)
Reward power
balanced

(e)
Reward power
imbalanced in
favor of B and D

Figure 6.1. Five exchange networks

In this interaction, actors are "using power" whenever they withhold rewards from another. Because B and D lose more from A and C's reward withholding than A and C lose from B and D's reward withholding, A and C have a structural advantage in the use of power. They incur lower costs than they impose. As a result, they are able to induce their partners to pay more (in opportunity costs) for their rewards. But these actors are not withholding rewards strategically, to influence the other's behavior. A and C's withholding of rewards from B and D is an *unintended by-product* of their preference for exchange with each other, produced by the structure of dependence.[5] In the same way, a business that favors one supplier may do so without any intent of decreasing another supplier's price for the same product, and a person who spends time with one friend may do so without any intent of acquiring another friend's favors at lower cost – but, nevertheless, their actions will have those effects if they are structurally advantaged in the relations.

The strategic use of power

Emerson's analysis did not rule out the strategic use of power, however. He argued only that it was unnecessary. Because structure – not intent – determines power use, he believed the end result would be much the same regardless of whether power use was structurally induced or strategically enacted.

To understand his logic, let us consider how, in the structure in Figure 6.1a, the two actors in the A–B relation might use their power resources *strategically* to improve their outcomes from the exchange. (I consider only the single relation to simplify the discussion.) Each can do so by selectively giving or withholding rewards for the other, contingent on the other's prior behavior. Their relative power positions determine the best outcomes they can hope to obtain, however, and the optimum strategies for achieving those outcomes.

Because A is power-advantaged in the relation, A should *never* reward B's failure to reward A and should only *intermittently* reciprocate B's rewards to A. The greater an actor's power advantage, the more intermittent the reciprocity can be. In the structure in Figure 6.1a, A must reward B every fourth time that B rewards A in order to provide the same value for B that B could receive by ignoring A and exchanging only with D (i.e., $\frac{1}{4} \times 8 = 2$, the value of B's rewards from D). Realistically, A

---

[5] The same logic applies if imbalanced power is created by varying the availability of alternatives rather than value. Assume, for example, that A has access to exchange with B and C, but B and C have access only to A (i.e., B–A–C), and all actors control resources of equal value. In the absence of information about the power structure, A will initiate exchange with *both* B and C, while B and C initiate exchange only with A. Whenever A exchanges with one partner, A necessarily – but inadvertently – withholds rewards from the other. B and C also can withhold rewards from A, but when they do so, they lose out on exchange altogether, while A can simply turn to the alternative partner. Power-dependence theory predicts that B and C will settle for only intermittent reciprocity from A, thus producing the predicted asymmetry in exchange.

probably needs to exceed that level of rewarding somewhat to maintain B's exchange.

The disadvantaged actor, B, might also use strategic action to minimize A's exchange advantage. Because symmetrical exchange is the *best* outcome that power-disadvantaged actors can hope to achieve (and, in most structures, even that is impossible), B should *always* reciprocate A's rewarding. In the structure in Figure 6.1a, B must do more than reciprocate: B must reward A at least two times in return for each of A's rewarding acts, in order to exceed the level of rewards that A could obtain by ignoring B and exchanging only with C. (On two exchange opportunities, A could receive 12 reward units from C; if A rewards B on one of those opportunities, and B rewards A on both, then A will receive 14 units – 6 from C, and 8 from B.) To minimize A's advantage, however, B should reward A *no more* than twice for every one of A's rewarding acts.

These two exchange ratios – the 4:1 ratio that A favors, and the 2:1 ratio that B favors – define the end points of the "profit latitude" of the relation, that is, the range of possible exchange ratios that will produce greater benefit for *both* actors than either could receive from alternative partners if they engaged in no exchange with each other (Michaels and Wiggins 1976). Within these boundaries, strategic power use by either actor can shift the distribution in one direction or the other; strategic power use by both actors will produce a power struggle that is likely to be resolved somewhere between the two end points.

Thus, within the limits set by structural power, strategic action can influence the distribution of exchange. Nevertheless, Emerson was correct in arguing that whether power is induced structurally or used strategically, the result in reward-based networks will be much the same. Power-imbalanced relations will produce asymmetrical exchange, in favor of the power-advantaged actor. The degree of asymmetry of that exchange can vary, within structurally constrained limits, but the basic pattern will not. As this example also shows, the effective use of power strategies requires that actors apply behavioral principles to influence others rather than merely following them (consciously or not) themselves. This task requires at least some information about the power structure, close monitoring of the other's behavior, and the consistent, contingent giving and withholding of rewards.[6]

---

[6] In addition, some researchers have suggested that influence strategies are of limited

At least in experimental settings, the strategies of real actors typically fall far short of this ideal (e.g., Molm 1987b). Although actors do respond contingently to one another, their contingencies (including those analyzed in Chapter 5) are rarely optimal for their structural positions and they seldom reflect planned influence strategies. Some subjects describe specific strategies in written postexperimental accounts (e.g., "I gave to X every time in exchange for his giving to me at least once every three times"), but most do not. Subjects are far more likely to indicate that they gave to exchange partners who controlled the more valuable resources, or to those who rewarded them more often.

To have power is *not* to use it: the case of coercive power

Now consider whether Emerson's analysis applies to networks in which actors have the power to both reward and punish one another. A structural advantage on punishment power provides the *capacity* to use coercion to obtain more rewards from an exchange partner. Does it also provide the *incentive* to use that power, as a reward power advantage does? Is coercion structurally induced, by punishment power advantage, without the need for actors to use power strategically?

My earlier comparison of reward and punishment power suggested that the answer to that question is no. For a more detailed look at why that is true, consider the three networks with dual power bases shown in Figure 6.1c–e. All three have the same structure of punishment power imbalance, with A and C advantaged relative to B and D, combined with three different conditions of reward power: (c) A and C advantaged on reward power, (d) reward power balanced, and (e) B and D advantaged on reward power.

Now assume, as before, that actors begin by exploring exchanges with all available partners. If actors follow the behavioral principles specified earlier, modified to apply to punishment as well as rewards (see Chapter

---

effectiveness in units larger than the dyad (e.g., Dawes 1980). Macy (1989) argues that this is less true when an operant, noncognitive model of the actor is assumed. In general, coercive strategies should be more difficult than reward strategies to apply to multiple partners. One can withhold rewards from multiple partners at the same time, but typically one can punish only one partner at a time. This distinction further supports the argument that reward withholding is more likely to be used by actors who are advantaged on reward power (if that advantage is derived from more available alternatives), and coercive strategies by actors who are disadvantaged on reward power.

3), they should initiate exchange by performing rewarding acts for those on whom they are dependent for *either* obtaining rewards or avoiding punishment. They should increase initiations that produce more rewards or fewer punishments, and decrease those that produce fewer rewards or more punishments.

These actions should result in distributions of exchange that reflect actors' relative dependencies, but they will not lead to the use of punishment. In Figure 6.1e, for example, B's greater reward dependence on D should lead B to increase reward exchange with D while decreasing exchange with A. In this network, as in networks (c) and (d), A has a punishment power advantage over B. *If* A uses her power advantage, and punishes B when B decreases the frequency of her rewards to A, then B will no longer derive greater benefit from exchange with D. B should once again increase her rewards to A, and the distribution of exchange will reflect both bases of power.

This scenario leaves the primary question unanswered, however: what causes A to use her power advantage? What makes A punish B, rather than, say, increasing her rewards to B? If the use of punishment power is structurally induced, then A's punishment power advantage must provide the impetus for its own use; that is, it must offer a direct incentive to inflict harm on B. But, as we saw earlier, it does not. Unless we bring in some notion akin to conflict spiral's concept of "temptation" (e.g., Deutsch 1973; Lawler 1986), the incentive to punish is not inherent in a structural advantage on punishment power. In fact, the act of coercion – punishing a partner's nonrewarding to make them give rewards – contradicts the reciprocity principle of exchange, of giving what one hopes to obtain in return. That principle suggests, instead, that punishment is likely to provoke reciprocal punishment.

Even if we assume that actors know which partners have more power to punish them (as they do in these experiments), and so can offer more rewards to those partners to deter their punishment (a pattern that should produce asymmetrical exchange, in favor of the actor advantaged on punishment power), it is unlikely that this behavior will be maintained over the course of a relation. If punishment is never used, deterrence effects are likely to decline. Consider, again, the example in Figure 6.1e. If B knows that A has strong punishment power over B, B may initially give more rewards to A to deter A's punishment. But if B also knows that D controls more valuable rewards than A, then B will initiate some exchange with D, as well. If A fails to punish that behavior, it will be differentially reinforced, and gradually increase. Thus, if A is to maintain B's rewarding, potential power is not enough – A must use that power.

In short, the use of coercion does not follow logically from the capacity to coerce, as an unintended by-product of actors following the behavioral assumptions that underlie exchange theory, in structures of imbalanced power. *In this respect, reward power and punishment power are fundamentally different.* The principle that a structural power advantage provides its own incentive for power use holds only for reward power. *If used*, the effects of punishment power imbalance should be comparable with those of reward power imbalance, because both affect an actor's ability to minimize his or her own costs while imposing cost on another. But the incentive to use coercion must come from the advantage that it offers the user: the opportunity to increase rewards.

As we saw earlier, the base of power that provides that incentive is reward power, not punishment power. In the networks in Figure 6.1c–e, A's incentive to coerce B (and C's incentive to coerce D) increases as we move from network (c) to (d) to (e); that is, the incentive to coerce increases with reward dependence and reward power disadvantage. A and C have the strongest incentive to use coercion in Figure 6.1e, the network in which A and C are disadvantaged on reward power. They have less incentive to use coercion when reward power is balanced (6.1d), and even less when they are advantaged on reward power (6.1c). In both of those structures, it is likely that B and D are already rewarding A and C with high frequency, and a form of power use that increases gains would be of little advantage. In addition, the opportunity costs of using punishment in those networks would make coercion an unprofitable strategy.

Reward power imbalance does not affect coercion directly (as it does reward withholding), however, but indirectly, through its effect on reward exchange. A structural imbalance in reward power reduces the advantaged partner's reward frequency, which in turn motivates the disadvantaged actor to try to change that behavior and increase the partner's rewarding. But that requires the use of contingent influence strategies. Rather than noncontingently giving in order to receive, actors must consistently and contingently punish a partner's failure to give. Reward power disadvantage does not automatically produce such strategies, any more than punishment power advantage does. Strategic power use is not structurally determined, although the structure of power can produce exchange outcomes that motivate the use of contingent influence strategies.[7]

In summary, this analysis suggests two reasons why punishment power is used less frequently. First, a structural advantage on punishment power provides no incentive to use that power. Second, the structural condition that does provide an incentive – reward power disadvantage – affects actors' motivations to change another's behavior, but it does not directly induce their use of coercive strategies. Unlike reward withholding, the use of coercion is never inherent in the structure of exchange.

Experiment 6: the structural inducement of power use

This analysis offers a theoretical explanation for the low use of punishment power: punishment power is used less often than reward power because reward withholding is structurally induced but coercion is not. That argument also implies, however, that *if* the use of both bases of power were structurally induced by a power advantage on the same base, then their effects would be equivalent. Are there conditions that allow us to test this inference and the validity of this argument – conditions under which the use of punishment power *is* inherent in a structural power advantage?

No such conditions exist naturally, but they can be created artificially, by designing networks that meet two assumptions. First, *the exchange advantage of using punishment power must be avoiding harm, not increasing rewards*. A network based solely on punishment power meets that condition; eliminating reward power changes the function of punishment from coercing gains to minimizing losses. In such a network, an actor minimizes losses by *not punishing* those on whom he is most dependent; that is, he avoids harm by not imposing it on another. Thus, we can test this argument by comparing networks in which actors have only punishment power with networks in which actors have only reward power.

Second, *all actors must initiate exchange with one partner on each opportunity*. That assumption is implicit in networks that offer the potential for rewards. Actors who are motivated to increase rewards should always

---

[7] In this sense, strategic power use is comparable with Emerson's power-balancing mechanisms (see Chapter 2). Those mechanisms, which include network extension and coalition formation, are also not structurally induced, but represent behavioral solutions to unsatisfactory exchange outcomes.

take the opportunity to initiate exchange when rewards are controlled by other actors and can be obtained solely through exchange. But networks based exclusively on punishment power offer only the potential of loss for everyone involved. If we assume that harm, like benefit, tends to be reciprocated, exchange relations would not be expected to form in such networks – actors should resist punishing one another. To create comparable conditions in networks based solely on reward power or punishment power, we must artificially impose the requirement that actors initiate exchange – with reward or punishment, whichever is available – on each opportunity.[8]

If these two conditions are met, then a punishment power advantage will provide both the *capacity* and the *incentive* to use power, just as a reward power advantage does, and power imbalance on either base should induce power use. To illustrate, consider the network in Figure 6.1b. This network structures the same dependencies among actors as the reward network in Figure 6.1a, but the dependencies are based on control over negative rather than positive outcomes. As in Figure 6.1a, actors A and C are both power-advantaged in their respective relations with B and D, but equal in power to each other.

Just as actors in the reward network were expected to increase exchange with the partners who rewarded them the most and to decrease exchange with the partners who rewarded them the least, actors in the punishment network should increase exchange with the partners who harm them the least and decrease exchange with the partners who harm them the most. An increase in losses, rather than a decrease in rewards, should prompt a change in their behavior.

If actors follow these principles, then the distribution of exchange that develops should be a mirror image of the distribution predicted in the reward network, again favoring the power-advantaged actors, A and C. Over time, A and C should increase the frequency with which they punish B and D and decrease the frequency of their exchange with each other (A and C lose less by initiating exchange with B and D than with each other). B and D should prefer to exchange with each other, and should decrease the frequency with which they punish A and C. That means, of course,

[8] Willer (1987: ch. 4) used a similar rule to create "strong" coercive structures in his experiments; that is, he required the coercer to transmit a negative sanction to at least one of three potential coercees (or two of four potential coercees) on each trial.

that A and C will punish B and D more often than B and D reciprocate. But any increase in B and D's retaliation of A and C's punishment should prompt a reciprocal increase in A and C's punishment and, in response, B and D's punishment should decrease. In time, the distribution of exchange should stabilize: A should punish B, and C should punish D, more often than B and D reciprocate, and exchange in the B–D relation should be more frequent than exchange in the A–C relation.

This process is completely parallel to the one proposed for the reward network in Figure 6.1a. In both networks, actors should pursue their own self-interest by initiating exchange with the partners who can benefit them the most or harm them the least. In both, these behaviors will inadvertently result in the power-advantaged actors (A and C) "using power" in their relations with B and D, by imposing costs on them through reward withholding or punishment. And in both, A and C will gain advantage in their respective relations because they incur lower costs than they impose. In the reward network, A and C will obtain their partners' rewards at lower opportunity cost; in the punishment network, A and C will receive fewer losses than they administer. The result, in both networks, should be asymmetrical exchange that favors the power-advantaged actors.

In summary, an experimental comparison of exchange networks based solely on reward power or punishment power provides a means to test the argument that *if* the use of both bases of power were inherent in a structural advantage on that base, then their effects on the frequency and distribution of exchange would be the same. Based on that logic, I conducted the experiment described here.

Design

The experiment compared the distribution of exchange in networks in which power is based solely on control over rewards (reward power), control over punishments (punishment power), or control over both (dual-base power), under conditions of both balanced and imbalanced power. Figure 6.2 shows the six networks produced by this 3×2 factorial design.[9]

In contrast to the experiments in Chapter 5, all four actors in these

---

[9] As in previous experiments, 10 networks were run in each of the six conditions and subjects exchanged with each other for 250 opportunities.

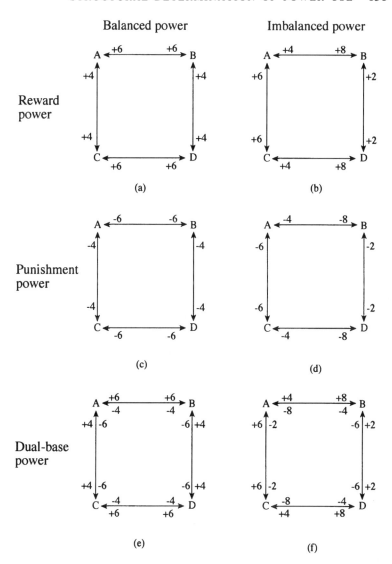

Figure 6.2. The exchange networks in Experiment 6

networks were real subjects. The strategies of the simulated actors in the previous experiments offered an alternative explanation for the low use of punishment that I wished to rule out: in those experiments, the simulated actors never initiated punishment, providing a model of noncoercive behavior that might have influenced subjects. Using real subjects eliminated any possible effects of the programmed strategies on subjects' behavior.

I manipulated the base of power by varying whether actors in the network could add to each other's earnings, subtract from each other's earnings, or both. Theoretically, the four single-base networks in Figure 6.2a–d are the most interesting. Subjects in these networks could choose between partners but not actions: subjects in reward networks could only add money; subjects in punishment networks could only subtract money. To meet the second condition for the structural determination of the use of punishment power, I required subjects to act toward one of their potential exchange partners on each opportunity, by adding to or subtracting from one of their partners' earnings. In the reward networks, subjects began with a small sum of money ($1) and gained money through exchange. In the punishment networks, they began with a large sum ($25) and lost money through exchange.[10]

Let me emphasize again that the purely punitive networks created in this experiment have no parallel in natural settings. Actors should avoid relations that offer only the potential of loss for everyone involved. Their use is an example of what Henshel (1980) calls "unnatural" experimentation – that is, the creation of conditions that would never exist in natural settings to answer certain kinds of theoretical questions. In essence, by forcing punishment networks to operate like reward networks, we can test predictions about why they typically do *not* act like reward networks.

The dual-base networks (Figure 6.2e,f) are included in the design primarily as a control. In these networks, both bases of power are available and subjects have a choice of both partners and actions toward them. Although the earlier experiments studied similar dual-base networks, it was necessary to show that the weak effects of punishment power could be replicated with the networks of four real actors used in this study. (Subjects in these networks began with $2.)

Within each base of power, I compared relations of balanced and imbalanced power. In the power-balanced conditions, each of the four actors in the network is in a balanced relation with each of the actor's partners. In the power-imbalanced conditions, two of the relations – A–B and C–D – have power imbalances of .4, with B and D more dependent and less

---

[10] These amounts were chosen so that subjects in different conditions would end the experiment with roughly similar earnings (about $15).

powerful than A and C, respectively. The other two relations (A–C and B–D) are balanced. The focal relations are the imbalanced ones, A–B and C–D.

The imbalanced, dual-base network (6.2f) places the two bases of power in opposition to one another so that their relative impact on reward exchange can be compared, and so that actors B and D have an incentive – the asymmetry in their reward exchange with A and C – to try to coerce rewards from A and C. Because actors in these networks lack a *structural* incentive to use punishment, however, the typical weak effects of punishment power should be observed.

As in the earlier experiments, measures of exchange frequency and exchange asymmetry serve as the dependent variables. In all networks, positive values for exchange asymmetry indicate that the power-advantaged actors benefit more (by gaining more or losing less) from the exchange.[11]

Hypotheses

Within conditions of balance or imbalance, the reward and punishment networks are identical except for the base of power. Because they provide equivalent structural incentives to use power, they should have parallel effects on behavior. When power is balanced (Figure 6.2a,c), stable, symmetrical relations should form between A and B, and C and D in the reward network (Figure 6.2a). In the punishment network (Figure 6.2c), relations should form between A and C, and B and D.

In the imbalanced networks (Figure 6.2b,d), asymmetrical exchange should develop in the imbalanced relations (A–B and C–D) in favor of the more powerful actors, A and C. In the reward network (Figure 6.2b), B should reward A, and D reward C, more frequently than A and C reciprocate. In the punishment network (Figure 6.2d), A should punish B, and C punish D, more often than B and D reciprocate. In both networks,

---

[11] The calculation of exchange asymmetry follows the rule of computing *reward* asymmetry by subtracting the less dependent partner's exchange from the more dependent partner's exchange, and *punishment* asymmetry by subtracting the more dependent partner's exchange from the less dependent partner's exchange. In the reward networks I compute reward asymmetry by subtracting A's exchange from B's exchange and C's exchange from D's exchange; in the punishment networks I compute punishment asymmetry by subtracting B's exchange from A's exchange and D's exchange from C's exchange. In the dual-base networks, I apply these same rules to both reward asymmetry and punishment asymmetry.

the more powerful actors – A and C – should incur lower costs than their more dependent partners, B and D. In the reward networks, A and C will obtain their partners' rewards at lower opportunity cost; in the punishment networks, A and C will receive fewer losses than they administer.

As a result, the patterns of exchange that develop in the reward and punishment networks should be mirror images of each other:

H1a. The average frequency of exchange in the A–B and C–D relations of the reward networks will equal the average frequency of exchange in the A–C and B–D relations of the punishment networks.

H1b. In the A–B and C–D relations, the asymmetry of exchange in the reward networks will equal the asymmetry of exchange in the punishment networks, with both favoring the power-advantaged actors (i.e., A and C will reward less frequently and punish more frequently than B and D).

H1c. In both the reward and punishment networks, power imbalance will affect behavior in comparable ways, by decreasing the average frequency of exchange and producing asymmetrical rather than symmetrical exchange.

These hypotheses are based on the assumption that *if* reward power and punishment power are used in comparable ways, they will have parallel effects on behavior; that is, actors will behave in ways that either increase rewards or decrease punishments. As we saw in Chapter 3, however, many theories of coercive power assume that actors respond emotionally to punishment and will retaliate another's punishment despite the costs. If so, then the patterns of exchange that result in the two networks should look quite different, particularly when power is imbalanced. In Figure 6.2d, if retaliating against the other is a stronger motivation than minimizing loss, then B and D should reciprocate A and C's punishment and asymmetry should be lower than in Figure 6.2b.

The dual-base networks (Figure 6.2e,f) are expected to produce the same patterns of exchange observed in previous experiments. Punishment power should rarely be used and, as a result, its effects should be minimal.

H2. The frequency and asymmetry of reward exchange in the dual-base networks will not differ significantly from the frequency and asymmetry of reward exchange in the comparable reward networks.

Table 6.1. *Mean values of exchange frequency and exchange asymmetry, Experiment 6*

| Exchange outcome | Network structure | | | |
	Balanced		Imbalanced	
a. Single-base networks	Reward	Punishment	Reward	Punishment
Exchange frequency				
A–B and C–D	.88	—	.46	—
A–C and B–D	—	.81	—	.46
Exchange asymmetry[a]				
A–B and C–D	.01	.03	.26	.20
b. Dual-base networks[b]	Dual		Dual	
Reward exchange				
Frequency	.65		.47	
Asymmetry	.03		.22	
Punishment exchange				
Frequency	.03		.04	
Asymmetry	.00		-.03	

[a] In the reward networks, exchange asymmetry is computed by subtracting A's exchange from B's exchange and C's exchange from D's exchange. In the punishment networks, it is computed by subtracting B's exchange from A's exchange and D's exchange from C's exchange.
[b] All means are for the high value relations, A–B and C–D. Reward and punishment asymmetry are computed by the same rules used for the single-base networks.

Results

To simplify the analysis, data for the A–B and C–D ("high value") relations, and for the A–C and B–D ("low value") relations, are combined by averaging measures of the two dependent variables, exchange frequency and exchange asymmetry.[12] Table 6.1 shows the mean values of these variables for the relations used in tests of the hypotheses.

To test Hypotheses 1a–c, I compared the appropriate measures of exchange frequency and exchange asymmetry for the four single-base net-

---

[12] The A–B and C–D relations are structurally equivalent in all of the networks. The A–C and B–D relations are structurally equivalent in the balanced networks, but differ on average power in the imbalanced networks. Mean average power in the two relations equals that in the balanced relations, however.

Table 6.2. *Analyses of variance on exchange frequency and exchange asymmetry, Experiment 6*

Source	df	Exchange frequency		Exchange asymmetry	
		MSS	F-ratio	MSS	F-ratio
a. *Single-base networks*					
Power base	1	0.01	0.76	0.00	0.92
Power balance	1	1.43	90.38***	0.44	95.41***
Base x balance	1	0.01	0.78	0.02	3.28
Explained	3	0.49	30.64***	0.15	33.20***
Residual	36	0.02		0.01	
b. *Reward and dual-base networks[a]*					
Power base	1	0.12	10.02**	0.00	0.04
Power balance	1	0.88	70.88***	0.49	104.03***
Base x balance	1	0.14	11.04**	0.01	1.54
Explained	3	0.38	30.65***	0.17	35.20***
Residual	36	0.01		0.01	

[a]Analyses are conducted on the frequency and asymmetry of *reward* exchange.
**$p < .01$ ***$p < .001$

works.[13] Results of analyses of variance strongly support all three hypotheses (Table 6.2a). The F-ratios show the predicted effects of power imbalance, but no effect of power base on either the frequency or the asymmetry of exchange. Within conditions of power balance or imbalance, the two bases of power produced frequencies and distributions of exchange that were virtual mirror images of each other (see Table 6.1a).

As expected, the dual-base networks produced patterns of exchange very similar to those observed in the earlier experiments (Table 6.1b). Compare, for example, the frequency and asymmetry of reward exchange in Table 6.1b with the frequency and asymmetry of reward exchange in Table 5.2, when reward power imbalance is .4. As before, subjects rarely used punishment power; they punished their partners on fewer than 5% of all exchange opportunities.

To test Hypothesis 2, analyses of variance compared reward exchange

---

[13] For the analyses of exchange frequency, I reversed the coding for high- and low-value relations in the punishment networks. The analyses of variance then compared the means for the high-value relations (original or recoded) in the punishment and reward networks.

in the high-value relations (A–B and C–D) of the reward and dual-base networks (Table 6.2b). This hypothesis implies that power balance but not power base should affect the frequency and asymmetry of reward exchange. As predicted, base has no significant main or interactive effect on the *asymmetry* of reward exchange. The distribution of reward exchange in the imbalanced dual-base network favors the actors with greater reward power (A and C), not the actors with greater punishment power (B and D), and reward exchange asymmetry is very similar in the reward and dual-base networks (see Table 6.1).

Contrary to Hypothesis 2, however, base does affect the *frequency* of reward exchange, in the balanced networks. Reward frequency is lower in the balanced dual-base network than in the balanced reward network, but equal in the imbalanced dual-base and reward networks. Consequently, both the main and interactive effects of power base on exchange frequency are significant. This finding suggests that in balanced networks, actors do provide rewards more frequently to partners who have greater power to punish them, as exchange theory predicts. Remember, in the balanced dual-base networks, partners with weaker reward power have stronger punishment power. Thus, the finding that reward frequency is reduced in the A–B and C–D relations of these networks implies that it is increased in the A–C and B–D relations, in which potential punishment power is stronger.[14] But in imbalanced networks, punishment power does not have this effect – subjects do not give rewards more frequently to partners who have greater power to punish them.

This interaction parallels findings of a deterrent effect of punishment in equal, but not unequal, power relations (Bacharach and Lawler 1981). Lawler's (1986) extension of bilateral deterrence theory suggests that deterrence effects should disappear when power is unequal. Although my results do not show increased use of punishment when punishment power is imbalanced, they do indicate that actors no longer give rewards to deter punishment when punishment power is imbalanced.

Finally, subjects' written accounts at the conclusion of the experiment provide additional support for the logic underlying the predictions. The

---

[14] Note, however, that variations in the strength of punishment power did not produce a deterrent effect in Experiment 3 (Chapter 5) when power was balanced, even though the manipulation of average punishment power in that experiment produced a greater difference in the magnitude of potential punishment than the presence or absence of punishment power in this experiment.

majority of subjects in the punishment networks described courses of action based explicitly on the principle of subtracting from the actor who could harm them the least. Very few reported behaviors based on getting mad or getting even. Subjects in the dual-base networks, however, rarely reported the use of coercive strategies (i.e., using punishment power to increase the other's reward frequency). Only 5 of the 20 subjects in the B and D positions of the imbalanced dual-base network stated that they used the strategy of punishing their partner's nonexchange, and only one of the 5 used punishment more than 5% of the time. That subject (in position B) used punishment coercively (i.e., punished A when A did not reward B on the previous opportunity) on 28% of all opportunities – a strategy that produced the highest level of rewarding by A in that condition.

Summary and conclusions

In this chapter, I argued that the weak effects of punishment power are the direct result of the low use of that power, and I began to develop a theory that explains why actors use coercion so infrequently. According to power-dependence theory, power use results from structural power advantage, regardless of actors' awareness of power or their use of influence strategies. Emerson argued that while voluntary modes of power use might affect the speed with which structure produces its effects, they would not alter the end result. The incentive to use power is inherent in the unequal dependencies of imbalanced relations.

My analysis shows that this tenet, which is one of the most basic and well known of all power-dependence principles, holds only for reward power. In a relation of imbalanced reward power, power use occurs as an *unintended by-product* of advantaged actors' more frequent exchange with alternative partners. Their greater access to alternatives both *reduces* their dependence and *induces* their use of power. In contrast, access to alternative sources of punishment reduces dependence but provides no incentive to use that power. Neither punishment power advantage nor any other structural condition directly induces actors to use punishment to coerce rewards. Structure can provide the motivation to coerce, by producing unequal or insufficient rewards from exchange, but it does not lead directly to coercive behaviors. I proposed that this difference between reward and punishment power is the major cause of differences in their use.

An experiment supported this analysis, by showing that when structural conditions are created that do induce the use of both bases of power, they have virtually identical effects on behavior. Actors who are faced with the task of simply distributing rewards or punishments among alternative partners, in networks based solely on reward power or punishment power, follow the same principles in doing so: they provide more frequent benefits (rewards or the withholding of punishment) to those on whom they are most dependent for obtaining rewards or avoiding punishment. Under these conditions, the hypothesis of structural equivalence is supported: equivalent structures of reward or punishment power produce equivalent frequencies and distributions of exchange. Actors in the punishment networks were not using coercion to obtain rewards, however; they were simply minimizing losses.

These highly similar patterns of exchange contrast sharply with the very different effects of reward and punishment power observed when both are available in networks of exchange. The dual-base networks in this experiment closely replicated the results of the earlier experiments: actors rarely used punishment, and only reward power influenced the distribution of exchange. These similar results occurred despite the methodological difference between the experiments of the first phase, which studied networks in which some actors were computer-simulated, and this experiment, which employed real subjects in all network positions. Apparently, the programmed strategies of the simulated actors in the earlier experiments were not responsible for the weak effects of punishment power.

What are the implications of this chapter for the theoretical integration of coercive power within the framework of power-dependence theory? Clearly, the principle that the use of power is inherent in a structural power advantage must be restricted to reward power. We have yet to analyze the *strategic* use of coercive power, however, and key questions remain unanswered. While the lack of structural determinism explains why coercive power is used less frequently than reward power, it does not explain why it is hardly ever used, or why its use declines over time. Chapter 7 begins to address those questions.

7. Dependence and risk: structural constraints on strategic power use

The preceding chapter developed the thesis that punishment power is less effective than reward power because its use is not structurally induced by power advantage. Unlike reward power, coercion is not an unintended by-product of actors seeking exchange with alternative partners. Instead, it must be used strategically, by actors punishing their partners' failure to reward. The effective use of power strategies requires more information, skill, and behavioral monitoring than structurally induced power use. On this basis alone, then, we would expect to observe some differences in the use and effects of the two bases of power.

But we would not expect to find the very low rates of punishment that all subjects, even those with a strong incentive to coerce, have repeatedly displayed in these experiments. Actors might use punishment ineffectively and inconsistently, but why should they use it so infrequently? And why does punishment always decline, before it has any chance to influence the partner's behavior?

This chapter begins to answer these questions, by developing and testing a theory of strategic power use. Although Emerson included voluntary modes of power use within the scope of his theory, he assumed that they were fairly irrelevant; structure would determine power use in any event. Consequently, he made few assumptions about the decision-making processes of individual actors.

In this chapter I draw on theories of choice and decision making to explain how the strategic use of both bases of power – but especially coercive power – is constrained by risk and fear of loss. I argue that loss aversion inhibits power use, and that actors who use coercive power risk greater loss than those who use reward power. The reason for this difference lies in the structure of dependence and its different effects on the relation between the capacity to use power and the incentive to use power for the two bases of power. Several experiments test hypotheses derived from this analysis.

Strategic power use

Two important differences distinguish strategic power use from the structurally induced use of power with which Emerson was concerned. First, actors do not merely respond to the consequences of their own behaviors; they *create* contingencies that *produce* consequences for *other* actors' behaviors (Thibaut and Kelley 1959). As the term "strategy" suggests, such actions are typically purposive. With few exceptions, actors who use power strategically impose cost knowingly.[1]

Second, strategic power use is based not on the principle of reciprocity that underlies power-dependence theory's assumption about the initiation of exchange, but on an application of behavioral principles. Rather than giving rewards to obtain benefits in return, actors administer rewards and punishments contingently. In particular, they impose cost (by administering punishment or withholding rewards) on partners who fail to provide sufficient benefits.

These distinctions have important implications for predicting when actors will use coercion. Developing their significance requires extending Emerson's model of the actor as *learner*, to a model of the actor as both *learner* and *teacher*. Actors who use power strategically respond to others' behaviors, but they also attempt to influence them.

Assumptions about strategic actors

In the reciprocal exchanges studied in this research program, actors know the *value* of the outcomes they can potentially receive from their exchange partners, but not the *probability* of their partners' behaviors. Actors may estimate those probabilities, based on knowledge of their partners' relative dependencies or past behavior, but such estimates still have some degree

---

[1] While coercive strategies are typically purposive, they are sometimes shaped without awareness – for example, when punishing actions are elicited emotionally and then maintained by their consequences. This process seems to explain the rapid development of coercive strategies employed by young children, who quickly learn to cry, whine, or throw tantrums to increase adults' attention (see Patterson 1982).

of uncertainty. Consequently, actors choose among alternative partners and alternative behaviors in a context of risk and uncertainty, conditions typical of many social interactions.[2]

Game theorists attempt to transform uncertainty (unknown probabilities) into risk (known probabilities), by making assumptions about other actors' preferences and motives that allow subjective probabilities to be attached to their behaviors (Luce and Raiffa 1957). Given knowledge of these subjective probabilities and the values attached to each, actors should then make choices that maximize expected utility. That is, they should choose the alternative that produces the highest expected utility, as estimated by multiplying the probabilities and values of the possible consequences of each alternative action (the "possible consequences" depending on the partner's behavior) and summing the products.

The normative predictions of game theory provide useful benchmarks for comparisons with actual behavior, and reasonably accurate predictions of aggregate tendencies in large markets. But experimental research by both economists and psychologists shows a rather poor fit between the theory's prescriptions and the actual behavior of most subjects. Most decisions appear to emerge from processes more typical of adaptation, or trial-and-error learning, than rational calculation (e.g., Gale, Binmore, and Samuelson 1995; Lucas 1986).

In response to these findings, many researchers have questioned the information-gathering and computing abilities assumed by the expected utility model (e.g., Herrnstein 1993; Macy 1993). Some, like Simon (1955, 1956), propose that actors "satisfice" rather than maximize, but still make rational choices within the bounds of time, information, and so forth. Others argue that actors are subject to systematic biases and heuristics in estimating probabilities (e.g., Tversky and Kahneman 1974, 1981, 1983). And some suggest that actors may not estimate probabilities at all (e.g., Machina 1987).[3]

For my assumptions about strategic actors, I draw on two theoretical

---

[2] Economists distinguish between decision making under *risk*, in which the probabilities of various outcomes are known but are less than 1.0, and under *uncertainty*, in which even the probabilities are unknown. Sociologists more commonly group risk and uncertainty together and contrast both with certainty (Heimer 1988).

[3] See Machina (1987:148–149) for a discussion of economic solutions to choice in the absence of estimated probabilities.

traditions that are more compatible with the learning model on which power-dependence theory has traditionally been based: Axelrod's evolutionary approach to strategic action, and Kahneman and Tversky's analysis of decision making under risk and uncertainty.

Axelrod's evolutionary theory. Axelrod's (1984, 1986) theory[4] of the evolution of cooperation and of norms is based on a dynamic model of strategic action in mixed-motive structures. The theory assumes conditions very similar to those of the reciprocal exchanges in this program. Actors engage in recurring interactions, make individual choices simultaneously, know what other actors have done in the past but not what they will do in the future, and communicate only through their behavioral choices. I adopt two of the core assumptions of this theory.

First, strategies are dynamic and adaptive. Both actors' expectations and their behavioral strategies evolve over time, as they experience the consequences of their own actions and observe their partners' actions. Initial expectations about others' behavior may be based on knowledge of the outcome structure or beliefs formed from past experiences, but these expectations are modified in the light of actual experience. As actors adapt to what each other is doing, they mutually shape each other's strategies. Effective strategies are kept, and those that work poorly are discarded or modified.[5]

Second, when the "shadow of the future" is sufficiently large, there is no single best strategy independent of the other actor's strategy (Axelrod 1984, prop. 1). In other words, when actors expect continued interaction for an indefinite period of time, and the value of future interactions looms large (i.e., the potential value from future interactions is much greater than the value from any single immediate action), there is no single "dominant" response or rational strategy.[6]

---

[4] As Axelrod (1986) notes, the evolutionary principle can be the product of any one of three different mechanisms: (1) natural selection, (2) trial-and-error learning, or (3) imitation. The second is clearly most compatible with this analysis.

[5] Heimer's (1985) analysis of risk in exchange relations is based on a somewhat similar idea. She argues that exchange relations involve *reactive risk*, that is, risk that changes once an actor has decided what to do, because both actors are dependent on each other and each actor's behavior may change as a result of the other's initial behavioral choice.

[6] In the prisoner's dilemma, for example, the game theoretic solution of defection as the best strategy, no matter what the other player does, holds only for one-shot games. In extended interactions, stable defection is rarely the best choice. (See, also, Luce and Raiffa 1957:97–102.)

Kahneman and Tversky's prospect theory. I draw on Kahneman and Tversky's prospect theory (Kahneman and Tversky 1979; Tversky and Kahneman 1992) for specific assumptions about the value function that governs actors' choices during the evolution of strategies. Prospect theory is a formal analysis of choice under risk and uncertainty, based on empirical generalizations derived from numerous studies of decision making (for overviews, see Kahneman and Tversky 1982, 1984; Tversky and Kahneman 1974, 1986). It is best known for its challenge to expected utility theory as a descriptive model of choice behavior.

Both prospect theory and the empirical research on which it is based suggest that actors evaluate outcomes of risky and uncertain choices by a value function that has three main characteristics: referent dependence, diminishing sensitivity, and loss aversion.

The first property, *referent dependence*, states that people evaluate outcomes as deviations from a reference point, typically the status quo (Kahneman and Tversky 1979; Markowitz 1952).[7] Outcomes count as gains if they improve the status quo and as losses if they worsen it. These evaluations are made sequentially; as the status quo changes, what constitutes a gain or loss also changes. While this process contradicts the economic assumption that people compare the expected utilities of final states, it supports the assumptions of behavioral psychology discussed in Chapter 2; that is, the reinforcing or punishing effects of behavioral consequences depend on the changes they produce in the value of outcomes the person is currently experiencing (Van Houten 1983).[8]

The second property, *diminishing sensitivity*, states that the marginal value of both gains and losses decreases with their distance from the reference point (e.g., Fishburn and Kochenberger 1979; Hershey and Schoemaker 1980; Kahneman and Tversky 1979; Payne, Laughhunn, and Crum 1980). This principle indicates, as I assumed in Chapter 3, that individuals become increasingly less sensitive to a given change in outcome as the stakes get larger, in either a positive or a negative direction. As a result, the value function is concave for gains but convex

---

[7] Although the reference state usually corresponds to the status quo, it can be influenced by aspirations, expectations, norms, and social comparisons (e.g., Easterlin 1974; van de Stadt, Kapteyn, and van de Geer 1985). I consider some of these effects in Chapter 8.

[8] This principle is shared, more generally, by all theories that posit some process of value adaptation. See, in particular, Thibaut and Kelley's (1959) analysis of the comparison level (CL) of exchange relations.

for losses, implying that individuals are risk averse for gains but risk seeking for losses.[9]

Third, and most important, the negative subjective value of a loss is greater than the positive subjective value of an equivalent gain, a phenomenon called *loss aversion*. While this principle is most closely associated with Kahneman and Tversky's own research (Kahneman and Tversky 1979, 1982, 1984; Tversky and Kahneman 1991), numerous studies by economists, psychologists, and sociologists support it (see, e.g., Fishburn and Kochenberger 1979; Galanter and Pliner 1974; Gray and Tallman 1987; Hershey and Schoemaker 1980; Payne et al. 1980). Studies typically report coefficients of loss aversion in the range of 2 to 2.5, indicating that the slope of the value function for losses is roughly twice the slope of the value function for gains (see Kahneman, Knetsch, and Thaler 1991; Tversky and Kahneman 1991).

Although the value function was originally proposed to account for patterns of decision making about future events, Tversky and Kahneman suggest it is equally valid for describing reactions to past experience: "organisms habituate to steady states, the marginal response to changes is diminishing, and pain is more urgent than pleasure" (1991:1057).

The properties of referent dependence and diminishing sensitivity have already been introduced, in slightly different form, in the discussions of behavioral principles in Chapters 2 and 3. The concept of loss aversion is the most important new introduction. It, too, is generally supported by behavioral studies, which suggest that punishment suppresses behavior faster and to a greater extent than reinforcement strengthens it (see Patterson 1982 and Van Houten 1983 for reviews). Nevertheless, most exchange theories implicitly assume that rewards and costs carry equal weight. The assumption that they do not has important implications for understanding the use and effects of coercive power.

Analyses of data from the earlier experiments in this project support the applicability of loss aversion to reactions to past experiences as well as choices of future events. Using the combined data set created for the process analyses in Chapter 5, I examined the effects of experienced rewards (gains) and punishments (losses) on subjects' affective evaluations

[9] This principle reverses for gains and losses of small probability (Tversky and Kahneman 1992). For example, people are willing to pay more for lottery tickets than their expected value, indicating risk seeking rather than risk aversion for gain (Kahneman and Lovallo 1993).

of their exchange partners' behavior (Molm 1991).[10] As prospect theory predicts, the negative affect produced by each additional unit of punishment was stronger than the positive affect produced by each additional unit of reward. Averaged across different power positions, the regression coefficients for punishment were 2.3 times the regression coefficients for reward – a magnitude of difference that is remarkably close to the coefficients of loss aversion reported in studies of decision making.

Implications for strategic power use under risk and uncertainty

The concept of the status quo as a moving reference point implies that actors in exchange relations evaluate the potential and actual consequences of power use in comparison with the current state of their relation – that is, the most recent outcomes they have received from the exchange.[11] While the status quo is known, the consequences of power use are uncertain. Actors must decide whether to use coercion without knowing how the partner will respond. Once coercion is initiated, its persistence or decline should depend on the partner's actual behavior. How the partner responds to coercion provides immediate reward or punishment for the actor, as well as information which can affect the actor's estimates of the partner's future behavior.

Consistent with the principles that underlie exchange theory, actors might initially expect the partner to follow one of two simple behavioral rules: (1) reciprocate in kind (the reciprocity principle), or (2) increase behaviors that are rewarded and decrease behaviors that are punished (the learning principle). Both principles are reflected in the behavioral assumptions of power-dependence theory. The reciprocity principle explains why actors initiate exchange in the first place, and the learning

---

[10] I measured affect with a five-item scale that included measures of overall satisfaction with the relation, positive–negative feelings toward the partner, and three items tapping the evaluative dimension of affect (good–bad, pleasant–unpleasant, nice–awful). Subjects evaluated these items on 7-point semantic differential scales in the postexperimental questionnaire; summing their responses produced a scale with an alpha reliability of .92. I estimated the effects of reward and punishment on satisfaction with unstandardized regression coefficients, after controlling for the effects of structural power. For further details see Molm (1991).

[11] Macy (1993) has modeled the status quo as an unweighted moving average of the three most recent exchange opportunities. While this particular rule (like any other) is arbitrary, limitations on memory suggest that actors' perceptions of the status quo are probably based on fairly recent experiences.

principle governs whether their initiations will increase or decrease over time.

But when applied to reactions to power use, these principles imply contradictory responses. Power use imposes cost on a partner. Consequently, the reciprocity principle predicts retaliation (i.e., repay harm with harm), whereas the learning principle predicts compliance (increase rewarding to reduce cost). The conflict between these two principles, and the alternative prospects they create, make power use risky. Power strategies might improve an actor's situation, by increasing the partner's rewarding, or worsen it, by provoking retaliation in the form of decreased rewards or punishment.

Because both consequences are based on reasonable behavioral rules that actors are likely to have used and experienced before, both have nontrivial probabilities of occurrence. Indeed, if the partner is also applying behavioral principles to influence the actor, she *should* retaliate to punish the other's coercion. Tversky and Kahneman (1992) suggest that people are relatively insensitive to differences in such middle-range probabilities (they overweight low probabilities, and underweight high ones). Therefore, to the extent that actors try to estimate the probabilities of their partners' actions, it is likely that they will judge both reactions to be of roughly equal probability.

When actions can produce either gain or loss and the probabilities of both outcomes are either equal or uncertain, the principle of loss aversion implies a bias toward the status quo. Empirically, choices favoring the status quo tend to dominate decision making under uncertainty (Kahneman and Tversky 1984; Knetsch 1989; Knetsch and Sinden 1984; Samuelson and Zeckhauser 1988; Thaler 1980). Therefore, actors are more likely to accept their current position in a relation rather than risk using power in an attempt to improve their lot. This constraint on strategic power use holds, in general, for both bases of power. Both reward withholding and coercion impose cost on a partner, and both entail risk.

The status quo bias increases as what actors stand to lose relative to what they stand to gain increases. Thus strategic power use, like structurally induced power use, should vary with the structure of dependence.

Dependence, risk, and coercion

Actors' dependencies affect the probability that they will initiate coercion, the probability that their partners will respond with compliance or retaliation, and the respective gains and losses attached to those alternative outcomes.

Actors' *relative* dependencies – their positions of power advantage or disadvantage – influence both the *probability of coercion* and the *probability of retaliation* against coercion. As we have seen, a position of reward power disadvantage provides the behavioral motivation to use coercion as a means of securing rewards from a less dependent (and less rewarding) partner. A punishment power advantage increases an actor's capacity to coerce, but it does not provide the incentive. Therefore, the probability that an actor will *initiate* a coercive strategy should increase with her relative disadvantage on reward power.

But power advantage or disadvantage also affects the probability that the partner will *retaliate* against coercion. Power-advantaged actors stand to gain more by retaliating, and lose more by complying, than power-disadvantaged actors. Consequently, the probability of the partner's retaliation should increase with the partner's power advantage. Presumably, both bases of power should affect retaliation; that is, a power advantage on either reward power or punishment power should increase the probability of the partner's retaliation. A partner who controls rewarding outcomes can retaliate by withdrawing those rewards; a partner who controls punishing outcomes can retaliate by administering punishment. A partner who controls both can do either.

Exchange partners can retaliate against the use of reward power as well as coercive power, of course, and for both bases of power, the risk of retaliation increases with the partner's power advantage. The partner's retaliation is unlikely to deter the use of reward power, however, because the same condition that increases the incentive to use reward power – reward power advantage – simultaneously reduces the chance of the partner's retaliation. It is likely, for example, that the senior worker in our example in Chapter 6 could establish a relation in which he offered only occasional advice to the new employee in exchange for frequent approval and deference. The chances of the junior worker withdrawing from the relation are slim; he is better off accepting the intermittent rewarding than losing the senior's rewards altogether.

For this reason, researchers studying reward-based networks have rarely analyzed how risk affects actors' decisions to use power.[12] Punitive retal-

---

[12] The focus of many researchers on explicitly negotiated exchanges with strictly binding

iation is impossible in these networks, and disadvantaged partners are unlikely to respond with reward withdrawal (and, if they do, the costs are low). Consequently, whether reward power is used strategically or induced structurally, its use should increase with power advantage.

But risk can, and does, constrain the use of coercion. Because the actors who are likely to initiate coercion are disadvantaged on one base of power – reward power – risk and incentive are not negatively correlated. The structural condition that provides the incentive to use coercion, reward power disadvantage, also increases the probability of retaliation. Even if A is advantaged on punishment power, thus reducing the probability of B's punitive retaliation, A still faces potential loss from B's reward withdrawal. If the new employee in our example attempts to coerce the senior worker into giving advice more frequently, he risks alienating the senior worker permanently, and losing whatever help and support he had been providing on an occasional basis.

This is the dilemma that constrains the use of coercive power in exchange relations: the actors who have the incentive to use coercive strategies are highly dependent on their targets. As Blalock (1987:13) observes, "substantial degrees of dependence will lead to both a high level of motivation to employ negative sanctions to the other party *and* high potential costs of such actions." He suggests that reward power disadvantage increases the risk of retaliation, in general, but also notes, "Where exchanges of positively valued goods accompany the punitive actions, the more dependent party is especially vulnerable to a cutoff of the exchange relation altogether."

To the extent that actors anticipate risk, this dilemma can keep them from ever initiating coercion. If they do initiate it, their reward power disadvantage increases the likelihood of retaliation. As we have already seen, most actors – regardless of power position – do initially retaliate a partner's punishment. And, as we shall see in the next chapter, actors who are advantaged on reward power retaliate *more* often, with *both* punishment and reward withdrawal, than do other actors.[13]

agreements has also reduced concerns with risk (e.g., Cook et al. 1983; Lawler 1992; Markovsky et al. 1988). Kollock's (1994) recent work is an exception. In the negotiated exchanges he has studied, actors can deceive one another about the value of what they are giving in exchange, and risk is an important consideration.

[13] The emphasis on risk as a key factor in power use is very similar, of course, to the logic of deterrence theory (e.g., Morgan 1977; Schelling 1960). But deterrence theory considers only the risk of retaliatory punishment, not the risk of losing valued rewards. It also

For actors who are uncertain how their partners will respond, and who adapt both expectations and strategies to their partners' behaviors over time, early retaliation is likely to suppress further coercion. Like all behavioral contingencies, coercive strategies take time to work. To be effective, they must be applied consistently, over repeated interactions. But in the face of immediate retaliation, loss-averse actors are unlikely to persist with a strategy whose long-term consequences are uncertain.[14] For that reason, of course, retaliation is not an irrational response. If an actor can effectively suppress a partner's attempts at coercion, by swift retaliation, she can avoid the costs of both continued coercion and compliance.[15]

Reducing risk

Although reward power disadvantage increases both the incentive to use coercion and the probability that the partner will retaliate, how much actors stand to gain or lose from coercive strategies depends on their individual dependencies and their current outcomes from the exchange. Analyzing these dependencies reveals that under some conditions, the actual *cost* of retaliation can be low enough to encourage coercion even if the *probability* of retaliation is high.

Assume that B is an actor whose disadvantage on reward power provides the incentive for him to coerce A. B's reward dependence on A determines the *range of potential outcomes* that A can produce for B by varying the frequency of his rewarding, in either direction. This range represents the rewards at stake for B. If B's reward dependence is high, the stakes are high: changes in A's behavior (for better or worse) can affect B's rewards substantially. If B's reward dependence is lower, increases or decreases in A's rewarding matter less.

Within this range, the outcomes that A is currently producing for B constitute the "status quo" of the relation for B – that is, B's *current outcome level*. Holding B's dependence constant, this outcome level

assumes that when power is imbalanced, the constraining effects of risk on punishment begin to erode (Lawler 1986).

[14] When actors know that long-term gains will outweigh short-term costs, they are more likely to adopt strategies of "self-control" that help them maintain strategies that are difficult in the short-run but important for long-range interests (see, e.g., Ainslie and Haslam 1992; Elster 1984).

[15] See Axelrod (1984: ch. 3, n. 6) for a comparison of retaliation with his concept of provokability. Both emphasize the strategic importance of punishing defections.

should increase with A's dependence on B. The greater A's dependence, the more frequently A should reward B. I assume that B uses this reference point to evaluate the consequences (potential or actual) of coercion. Increases from A's current level of rewarding count as potential gains, and decreases as potential losses. Consequently, B's potential gains from coercion increase, and potential losses decrease, as A's dependence on B decreases.

Together, the range of outcomes that A can potentially produce for B, and the level of outcomes that A is currently producing, determine how much B can potentially gain from A's compliance or lose from A's retaliation. To illustrate, conceptualize the potential frequency of A's rewards to B (standardized by A's opportunity to reward B) as a continuum, varying from 0 (A never rewards B) to 1 (A always rewards B):

Assume that A's current level of rewarding is at the point indicated by the arrow, that is, A rewards B on .4 of all opportunities. At that point, B's potential gain from an increase in A's rewarding is .6 (1 − .4), and B's potential loss from a decrease in A's rewarding is .4 (.4 − 0). Because loss aversion roughly doubles the negative value of any losses, however, potential losses (2 × .4) still outweigh potential gains (.6) at this point on the scale. At lower frequencies of A's rewarding, B's potential gains increase and B's potential losses decrease; at higher frequencies, the opposite is true.

Thus, holding constant B's dependence on A, the probability of B's coercion should increase as A's dependence on B, and the frequency of A's rewarding, decrease. This inference is consistent with the prediction that the probability of B's coercion should increase with B's reward power disadvantage. But what this analysis reveals is that even though the probability of A's retaliation also increases as A's dependence declines (and A's power advantage increases), *the costs of A's retaliation also decrease.* As Emerson (1972b) observed, when advantaged actors use reward power, by imposing higher costs on the partner in return for fewer rewards, the *additional* costs they can impose decline. Because of loss aversion, however, the frequency of A's rewarding must be below .3 before potential gains begin to outweigh potential losses. At that point, gains (.7) just outweigh losses when weighted for loss aversion (.3 × 2 = .6).

Even that figure is conservative, of course; it represents the *minimal* condition that must be satisfied before we can anticipate an increase in B's coercion. It does not take account of B's potential losses from A's punitive retaliation, which can independently affect B's coercion, nor does it adjust gains and losses for the higher probability of retaliation (and lower probability of compliance) that we would expect from a power-advantaged actor. Furthermore, it assumes a potential gain (from A's current frequency of rewarding to the maximum possible) that is highly unlikely; a small or moderate increase in A's rewarding is more probable than a large increase. Nevertheless, as the frequency with which A rewards B approaches zero, the amount that B could lose from A's reward withdrawal eventually becomes trivial – even if the probability of A's retaliation is high, and B's structural dependence on A is high. As this risk decreases, B's coercion should increase.

This analysis implies that coercion is likely to be used only when a relation is so unrewarding for an actor that he has little to lose from the prospect of the partner's withdrawal from the exchange. Structurally, this means that coercion becomes probable only when the partner's reward dependence is so low, and power imbalance so high, that it is difficult to sustain any pattern of mutual exchange, even one that is highly asymmetrical.[16] And, indeed, many of the classic examples of coercion, such as mugger and victim, consist of purely coercive relations in which the reward dependence of the target of coercion on the coercer is zero.[17]

Thus, as many theorists have argued (see Chapter 3), coercion is likely to be a tool of last resort – not because of normative constraints (although, in Chapter 8, we shall see that they also play a role), or because coercion is ineffective, but because dependence and loss aversion constrain actors from using coercion until they have little to lose. It is not surprising, then, that we commonly see coercive tactics employed by workers who are about to be laid off, individuals whose marriage partners have ceased to

[16] As Michaels and Wiggins (1976) have shown, mutual reward exchange – whether symmetrical or asymmetrical – is not profitable when average reward power is less than .5. When mutual dependence is that low, no ratio of exchange exists that will make the relation more rewarding for both partners than withdrawing from it altogether and exchanging with alternative partners.

[17] These are the forms of coercion discussed by Willer and Anderson (1981) and studied by Willer (1987).

care for them, or political factions who have lost all clout with mainstream parties. The irony of this behavior, of course, is that coercion should then have less chance of success: the lower the partner's reward dependence, the more difficult it becomes to coerce the partner into reward exchange.

Experiment 7: manipulating the risk of coercion

This analysis implies that risk constrains coercion in many exchange relations. If risk is reduced while maintaining the structural incentive to coerce, however, coercion should increase. Experiment 7 tested this thesis by manipulating (1) the risk of loss from the partner's punishment (risk of retaliatory punishment), and (2) the risk of loss from the partner's reward withdrawal (risk of reward loss), in structures that provide the necessary incentive to coerce – imbalanced reward power.

Both sources of risk should independently affect the use of coercion. Only the risk of reward loss, however, distinguishes coercive power from reward power. Actors who use either reward power or punishment power might face retaliatory punishment from the partner; that risk depends on the structure of punishment power and the actor's position within that structure. It is the greater risk of reward loss, produced by the high reward dependence of those who have the incentive to use coercion, that makes the use of coercive power riskier than the use of reward power.

Design

The experiment manipulated the risk of coercive power use within a basic structure in which two actors, B and D, were highly dependent on A and C (respectively) for rewards, reward power was imbalanced in the A–B and C–D relations in favor of A and C, and punishment power was imbalanced in these relations in favor of B and D (Figure 7.1). This basic structure provides both the incentive (reward power disadvantage) and the capacity (punishment power advantage) for B and D to use coercion to obtain increased rewards from A and C. The 2 × 2 factorial design manipulates the risks that B and D incur if they do so, by crossing two levels of the risk of retaliatory punishment from A and C with two levels of the risk of reward loss from A and C. As in Experiment 6 (Chapter 6), all four actors in these networks were real subjects, and they exchanged with one another for 250 opportunities.

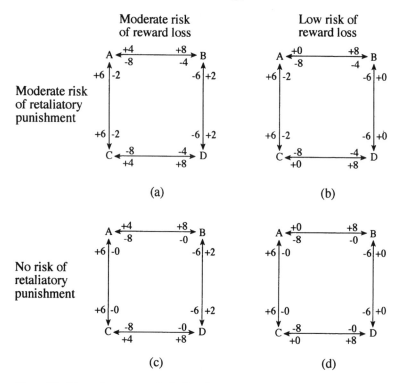

Figure 7.1. The exchange networks in Experiment 7

The risk of retaliatory punishment increases with an actor's dependence on a partner for avoiding punishment and with disadvantage on punishment power. I manipulated this source of risk by varying A and C's capacity to punish B and D, while holding B and D's punishment power constant. This risk is present and moderate in the networks in Figure 7.1a and b, in which A and C have moderate (.4) punishment power over B and D, and zero in the networks in Figure 7.1c and d, in which A and C's punishment power over B and D, and hence the risk of their retaliatory punishment, is reduced to zero.[18]

---

[18] In one of the earlier experiments (Experiment 2, in Chapter 5), I reduced the risk of retaliatory punishment by increasing the actor's punishment power advantage in the relation, thus reducing (but not eliminating) the partner's capacity to retaliate. Retaliation persisted, although the amount of loss imposed was reduced. Because people tend to overweight not only losses relative to gains, but outcomes that are considered certain relative to outcomes

The high reward dependence that provides B and D with the incentive to coerce rewards from A and C also increases risk. To reduce potential reward loss and increase potential gain, I reduced A and C's reward dependence on B and D, which, in turn, should reduce the frequency of their respective rewards to B and D. In the networks in Figure 7.1a and c, A and C's reward dependence is moderate (.4); in Figure 7.1b and d, their reward dependence is reduced to zero (B and D have no reward power over A and C). When A and C's reward dependence is zero, the frequency of their rewards to B and D should be minimal, and B and D's potential losses from withdrawal of those rewards should be lower than their potential gains from an increase in them.

Both manipulations vary actors' reward or punishment power over *both* of their potential partners. When the risk of retaliatory punishment is zero, A and C can punish neither of their partners. Similarly, when the risk of reward loss is low, B and D can reward neither of their partners. To make coercion voluntary, actors who could only punish (or only reward) were given a "no action" option. Thus, when B and D had only punishment power (Figure 7.1b,d), they could choose to punish one of their two partners, *or* to perform a behavior that affected neither partner.

The network in which both sources of risk are moderately high (Figure 7.1a) is identical to the dual-base, imbalanced network in Experiment 6 (Figure 6.2f). It is in this and similar structures that the low use of coercion has been the most puzzling, because actors B and D do have both the capacity and the incentive to coerce and neither source of risk is at its maximum. However, in this network and in similar networks in earlier experiments (Experiments 2, 4, and 5 in Chapter 5), the reward-advantaged actors have consistently rewarded their disadvantaged partners about 35% of the time. As a result, the potential loss from A and C's withdrawal of rewards (weighted by loss aversion) is higher than the potential gain from an increase in their reward frequency – even if we generously assume that compliance is as likely as retaliation, and even if we ignore the additional loss that might result from A and C's retaliatory punishment. In reality, of course, A and C's position of reward power advantage makes the probability of their retaliation higher than the prob-

that are merely probable (Allais 1953; Kahneman and Tversky 1979), completely eliminating the partner's capacity to punish should provide a stronger test of the effect of this source of risk.

Table 7.1. *Mean frequency of B's and D's punishment, Experiment 7*

	Risk of reward loss	
	Moderate	Low
Risk of punishment		
Moderate	.06	.18
Zero	.04	.23

Note: Means are averages of the frequencies with which B punished A and D punished C.

ability of their compliance, and they can (and do) retaliate with both punishment and reward withdrawal.

Hypotheses

The experiment tests the prediction that both sources of risk will independently affect the frequency with which B and D punish A and C, respectively:

H1. B and D will punish A and C more frequently when the risk of retaliatory punishment is zero than when it is moderate.
H2. B and D will punish A and C more frequently when the risk of reward loss is low than when it is moderate.

Results

The mean frequency with which B and D punished A and C, averaged together as a single variable, served as the main dependent variable (see Table 7.1). An analysis of variance on these means found a strong and significant effect of the risk of reward loss ($F_{1,36} = 19.77$, $p < .001$), in the direction predicted, but no effect of the risk of retaliatory punishment ($F_{1,36} = .33$) and no interaction between the two.

The risk of retaliatory punishment did have some effect on the use of punishment over time, however. A repeated-measures analysis of variance, which examined trends across five 50-trial blocks, revealed a three-way interaction between both sources of risk and trial block ($F_{4,144} = 3.13$, $p < .05$). Removing the risk of retaliation enhanced the use of punishment

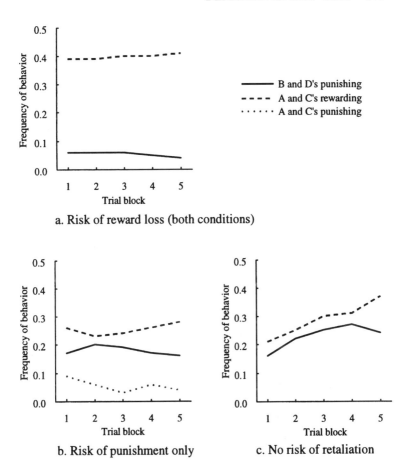

a. Risk of reward loss (both conditions)

b. Risk of punishment only

c. No risk of retaliation

Figure 7.2. Behavioral frequencies by trial block, Experiment 7

over time when the risk of reward loss was also low, but had no effect when the risk of reward loss was moderate.

Figure 7.2a–c illustrates this interaction and also shows the evolving, adaptive relationship between A(C)'s behavior and B(D)'s behavior over time. Figure 7.2a shows that when the risk of reward loss was moderate (the conditions shown in Figure 7.1a and c), B and D rarely used punishment and its use decreased over time, as we have observed before. In these conditions, A and C consistently rewarded B and D about 40% of the time. The potential loss of their rewards was too costly to risk using coercion; whether A and C also had the capacity to punish made no difference.

The graphs in Figure 7.2b and c show the effects of reducing the risk of reward loss, by reducing A and C's reward dependence and, consequently, their reward frequency. In 7.2b, A and C can still retaliate punitively; in 7.2c, that source of risk is also removed. Initially, A and C reward B and D no more than 20% to 25% of the time in both conditions, and B and D respond in both with substantially higher levels of punishment than in Figure 7.2a. Both graphs show a close correspondence between A(C)'s rewarding and B(D)'s punishing. What distinguishes the two is that when the risk of punitive retaliation is also eliminated (7.2c), B(D)'s use of coercion continues to increase over time and, as a result, it nearly doubles A(C)'s rewarding (from .20 to .37). B(D)'s punishment declines only in the last trial block, in response to the final, sharp increase in A(C)'s rewarding. In 7.2b, in contrast, the upward trajectory of B(D)'s initial punishment is not maintained beyond the first trial block; after that, it levels off and returns to its original level. Although this pattern appears to mirror the changes in A(C)'s rewarding, it is likely that A(C)'s capacity to punish, and periodic use of that capacity (see the bottom dotted line in Figure 7.2b), deterred B(D) from risking higher frequencies of punishment.

By the last two trial blocks, the condition that reduced both sources of risk (Figure 7.2c) produced a fourfold increase in the use of punishment when compared with the condition in which both sources of risk were moderate (7.2a). This condition is also the only one of the four in which the average frequency of A and C's rewards to B and D increased over time ($F_{4,36} = 4.52$, $p < .005$).

Implications

These results show that the primary constraint on the use of coercion is not the risk of retaliatory punishment, but the risk of losing the partner's rewards. However unequal or insufficient the partner's rewarding may be, as long as actors stand to lose more than they can gain – with losses weighted for loss aversion – their use of coercion is constrained. Reducing A and C's reward dependence on B and D from .4 to 0 did not reduce their reward frequency to 0, but it did reduce it enough (from .39 to .23, based on means during the first 100 trials) that B and D's potential losses from a decrease in their partners' rewarding were well below the potential gains from an increase in their rewarding, even with losses weighted for loss aversion. Unless B and D estimate reward loss to be substantially more likely than reward gain, we would expect coercion to increase as A and C's reward frequency declines. And it did.

Although removing the risk of retaliatory punishment had little effect by itself, it enhanced the effects of reducing the risk of reward loss over time. Reducing *both* sources of risk produced the highest frequency of punishment, increased (rather than decreased) punishment over time, and increased the reward exchange of the target of coercion over time. No other structure produced all of these effects. Note, however, that reducing both sources of risk – by removing A and C's punishment power, and B and D's reward power – created a structure of pure coercion, in which neither mutual reward exchange nor mutual punishment was possible. In the structures that are the focus of this research program – networks in which actors can engage in the mutual exchange of *both* rewards and punishments – risk constrains the use of coercion.

The lack of an overall effect of the risk of punitive retaliation is surprising in some respects, but consistent with the earlier experiments that found few effects of manipulations of punishment power advantage. The interaction between the two sources of risk and trial block suggests the two may affect the use of coercion at different times. Because the partner's insufficient rewarding motivates coercion in the first place, the prospect of changes in those rewards – for better or worse – may be the only salient factor in the initial decision to use coercion. Once initiated, the actual consequences of coercion, including punitive retaliation, determine its subsequent use.

Experiment 8: an alternative interpretation

My analysis explains the effect of the manipulation of potential reward loss by its impact on reward frequency. Eliminating A and C's reward dependence on B and D reduces the frequency with which they reward B and D, which in turn reduces the potential for reward loss relative to reward gain. As a result, B and D's use of punishment increases.

But an alternative interpretation of these effects is also possible: actors prefer to use rewards rather than punishment to influence their partners (even when their reward power is weaker), but they prefer some form of

Table 7.2. *Mean frequency of B's punishment, Experiment 8*

	B's reward power over A	
	Moderate	None
A's reward frequency		
.1	.08	.15
.3	.07	.10
.5	.03	.06

influence to not acting at all. According to this account, B and D increased their use of punishment not because A and C rarely rewarded them, but because it was the only base of power they had.

In Experiment 7, however, B and D's lack of reward power *determined* the frequency of A and C's rewarding; therefore, these alternative explanations are confounded. To disentangle them, I conducted an experiment using computer-simulated actors in which the frequency of A and C's rewarding was independent of whether B and D had reward power over them.

Experiment 8 studied two of the network structures from Experiment 7, those in which the risk of retaliatory punishment was removed and the risk of reward loss was manipulated (Figure 7.1c and d). But this time, only the actor in position B was a real subject; B's partners – A and D – were computer-simulated actors, and C was a hypothetical partner for A and D. I manipulated the frequency of A's rewarding. A rewarded B on 10%, 30%, or 50% of all exchange opportunities, with the distribution of A's rewards determined randomly. D's behavior was controlled; D rewarded B on 30% of the exchange opportunities in all conditions. This 2 × 3 factorial design, which crossed B's reward power over A (power or no power) with the frequency of A's rewarding (10%, 30%, or 50%), made A's reward frequency independent of A's reward dependence on B. Thus, I could determine whether B increased punishment in response to A's infrequent rewarding, or in response to B's lack of reward power.

The results of an analysis of variance on B's punishment frequency (see Table 7.2 for the means) show significant effects of both variables. B punished A more frequently when A's reward frequency was lower ($F_{2,54}$ = 5.01, p < .01) *and* when B had no reward power ($F_{1,54}$ = 4.46, p < .05). The effect of reward frequency was the stronger of the two (eta = .38 for A's reward frequency and .25 for B's power).

These results partially support the theoretical analysis. They show that the primary determinant of B's increased punishment is A's lower reward frequency, which reduces the risk of reward loss. At the same time, they also suggest that actors are less likely to punish, regardless of risk, when both bases of power are available. Disadvantaged actors who have some amount of reward power are more likely to try to influence their partner through positive rather than negative incentives, relying on the principle of reciprocity – give what you hope to receive – rather than on the use of contingent sanctions.

These conclusions must be qualified, however, by an important caveat: they were obtained under conditions in which the subject's behavior had no effect on the partner's behavior. The simulated partner continued to reward the subject at the programmed frequency regardless of whether the subject offered reward or punishment. Thus, the preference for rewarding over punishing is obtained under conditions in which both are equally effective – or ineffective – strategies. Differential experiences with the relative effectiveness of these two bases of power are likely to affect their use.

Experiment 9: the effects of punishment power under low risk

Experiments 7 and 8 showed that reducing risk, particularly by reducing the potential for reward loss relative to reward gain, increases the use of coercion. These experiments could not examine how increased *use* of coercion affects the impact of variations in the structure of punishment power, however. Apart from the manipulation of risk, neither experiment varied the absolute or relative strength of punishment power. Experiment 9 was designed to address that question.

Experiment 9 tests how the target of power use responds to varying levels of reward and punishment power when the risks of using both forms of power are equivalent for the power user. With risk reduced and frequency of coercion increased, the effects of punishment power should also

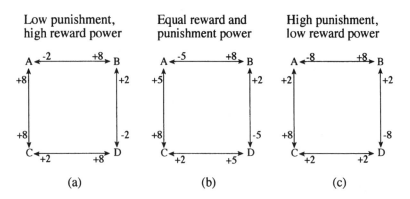

Figure 7.3. The exchange networks in Experiment 9

increase. Actors with relatively greater punishment power should be more successful than those with weaker power at increasing their partners' reward exchange.

Design

Because the experimental reduction of the risk of reward loss leaves actors with only punishment power over their partners, this experiment cannot compare the effects of reward and punishment power in networks in which actors have both. Instead, I compared the effects of the two bases when each is an actor's sole source of power, by placing an actor with only punishment power (B) and an actor with only reward power (C) in direct competition with each other for exchange with a third actor, A, who had only reward power (Figure 7.3). (For ease of reading, both rewards and punishments are displayed on the outer perimeters of these networks.) The fourth actor in the network, D, provided an alternative for B and C, but D's behavior was not of interest for its own sake. All four actors were real subjects.

In all conditions, both B and C are highly and equally dependent on A for rewards, giving both actors a strong (and equal) incentive to secure A's rewards through strategic power use. And, in all conditions, both sources of risk for B's use of coercion are equal to those in the lowest risk condition of Experiment 7 (Figure 7.1d). A has no power to punish and no reward dependence on B. Thus, both the incentive to use power and the risks of power use are equal for the two bases of power, and both bases must be used strategically. Just as B can try to coerce A's rewarding through contingent punishment, C can try to induce A's rewarding through contingent reward.

The completely randomized design compares three conditions that vary B's power over A relative to C's power over A: (1) B with lower power than C (low punishment, high reward power, Figure 7.3a), (2) B and C with equal power (Figure 7.3b), and (3) B with greater power than C (high punishment, low reward power, Figure 7.3c). Subjects exchanged for 200 opportunities.

The main dependent variable is the relative frequency with which A rewarded B, computed by dividing the frequency of A's rewards to B by the total frequency with which A rewarded both B and C.

Hypotheses

Initially, A should prefer to exchange with C, the actor with the power to reward A, in all conditions. But over time, if B punishes A when A fails to reward B, A's rewards to B should increase in proportion to B's relative power over A. The initial effects of the base of power that B and C control should disappear; only their relative power should matter.

H1. The relative frequency with which A rewards B rather than C will vary directly with B's relative power over A.

H2. Support for Hypothesis 1 will increase over time.

H3. By the last trial block, the frequency of A's rewards to B when B's punishment power is high will equal the frequency of A's rewards to C when C's reward power is high (and B's punishment power is low).

Results

In all conditions, B punished A an average of 27% of the time, a frequency comparable with that in the lowest risk condition of Experiment 7. What effect did B's increased use of punishment have on the effectiveness of B's punishment power?

Figure 7.4 shows the relative frequency with which A rewarded B, by condition, across the four 50-trial blocks of the exchange. As expected, A

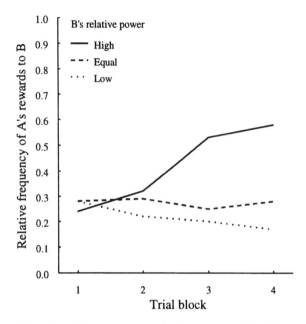

Figure 7.4. Relative frequency of A's rewards to B, by B's relative power and trial block, Experiment 9

initially preferred to exchange with C, the partner with the power to reward A, in all three conditions. But over time, the relative structural power of A's two partners assumed greater influence over A's behavior. A repeated-measures analysis of variance, using B's relative power as a between-subject variable and trial block as a within-subject variable, shows a significant interaction between these two variables as predicted by Hypothesis 2 ($F_{6,81}$ = 12.14, p < .001). A's preference for exchange with B increased over time when B's punishment power was stronger than C's reward power, decreased when it was weaker, and did not change when both were equal.

By the third trial block, the effect of B's relative power on A's relative rewarding was significant ($F_{2,27}$ = 5.76, p < .01). And by the fourth (last) trial block, as Hypothesis 3 predicts, the frequency of A's rewards to B in the high punishment power condition did not differ significantly from the frequency of A's rewards to C (not shown in Figure 7.4) in the high reward power condition (t = .40).

The contingency of punishment. These results show, as predicted, that punishment power is more effective when it is used more frequently. But frequency per se is a poor measure of coercion. To use punishment to coerce rewards, actors must make their punishment contingent on the other's failure to reward.

To examine whether the effectiveness of B's punishment power did result from an increase in the use of contingent punishment, rather than random or noncontingent punishment, I regressed the relative frequency with which A rewarded B during the last 50-trial block on the frequency and the contingency with which B punished A during the entire 200 trials. For comparison, I also included the frequency and contingency with which C rewarded A. The effects of the frequency and contingency of reward and punishment were estimated after controlling for the effects of the experimental manipulation of power (represented by two dichotomous variables).

I computed each measure of contingency by the difference between two conditional probabilities:

$$\text{Contingency of B's punishing} = p(P_B|\overline{R}_A) - p(P_B|R_A), \text{ and} \tag{1}$$
$$\text{Contingency of C's rewarding} = p(R_C|R_A) - p(R_C|\overline{R}_A), \tag{2}$$

where P_B = punishment from B to A at time t, R_C = reward from C to A at time t, R_A = reward from A to the designated partner at time $t - 1$, and $\overline{R}_A$ = no reward from A to the designated partner at time $t - 1$. Overall, the mean contingency of C's rewarding was .25 and the mean contingency of B's punishing was .33. These means do not differ significantly from each other, nor do they vary by power condition.

The results, summarized in Table 7.3, show the strong effect of coercive, contingent punishment. Not only does the contingency of B's punishment have an independent effect on the distribution of A's rewards, but the contingency of B's punishment is the strongest predictor of A's relative rewarding. The greater the contingency of B's punishment on A's nonrewarding, the more likely A was to reward B rather than C. With contingency controlled, the frequency of punishment had a negative effect on A's rewarding, replicating the results of the strategy analyses in Chapter 5. As those analyses also found, neither the frequency nor the contingency of C's rewarding had a significant effect on the relative frequency of A's rewarding.

Table 7.3. *Regression of A's relative frequency of rewarding B, on B's relative power and the frequency and contingency of B's punishment and C's rewards, Experiment 9*

Variables	b	SE	T
Intercept	0.16	.17	0.90
Punishment power[a]	0.16	.10	1.65
Reward power[a]	0.02	.10	-0.23
B's punishment frequency	-1.55	.48	-3.25**
C's reward frequency	0.16	.21	0.77
B's punishment contingency	1.42	.36	3.97***
C's reward contingency	-0.02	.21	-0.09
$R^2 = .64$			

[a]Punishment power is a dichotomous variable for the high punishment (low reward) power condition; reward power is a dichotomous variable for the low punishment (high reward) power condition. The equal power condition is the omitted category.
**$p < .01$ ***$p < .001$

Implications

Experiment 9 shows that the effectiveness of coercive power increases when a reduction in risk increases its use. Because low risk could be created only by altering the structure of power itself, I tested the effectiveness of punishment power under conditions in which actors had no power to reward. Remarkably, the effectiveness of punishment obtained even in a relation that was purely coercive; that is, B could respond to A's rewarding only by withholding punishment, not by reciprocating A's rewards.

The results of the contingency analyses confirm the theoretical arguments and empirical results developed in Chapter 5. The effectiveness of punishment power increased with the contingency of its use; in fact, the contingency of punishment had a stronger effect than structural power on the partner's rewarding. This finding, together with the finding that the contingency of rewarding had no effect once structural power was controlled, confirms one of the main conclusions of Chapter 5: how actors use punishment power is more important than how much power they have, whereas the opposite is true for reward power.

Summary and conclusions

This chapter examined how risk and fear of retaliation constrain the strategic use of power in exchange relations. Theories of choice under risk and uncertainty, particularly Axelrod's evolutionary theory and Kahneman and Tversky's prospect theory, help to explain why actors rarely use coercive power even when both their capacity and their incentive to coerce are high. Power use is risky (it may produce either gain or loss), and actors fear loss far more than they value gain. Consequently, disadvantaged actors in imbalanced exchange relations will accept insufficient and unequal rewards rather than risk the unknown consequences of power use, and they will reduce the use of power strategies that produce immediate retaliation, sometimes at the cost of long-term gains.

In general, a structural advantage on either base of power reduces risk because it reduces both the likelihood and magnitude of loss from the partner's retaliation with that same base of power. Thus, actors with greater coercive power face less risk of loss from the other's punitive retaliation, and actors with greater reward power face less risk of loss from the other's reward withdrawal. But because the incentive to use coercion comes not from the power to coerce, but from dependence on another for rewards, coercion is still risky, even for actors who are advantaged on punishment power. Reward dependence creates the desire to make the partner give more, but it also creates the fear that what the partner is currently giving might be lost. This conflict between potential gain and potential loss constrains coercion until the partner's reward frequency is low enough that potential losses from the partner's reward withdrawal, even when weighted by loss aversion, are lower than potential gains.

The implications of this analysis, supported by the experiments, is that higher frequencies of coercion are more likely to be found in relations in which one member is highly dependent on the other for rewards, but the partner's reward dependence is so low that few rewards are forthcoming. This might occur, for example, when individuals remain in relations even after one partner's reward dependence has declined, because of contractual or normative obligations (e.g., marriage or business relations), or when the constraints of structure or stratification create highly asymmetrical relations for which there are few alternatives (e.g., tight job markets, friend-ships in small closed communities).[19]

Under these conditions, however, the structural basis for *mutually* ben-eficial exchange is either weak or absent. The coercer must rely solely on the threat of punishment to maintain the other's rewarding, rather than using coercion as a tool to establish a relation of mutual reward exchange that is more favorable to the coercer. As a result, disadvantaged actors in stable but unequal relations will use coercion occasionally, but not fre-quently enough to have much impact on their advantaged partners. Co-ercion increases to effective levels only when an actor literally has nothing to lose. This is true, of course, of many of the classic examples of coercion (e.g., mugger and victim), in which there is no relation of mutual reward exchange to risk losing.

This principle helps to explain the puzzling finding, observed repeatedly in the earlier experiments, that even when actors who were disadvantaged on reward power had an equal and opposing punishment power advantage, they still used coercion rarely. Although nearly all of the earlier experi-ments studied coercion in exchange relations in which average reward dependence was high enough (i.e., greater than .5) to maintain mutual but asymmetrical reward exchange, this analysis shows that coercion is un-likely to be used much in those structures. The conflict between the po-tential gains and potential losses from power use is simply too great. Consequently, although reward power disadvantage sometimes increased the use of punishment, the results were inconsistent and the effects were small (see Chapter 5).

The concept of the status quo bias also helps to explain why punishment always declined over time in the experiments in Chapter 5. In the early stages of exploratory interaction, there is little to lose from the partner's potential withdrawal of rewards because no stable pattern of rewarding has been established. Consequently, actors are more likely to attempt co-ercion. But because these attempts typically provoke retaliation, they are suppressed. Then, as the relationship progresses and some level of reward exchange is established, attachment to the status quo increases, even if it is less than optimal (Kahneman and Varey 1991). The negative value

---

[19] An additional set of conditions, beyond the scope of this program, could also reduce the risk of reward loss: if the partner cannot leave the relation, and in fact is compelled by law or normative obligation to continue providing some level of rewards, the risk of the partner's reward withdrawal is reduced.

attached to losing the partner's rewards escalates, and coercion becomes riskier. In general, actors should be more likely to risk power use in the early stages of relationships than later on, unless the benefits from the relation have declined to such a level that an actor has little to lose.

There are two interesting ironies to this analysis. First, the same principle that should make punishment power highly potent when it is used – the preference for minimizing loss over maximizing gain – instead constrains its use. Second, the structural conditions that encourage the use of coercion, by reducing risk, probably decrease its effectiveness and contribute to the widespread belief that it *is* ineffective. The lower the partner's reward dependence, the more difficult it becomes to coerce the partner into reward exchange. Coercion can still be effective even under these conditions, as Experiment 9 illustrated. But punishment should be far more effective when combined with rewards and used in a structure that supports mutually beneficial exchange. I test this assertion in Chapter 9.

Finally, the analysis in this chapter demonstrates that even though the study of strategic power use departs from Emerson's original focus, the cornerstone of power-dependence theory – the concept of dependence – is as central to coercive power as to reward power. Dependence on others for gaining rewards both induces and constrains the use of coercive power, and dependence on others for avoiding punishment determines how effective coercive power will be once used.

This chapter has examined how the structure of dependence increases the risk of coercive power use. But actors also may avoid using punishment because it violates norms of justice and ''fair exchange'' (Blau 1964). Concerns with justice and equity have long been a theme in theories of exchange; Chapter 8 explores how these norms affect the use of power and responses to that use.

8. Injustice and risk: normative constraints on strategic power use

The classical exchange theorists (Blau 1964; Homans [1961] 1974; Thibaut and Kelley 1959) believed that social exchange is governed not only by the actual benefits actors obtain from one another, but by the expectations they bring to the relation as a result of past experiences or social norms. These expectations, like the status quo, provide a reference point for evaluating the rewards received from exchange. Rewards that either exceed or fall short of expectations produce emotional reactions, such as satisfaction or anger, and these emotions can influence behavior.

When expectations are based on *social* comparisons of some kind – what you receive in comparison to another person or reference group – questions of fairness or justice arise.[1] Because such comparisons are an inevitable result of social exchange, power and justice are considered, by many, to be the two most important concepts of social exchange theory.

Nevertheless, the role of justice in the classical theories is something of an aberration. The concept of justice is found in neither of the root theories of social exchange (behavioral psychology or microeconomics), and its inclusion in exchange theory requires that we import concepts from other theories, either normative or cognitive. While Blau (1964) emphasized the former, contemporary justice theories tend to give more weight to the latter. Principles of justice have a normative base, but because perceptions of justice are in the eye of the beholder, they are subject to some of the same kinds of cognitive biases (e.g., loss aversion) discussed in the preceding chapter.

In this chapter I examine whether and how norms of justice affect reactions to an exchange partner's use of power. I begin by reviewing and assessing theories of justice. Then, drawing on principles of loss aversion and attribution, I show that coercion is more likely than reward withhold-

---

[1] I use these two terms interchangeably.

ing to provoke feelings of injustice. These feelings should increase the partner's tendency to resist or retaliate, according to justice theories, and therefore increase the risks of using coercion. These risks are greater for actors in disadvantaged positions.

Two experiments test these predictions by examining how subjects evaluate and respond to power strategies based on reward or coercive power and how the structure of power modifies these responses. As they show, rather than providing a moral counterforce to structural power, justice norms reinforce the effects of structure on risk and contribute to the low use of coercion.

Theories of justice and social exchange

Early theories of equity were influenced by Homans's ([1961] 1974) concept of distributive justice and Blau's (1964) discussion of fair exchange. Homans proposed that individuals follow a rule that prescribes proportionality (i.e., equity) between the rewards one receives from exchange and one's costs. Blau (1964) emphasized the normative basis of justice rules and the societal needs from which they derive.

Equity theorists proposed, much like Homans, that actors compare either ratios or differences of exchange *inputs* and reward *outcomes* with those of other actors (e.g., Adams 1965; Harris 1976; Walster, Walster, and Berscheid 1978). When actors' outcomes are proportional to their inputs, equity is said to obtain. Discrepancies between what is expected, based on this rule, and what is actually received produce psychological distress and motivate individuals to reduce distress and restore equity.

Equity theories emphasize "local" comparisons, in which individuals compare their own input–outcome ratios to those of particular other individuals, presumably exchange partners. As Cook and Hegtvedt (1983) and McClintock and Keil (1982) have noted, however, there is a curious gap between the exchange terms in which these theories are couched and the empirical settings in which they have been tested. Most of the research was conducted in allocation settings, especially industrial settings (natural or experimental), in which employees compared ratios of work-to-pay with other employees with whom they were not in a direct exchange relation (Walster et al. 1978). Even Homans's ([1961] 1974) original formulation of distributive justice was based on examples drawn from this kind of setting.

Recent formulations of distributive justice (e.g., Jasso 1980; Markovsky 1985) have moved away from a focus on justice in direct exchange relations to more general models in which actors compare their actual outcomes to some justice standard – that is, what they think they ought to receive. This standard may be based on the outcomes that a specific other receives (an exchange partner or another recipient of an allocation such as a fellow employee), or on a general referential structure, such as "what all class II secretaries make" (Berger, Cohen, and Zelditch 1972). Perceptions of injustice increase as an actor's actual rewards depart from this justice standard.[2]

Virtually all theories of justice assume that perceptions of injustice create distress and lead to either cognitive or behavioral efforts to restore justice. Inequity can induce such reactions as uncooperativeness (Marwell and Schmitt 1975), withdrawal (Schmitt and Marwell 1972), and the formation of revolutionary coalitions (Lawler 1975; Webster and Smith 1978). But because the perception of injustice is subjective, individuals can also construe events in ways that allow them to believe that individuals get what they deserve (e.g., victims of crime deserve their fate). Self-interest plays a substantial role in this process. Thus, while early equity theories proposed that *both* overrewarded and underrewarded actors would feel distressed and would try to restore equity to the relation, most contemporary theorists restrict such efforts to the underrewarded. Those who benefit from inequalities are more likely to restore justice cognitively, by convincing themselves that their greater benefits are deserved and fair (e.g., Hegtvedt 1990; Leventhal and Anderson 1970; Michaels, Edwards, and Acock 1984). It is the victims of injustice who are most likely to initiate behavioral efforts to restore justice or seek retribution.

More recently, work on procedural justice has proposed that judgments of fairness are a function not only of outcomes in relation to some standard of justice, but of the process or procedures through which those outcomes are obtained (e.g., Leventhal, Karuza, and Fry 1980; Lind and Tyler 1988; Thibaut and Walker 1975). This perspective is particularly relevant to judgments about power use in exchange relations. Conceptions of process in this literature have been fairly limited, though, with most work address-

---

[2] All of these theories assume that cognitive calculations of justice precede emotional reactions to injustice. For an interesting challenge to this perspective, see Scher and Heise (1993). They propose that emotional reactions precede cognitive work, and that actors do not calculate justice unless they feel a justice-related emotion (i.e., anger or guilt).

ing third-party procedures for settling legal disputes, or rules and procedures in bureaucratic decision making – for example, the rules that
university committees use to allocate internal research grants.[3]

Theories of both distributive and procedural justice focus almost exclusively on the fair distribution of rewards. The study of retributive justice,
or the fair use and distribution of punishments, has received little attention
outside the framework of criminal behavior (e.g., Austin, Walster, and
Utne 1976; Hamilton and Rytina 1980; Miller and Vidmar 1981).[4]

Assumptions about justice processes

Despite their roots in social exchange, most theories of justice rely on a
rather different set of assumptions, derived from theories of social comparison and cognitive consistency. Perceptions of justice, like evaluations
of outcomes, are referent dependent. But the reference standard (i.e., the
justice standard) is some function that *compares* the actor's own outcomes
with those of another actor, group, or referential structure (Hegtvedt and
Markovsky 1995), not the status quo. The assumptions that departures
from this standard will produce emotional distress, and that actors will
attempt to reduce distress either cognitively or behaviorally, are based on
principles of cognitive dissonance (e.g., Adams 1965).

The forms of interaction that most justice theories assume also differ
from relations of direct exchange. Both distributive and procedural justice
theories are concerned with settings in which resources are allocated to a
set of actors, rather than exchanged between actors – settings in which,
for example, employers allocate pay to workers, criminal justice systems
allocate punishment to offenders, or committees allocate benefits to ap-
plicants.

But allocation and exchange settings differ in fundamental ways. In
allocation settings, shares of a ''whole'' – a resource pool – are distributed
to members of a group (e.g., a workplace, a family, an organization, or

---

[3] For comprehensive reviews of social psychological theories of justice, see Cook and
Hegtvedt (1983) and Hegtvedt and Markovsky (1995).

[4] See Hogan and Emler (1981) for an argument that retribution, not distribution, is the
most fundamental principle of justice. See, also, Marwell and Schmitt's research on inequity
in cooperative relations, which examines both reward- and punishment-based responses to
inequity (Marwell and Schmitt 1975; Schmitt and Marwell 1970, 1972). Recently, a body
of research comparing positive and negative outcome allocation has begun to emerge, particularly in Europe (see Tornblom 1988 and Griffith 1989 for reviews of this literature).

even a society), who merit consideration by virtue of their contributions to the group. In such a setting, it is appropriate for actors to compare their resource shares either with those received by members of the group who are most like themselves, or with some "generalized other" (Berger et al. 1972), and to apply some principle of equal treatment based on this comparison. In exchange settings, in contrast, separate resources are transmitted in a two-way exchange between two actors. The actors are not members of a group, and the resources are not shares of a whole. Instead, the benefits that are given and received in exchange are related to one another through their *contingency* on each other.

As Eckhoff (1974) (and, much earlier, Aristotle) has observed, these differences between allocation and exchange call for different conceptions of justice. In exchange settings, principles of reciprocation rather than distribution should underlie conceptions of justice; that is, actors should compare what they get with what they give. This principle corresponds to the scope condition that defines social exchange: "benefits obtained . . . are contingent on benefits provided" (Emerson 1981:32). When transformed from a description of social exchange to a prescription for fair exchange, this "norm of reciprocity" (Gouldner 1960) specifies that outcomes received should be contingent on, and functionally equivalent to, outcomes given (i.e., good should be repaid by good, and harm by harm) (Molm, Quist, and Wiseley 1993).[5]

In structurally balanced relations, I assume that reciprocity is the justice standard that actors use to evaluate whether exchange is fair or unfair. (Later, I consider how structural imbalance affects this standard.) As discrepancies between this standard and actual exchange increase, those whose exchange is not reciprocated equally will be more likely to feel distress and to perceive the exchange as unfair. These feelings of injustice can provoke behavioral reactions, leading actors to reduce their rewards or punish their partners.

Justice, power use, and risk

Even though power and justice were two of the central concerns of classical exchange theorists, contemporary analyses have rarely examined their

---

[5] Some degree of reciprocity is an attribute of social exchange relations *by definition* (Emerson 1972b; Gouldner 1960). Reciprocity can vary, however, on the dimensions identified here.

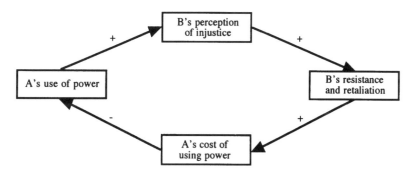

Figure 8.1. Causal model linking justice and power use in an exchange relation between actors A and B

relations to each other.[6] Emerson (1972a, 1972b) omitted justice altogether from his theory (but reintroduced it in his empirical work with Cook [Cook and Emerson 1978]), and most justice theories ignore the potential effects of power on perceptions of justice and reactions to injustice.

I propose that the use of power and norms of justice are linked in a control model, shown in Figure 8.1, in which A's power strategies provoke normative reactions from B that potentially feed back on and constrain A's use of power. This model connects justice norms with the analysis of risk in Chapter 7 through four causal paths: (1) A's use of power provokes feelings of unfairness and injustice in B, (2) B responds with behavioral efforts to restore justice, by *resisting* or *retaliating* rather than complying with A's power use, (3) these reactions make A's use of power costly, and (4) increased costs constrain A's power use.[7]

According to this model, to the extent that justice norms constrain power use, they do so indirectly, through their effects on the target of power use. Alternatively, of course, actors might constrain their power use because of the moral weight of justice norms (Blau 1964) or because of a preference for acting fairly (Kahneman, Knetsch, and Thaler 1986). Although there is evidence that actors sometimes do restrict their use of power when they learn that it produces inequality (e.g., Cook, Hegtvedt, and Yamagishi 1988), most research suggests that actors in powerful positions are able to convince themselves that they deserve greater benefits

---

[6] For exceptions, see Austin and Hatfield (1980), Cohen (1986), Cook and Emerson (1978), Cook and Hegtvedt (1986), Cook et al. (1988), and Stolte (1983, 1987a, 1987b).

[7] Homans ([1961] 1974) proposes much the same process.

(e.g., Cook and Hegtvedt 1986; Stolte 1983). Thus, although I do not rule out the possibility that actors reduce their use of power because it violates their own standards of fairness, it seems more likely, as Figure 8.1 suggests, that they do so because it violates their *partners'* standards of fairness.

This model provides a general framework for analyzing the relation between justice norms and the use of power. My primary interest is in how the first two relations in the model – the effects of power use on exchange partners' perceptions of injustice, and their behavioral reactions to injustice – are affected by the base of power used and the structural power in the relation. The third link, between retaliation and risk of loss, is logically true, and the fourth link, between risk of loss and power use, was tested and supported in Chapter 7.

I examine two separate but related issues. First, is the use of coercive power perceived as more unjust than the use of reward power, even when both represent equal departures from reciprocity, and does it provoke stronger behavioral reactions to injustice? Second, how does the structural context in which power is used affect these perceptions and reactions? As we have seen, reward power and coercive power are likely to be used by actors in different structural positions; therefore, how structure modifies justice evaluations can affect actors' use of these two bases of power. These two questions are the focus of the theoretical analysis in this chapter, and each is the subject of an experiment.

Experiment 10: the unjust use of power

The use of either reward power or coercive power violates the principle of reciprocity. Actors who withhold rewards reciprocate the other's reward exchange only part of the time; those who punish coercively respond to the partner's failure to reward with punishment. Consequently, the use of *either* base of power should be judged less fair than reciprocal exchange by the targets of power use.

Of the two power strategies, however, coercion is more likely to be judged unfair. This prediction is not based on any objective differences between the two. If actors withhold rewards or punish nonexchange with equal frequency, and if the values of the punishments and rewards that they give or withhold are equal, then the two forms of power use are equally nonreciprocal. In both cases, the actor follows the partner's behavior with a less desirable response, by responding to rewards with non-exchange (reward withholding) or to nonexchange with punishment (coercion).

Despite this objective equality in the justice – or injustice – of the use of reward and coercive power, two psychological tendencies suggest that coercion will be judged less fair than equivalent reward withholding: (1) the principle of loss aversion discussed in Chapter 7 – that is, the tendency for actors to perceive losses as more negative than equivalent gains are perceived as positive (see Kahneman et al. 1986, 1991) – and (2) differences in the imputed intentionality of power strategies based on reward withholding or coercion.

The principle of loss aversion implies that individuals will perceive the difference between punishment and nonexchange as greater than the difference between reward and nonexchange. If so, responding to a partner's nonexchange with punishment (coercion) will be evaluated as more nonreciprocal – and less fair – than responding to a partner's rewards with nonexchange (reward withholding), even if the differences between the values of reward and nonexchange, and of nonexchange and punishment, are objectively the same.

Attribution theorists argue that the intentionality of acts also influences perceptions of justice. The same act is more likely to be judged unfair (Cohen 1982; Utne and Kidd 1980), and to provoke behavioral efforts to restore justice (Garrett and Libby 1973; Hassebrauck 1987), if its negative consequences are viewed as intentional. Because reward withholding is an act of omission rather than commission, its intentionality is ambiguous. As I discussed in Chapter 6, intermittent rewarding may represent the strategic use of power (withholding rewards until the other gives more), or it may be an unintended by-product of exchanging with another, more desirable partner. No such ambiguity is involved in the use of punishment. It is an act of commission, directed at a specific target. As such, it is more likely to be judged intentional, and unfair. Research suggests, in general, that individuals hold actors responsible for the consequences of their commissions but not their omissions (Ritov and Baron 1992; Spranca, Minsk, and Baron 1991).

The second link in the causal model (Figure 8.1) proposes that perceptions of injustice lead to behavioral reactions and attempts to restore justice. Actors can respond to the perceived injustice of their partner's power use by *resisting* or *retaliating*, behaviors comparable to the two

forms of retaliation discussed in Chapter 7. Actors resist by not rewarding the partner, and they retaliate by punishing the partner.[8] If both
power strategies (reward withholding and coercion) are judged unjust,
then both should prompt one or both of these reactions. But because
greater injustices typically provoke more severe responses (Hamilton
and Rytina 1980), reactions to coercion should be stronger than reactions to reward withholding.

This analysis suggests three hypotheses, which are tested in Experiment 10:

H1. The targets of coercion and reward withholding will perceive both
strategies as less fair than reciprocal exchange.

H2. Actors will perceive coercion as less fair than reward withholding
even when both strategies represent equal departures from reciprocal exchange.

H3. Actors' resistance and retaliation will increase with their perceived
injustice of their partner's exchange behavior; consequently, coercion should provoke stronger reactions than reward withholding.

Design

The experiments in this chapter and the next introduce several new procedures and manipulations. Because the focus of these experiments is on
the reactions of individual actors to a partner's use of power, they are
conducted on exchange networks in which only one of the four actors is
a real subject (see Figure 8.2). That subject interacts with two computer-
simulated actors (POs) who are programmed to follow particular behavioral strategies. The fourth actor in the network (HYP) exists only as a
hypothetical partner for the POs. The use of computer-simulated actors
makes it possible to create strategies of reward and coercive power use
that are comparable on every dimension but the base of power. In both

---

[8] These behaviors differ in one important respect from those in Chapter 7, however: here,
resistance implies a *failure to increase* rewards in response to a partner's power use; in
Chapter 7, reward loss implied a *decrease* in rewards from an established level of exchange.
This shift is made for empirical rather than theoretical reasons. Because the experiments in
this chapter impose a constant rate of power use (by a computer-simulated actor) throughout
the exchange period, there is no opportunity to establish a reference point for exchange
before power is used. Thus, resistance is defined as a lower-than-expected frequency of
rewarding to the partner, and the term retaliation is reserved for punishment.

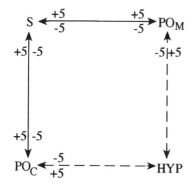

Figure 8.2. The exchange network in Experiment 10

experiments, I manipulate one PO's strategy (PO$_M$) while holding constant the strategy of the other (PO$_C$).

Experiment 10 employed a 2×2 factorial design that crossed PO$_M$'s use of reward power (the presence–absence of reward withholding) with PO$_M$'s use of coercive power (the presence–absence of coercion) to create four experimental conditions. I compared the effects of these strategies in an exchange network in which structural power was balanced on both bases (see Figure 8.2). Theoretically, of course, we are interested in the use of power in imbalanced networks, not balanced ones. But an unbiased test of the relative fairness of coercion and reward withholding requires comparing them within a single, neutral structure. In a power-balanced network, equivalent strategies of coercion and reward withholding represent equal departures from the behavior that is expected and modal in that structure: reciprocal exchange.

Thus, the logic of the research was first to test the relative fairness of reward withholding and coercion in a balanced structure (Experiment 10), and then to examine how variations in structural power affect perceptions of their fairness (Experiment 11).

All actors in the network had equal power: each could add 5 points to, or subtract 5 points from, either of their potential partners on each opportunity. Thus, actors were equally dependent on their two partners and, on structural grounds, indifferent between them. Their equal dependence assured that the probabilities that they would perform the behaviors on which the nonreciprocal power strategies were contingent (exchange or

Table 8.1. *The power strategies, Experiment 10*

Experimental condition	Probability of PO_M's behavior, conditional on S's prior behavior[a]		
	Conditional on reward	Conditional on nonexchange	Conditional on punishment
Reciprocal strategy[b]	R|R = .9	R|N = .1	R|P = 0
(modified tit-for-tat)	N|R = .1	N|N = .9	N|P = .1
	P|R = 0	P|N = 0	P|P = .9
Reward power strategy	R|R = .4	R|N = .1	R|P = 0
(nonreciprocal reward-	N|R = .6	N|N = .9	N|P = .1
withholding)	P|R = 0	P|N = 0	P|P = .9
Coercive power strategy	R|R = .9	R|N = .1	R|P = 0
(nonreciprocal punishment)	N|R = .1	N|N = .4	N|P = .1
	P|R = 0	P|N = .5	P|P = .9
Combined power strategy	R|R = .4	R|N = .1	R|P = 0
(nonreciprocal reward-	N|R = .6	N|N = .4	N|P = .1
withholding and punishment)	P|R = 0	P|N = .5	P|P = .9

[a] $i|j$ = the conditional probability of PO_M's behavior i at time t, given the occurrence of S's behavior j at time t − 1, where i and j = R (reward), N (nonexchange), and P (punishment).
[b] PO_C used this strategy in all conditions.

nonexchange with a particular partner) were equal, and the probabilities of experiencing the nonreciprocal strategies were equal. Actors exchanged for 100 opportunities.[9]

Manipulation of strategies. The simulated partner whose behavior was manipulated (PO_M) used one of four programmed strategies: a *reciprocal* strategy, a *reward power* strategy, a *coercive power* strategy, or a *combined power* strategy (reward withholding *and* coercion).

The conditional probabilities that comprise these strategies are shown in Table 8.1. On each opportunity each actor could reward, punish, or not act toward a given partner. Consequently, the description of each PO's

[9] This is a much shorter exchange period than used in the previous experiments. Because the manipulated strategies influenced subjects' preferences for exchange partners, a longer period would eventually have produced near extinction of exchange with one partner or the other. The 100-period length, selected after pretesting, assured that subjects' evaluations would be based on recent, salient experiences with both partners.

strategy consists of nine conditional probabilities, specifying the probabilities with which the PO responded with each of these three actions, given each of the three actions by the subject (S) on the previous exchange opportunity.[10]

In the reciprocal condition, PO_M used a modified tit-for-tat strategy, reciprocating S's prior behavior 90% of the time.[11] (The second simulated actor, PO_C, used this strategy in all four conditions.) For the reward and coercive strategies, PO_M responded nonreciprocally to *either* S's rewards (with nonexchange, the reward strategy) *or* S's nonexchange (with punishment, the coercive strategy), and reciprocally to S's other actions. The probabilities in these conditions represent equal departures from the probabilities in the reciprocal strategy; in both, reciprocal responding was reduced (and nonreciprocal responding increased) by .5.[12] In the combined power strategy, PO_M responded to S's rewards with the reward strategy and to S's nonexchange with the coercive strategy, while reciprocating S's punishment.

Measures of perceived justice. At the end of the exchange period, subjects evaluated the fairness of their partners' behavior toward them on a series of 7-point semantic differential scales presented on their computer screens. Responses to three of these items – fair–unfair, just–unjust, and equitable–

---

[10] All probabilities were randomized over blocks of 10 actions of the specified type by the subject. In all conditions, both POs were programmed to reward the subject on the first opportunity.

[11] That is, 90% of the time, PO_M responded to S's rewards with rewards, to punishment with punishment, and to nonexchange with nonexchange. The remaining 10% of the time, PO_M responded to S's rewarding with nonexchange, to S's nonexchange with rewarding, and to S's punishment with nonexchange.

[12] For the reward strategy, the probability with which PO_M reciprocated S's rewarding (R|R) was reduced by .5 (from .9 to .4), and the probability with which PO_M responded to S's rewarding with nonexchange (N|R) was increased by .5 (from .1 to .6). For the coercive strategy, the probability with which PO_M reciprocated S's nonexchange (N|N) was reduced by .5 (from .9 to .4), and the probability with which PO_M responded to S's nonexchange with punishment (P|N) was increased by .5 (from 0 to .5). Although these probabilities represent equal departures from the probabilities in the reciprocal strategy, they are not equal to one another in an absolute sense. Pretesting suggested it was necessary to have PO_M occasionally respond to S's nonexchange by initiating reward exchange in order to assure some interaction with S in all conditions. Consequently, p(R|N) was set at .1 and p(P|N) at 0 in the reciprocal strategy, and a .5 increase in p(P|N) in the coercive strategy produced a conditional probability of .5, rather than .6 – the probability of (N|R) in the reward strategy. To examine whether this difference in absolute probabilities affected the results, an additional coercive condition studied probabilities of p(R|N) = 0, p(N|N) = .4, and p(P|N) = .6. This condition produced results that were virtually identical to those reported for the coercive strategy in this experiment.

Table 8.2. *Mean perceptions of fairness and intentionality and mean behavioral reactions toward* PO_M *, Experiment 10*

	PO_M's strategy			
	Reciprocal	Reward	Coercive	Combined
Perceptions of fairness				
Fairness of PO_M's behavior	16.80	14.60	10.20	7.50
Fairness of PO_C's behavior	17.20	17.50	18.30	19.50
Fairness of structure	6.10	5.80	5.90	6.40
Perceptions of PO_M's intentionality				
Intentional-unintentional	5.30	4.70	5.90	6.30
Active-passive	4.30	3.80	5.20	6.20
Behavioral reactions toward PO_M				
Rewarding	0.49	0.28	0.51	0.30
Resistance	0.00	0.02	0.12	0.13
Retaliation	0.01	0.05	0.06	0.12

Note: Scale values for the fairness of POs' behavior range from 3 to 21. Those for fairness of the structure and perceptions of intent range from 1 to 7.

inequitable – were summed to form a justice scale with an alpha reliability of .81 for the fairness of PO_M's behavior. Scale values range from 3 (very unfair) to 21 (very fair), with a midpoint of 12.[13]

Subjects also evaluated the fairness of the earnings schedule – that is, the structure of power in the network – on a single item, fair–unfair. Because structural power was identical in all conditions, responses to this item indicate whether subjects were able to separate evaluations of the fairness of the strategies from the fairness of the structure. Two additional items on the questionnaire, measuring subjects' assessments of their partners' behavior as intentional–unintentional and active–passive, were used to test the relation of these variables to perceived fairness. Each of these items has a range of 1 (very unfair) to 7 (very fair). The mean values of all items are shown in Table 8.2.

[13] Experiments that study the fairness of exchange outcomes typically inform subjects of the total amounts of money that they and their partners receive from one another. Because the focus here is on the fairness of the partner's use of power, not exchange outcomes, the trial-by-trial account of what actors gave and received on each exchange opportunity served the same purpose.

Measures of behavioral reactions. Subjects in the experiment could respond to perceived injustice by resisting (withholding rewards) or retaliating (punishing) PO_M's power use. The mean frequencies of those behaviors are also shown in Table 8.2.

Because the frequencies with which subjects gave or withheld rewards should be a function not only of injustice, but of the actual consequences of rewarding PO_M and PO_C, the measure of resistance must take into account the differences in expected values across the four conditions.[14] Therefore, I computed S's resistance to PO_M by subtracting the actual frequency of S's rewards to PO_M (also shown in Table 8.2) from the expected frequency.[15] Because the expected values for S's punishing PO_M are identical in all conditions, the measure of retaliation requires no such adjustment.

Results

Perceptions of fairness. An analysis of variance on the perceptions of the fairness of PO_M's behavior (see Table 8.2) supports both of the first two hypotheses. As Hypothesis 1 predicts, subjects evaluated both the reward and coercive strategies as significantly less fair than reciprocal responding. Each power strategy independently decreased perceived fairness, relative to reciprocal responding ($F_{1,36} = 6.51$ for the reward strategy and 50.86

[14] Expected values can be estimated because the probabilities of the simulated actors' behaviors are known. The expected value of S's return for rewarding PO_i is computed by multiplying the probability with which each PO responds to S's rewards to PO_i with reward or punishment, by the value ($+/- 5$) of that response. The expected values (per opportunity) for rewarding PO_M are 5 points in the reciprocal and coercive strategy conditions and 2.5 points in the reward and combined strategy conditions. For rewarding PO_C, they are 5 points in the reciprocal and reward strategy conditions and 2.5 points in the coercive and combined strategy conditions.

[15] To compute S's resistance to PO_M, I first calculated the expected proportion of S's rewards to PO_M by assuming that subjects distribute their total reward exchange to both partners in proportion to the expected value of their returns for rewarding each partner (see note 14). This is a conservative assumption, based on matching (Herrnstein 1970) rather than maximizing. I then subtracted the *actual* proportion of S's rewards to PO_M from this *expected* proportion to produce the measure of resistance. For example, when PO_M used the reward strategy, S's expected value for rewarding PO_M on each opportunity was 2.5 points, and S's expected value for rewarding PO_C was 5 points. S's expected distribution of rewards to both POs was therefore one-third to PO_M and two-thirds to PO_C. If p represents the total proportion of exchange opportunities on which S rewarded either PO, then 1/3(p) represents S's expected rewards to PO_M in that condition. The difference between this value – S's expected rewards to PO_M – and S's actual rewards to PO_M is my measure of the subject's *resistance* to PO_M.

for the coercive strategy, p < .05 and .001, respectively). The combination of the two had an additive rather than an interactive effect.

As Hypothesis 2 predicts, subjects evaluated the coercive strategy as less fair than the reward strategy (t = 3.24, p < .01). The effect of the coercive strategy was nearly three times as strong as that of the reward strategy (eta = .74 versus .26). As the means in Table 8.2 indicate, subjects evaluated both the reciprocal and reward strategies as "fair" (i.e., above the midpoint value of 12) and the coercive and combined power strategies as "unfair" (below 12).

Analyses of subjects' perceptions of PO_M's behavior as active–passive and intentional–unintentional support the assumption that reward and coercive strategies differ in perceived intentionality, and that this difference affects their relative fairness. Subjects evaluated a partner's coercive strategy as significantly more intentional and active than a partner's reward strategy (t = 2.21 for intent and 1.97 for activity, both p < .05). Controlling for evaluations of intent and activity (as covariates) reduced the eta for the coercive strategy from .74 to .58 but had no effect on the eta for the reward strategy.

Other analyses show that subjects cognitively separated their evaluation of the structure, which was identical and balanced in all conditions, from their evaluation of their partners' strategies. Subjects evaluated the exchange structure as very fair regardless of which strategy PO_M used. Similarly, their evaluations of PO_C's behavior were always high and were unaffected by PO_M's behavior.

Behavioral reactions. I divided the exchange period into two 50-trial blocks for a repeated-measures analysis of variance on subjects' resistance and retaliation. The results showed that coercion produced greater resistance than reward withholding, as Hypothesis 3 predicts, but no greater retaliation. *Both* strategies increased subjects' punitive retaliation, with roughly equal effects ($F_{1,36}$ = 6.38 for the reward strategy and 7.66 for the coercive strategy; p < .05). But only coercion increased resistance ($F_{1,36}$ = 12.95, p < .001).

Retaliation declined over time ($F_{1,36}$ = 8.94, p < .01), mirroring the consistent finding of past experiments. Changes in resistance depended on the base of power used: resistance to reward withholding increased over time while resistance to coercion decreased. These changes show predictable responses to the consequences of the reactions. It was profitable for subjects to cease exchanging with PO_M when PO_M used a reward strategy, but costly when PO_M used a coercive strategy (see note 14). As a result, by the last 50-trial block, resistance to coercion did not differ significantly from resistance to reward withholding.

The finding that coercion produced no greater retaliation than reward withholding is unexpected and raises questions about the underlying assumption of Hypothesis 3 and Figure 8.1, that perceptions of justice mediate reactions to partners' power strategies. To test this assumption, I entered perceived fairness as a covariate before estimating the effects of the strategies on resistance and retaliation. If perceived fairness mediates these relations, they should decline when fairness is controlled. The effect of coercion on resistance does decline substantially (the F-ratio becomes nonsignificant and eta decreases from .51 to .17), but the effects of the two strategies on retaliation do not change.

Implications

This experiment shows that while individuals perceive power use, in general, to be more unfair than reciprocal exchange, they judge coercion as far more unfair than reward withholding, even when both bases of power use represent equal departures from reciprocity. In addition, the results support the thesis that loss aversion and intentionality jointly account for these different perceptions. As predicted, subjects perceived coercion as more active and intentional than reward withholding. When the effects of perceived intent are controlled, the difference that remains in the perceived justice of the two strategies is comparable with the effect of loss aversion reported in other studies (e.g., Kahneman et al. 1991; see Chapter 7). That is, reactions to coercion are roughly twice as strong as reactions to reward withholding.

The proposed link in Figure 8.1 between perceptions of injustice and reactions to injustice is only partially supported. These perceptions do account for the increased resistance to coercion, but actors engage in some punitive retaliation for a partner's use of power regardless of their perceptions of fairness. The amount of retaliation and its decline over time are comparable with the patterns observed in virtually all of the experiments in this program in which subjects have mutual punishment power. Not only did the coercive strategy produce no greater retaliation than reward withholding, it produced no greater retaliation than the infrequent coercion used by real subjects.

Even though the effect of injustice on behavior is limited to reducing the partner's rewarding below its expected level, this finding has important implications for risk. As we saw in Chapter 7, the primary risk of using coercion is not the partner's punishment but loss of the partner's rewards. Perceptions that coercion is unjust increase that risk.

This analysis compared reactions to coercion and reward withholding in structures of balanced power. But actors typically use power strategies when power is imbalanced. And, as we have seen in previous chapters, actors who use these two strategies tend to occupy different structural positions in imbalanced relations. Experiment 11 examined how the structure of power modifies actors' perceptions of the injustice of their partners' power strategies.

Experiment 11: justice in structural context

When actors use reward or coercive power, they do so in the context of a structural relation. While the structure of power does not alter the extent to which power use departs from reciprocal exchange, it can alter perceptions of justice, either by providing a context within which departures from reciprocity are more or less justified, or by modifying the standard of justice itself.

Justice as a moral counterforce to power

Many exchange analyses assume that norms of justice act as independent social forces that counter and oppose the effects of structural power, either by constraining powerful actors' use of power or by encouraging disadvantaged actors to resist its use (e.g., Blau 1964). Several experiments on negotiated exchange have shown, for example, that when actors in power-imbalanced relations are informed of the inequality of their rewards, power use declines and exchange becomes more equal (Cook and Emerson 1978; Cook and Hegtvedt 1986; Cook et al. 1988).

If justice norms do act as a moral counterforce to structural power, then we might also expect that power strategies would be evaluated more favorably when used to oppose the structurally advantaged rather than to exploit the structurally disadvantaged. Individually, imbalanced structures and nonreciprocal strategies are both unfair, but when judged in the context of structure, a nonreciprocal strategy that attempts to counter the effects of an imbalanced structure should be perceived as more fair than one that reinforces it. If so, then an advantaged actor who withholds rewards should be judged as more unfair than a disadvantaged actor who engages in the same behavior, even though both might be judged unfair when compared with an actor who reciprocates rewards. Similarly, punishment should be perceived as more justified when used by a disadvantaged actor to coerce rewards from an advantaged partner, than when used by an advantaged actor to subjugate a weak partner.

The latter inference is particularly important, of course, because of its implications for the risks of using coercion. As we have seen, the actors who have the strongest incentive to use coercion are disadvantaged on reward power. If justice norms support their use of coercion, by reducing the perceived injustice of the behavior, they should reduce the risk of retaliation (Figure 8.1).

Justice as a legitimating tool of power

The cognitive processes that underlie justice judgments, however, imply a rather different outcome. The highly subjective nature of these judgments suggests that norms of justice are not independent of power, and consequently their ability to counter the effects of power is limited. It is likely that power, in addition to determining the distribution of rewards, also influences expectations about what rewards are deserved and what behaviors are legitimate (Berger et al. 1972; Cook 1975). If so, then justice norms are more likely to legitimate the actions of the advantaged than to support the efforts of the disadvantaged. Structures of power and norms of justice will be mutually reinforcing rather than opposing.

Several theories propose some version of this basic process. Equity theorists (Austin and Hatfield 1980; Homans 1976) argue that the powerful have resources to persuade others that their inputs are deserving of greater reward, and that this process is buttressed by people's need to believe in a fair and equitable world (Lerner 1980). Della Fave (1980), drawing upon Mead's (1934) theory of the self and Bem's (1967) theory of self-perception, proposes that over time individuals develop self-evaluations that are consistent with the rewards they receive from society; these self-evaluations legitimate the unequal distribution of rewards in society. Finally, work in the expectation states tradition suggests that people come to expect consistency between certain status characteristics of individuals and their reward levels (e.g., Berger et al. 1972; Cook 1975). If so, then power – which exchange theorists consider to be the primary source of status – should operate in a similar manner.

Based on this logic, actors' structural positions will affect their expectations of the process and outcomes of exchange. In imbalanced relations, these expectations should shift the standard of justice away from reciprocity, in a direction that is congruent with actors' relative positions of power. Actors who are structurally advantaged are expected to initiate nonreciprocal exchange, but disadvantaged actors are not. When a disadvantaged actor withholds rewards or uses coercion, he violates the expectations attached to his structural position. Consequently, power strategies are more likely to be judged unfair when used by a disadvantaged actor against an advantaged partner, than when used by an advantaged actor against a disadvantaged partner.

The implications of these predictions for the use of coercion are directly opposite to those derived from assuming that norms are independent of power. They suggest that norms of justice will increase, not decrease, the risk of retaliation for disadvantaged actors who use coercion against their advantaged partners, thus reinforcing the effects of reward dependence.

Departures from reciprocal exchange may still be judged unfair, of course, by those who are on the losing end of such exchanges. Empirical evidence suggests they will be; in imbalanced relations, disadvantaged actors typically evaluate the distribution of rewards as unfair (Cook and Hegtvedt 1986; Stolte 1983, 1987b). Nevertheless, targets of power use should judge their partners' nonreciprocal strategies as *more* unfair when they themselves are structurally advantaged than when they are disadvantaged.

Implications for the base of power

So far, I have considered the effects of structural power on the perceived injustice of power strategies without regard to the base of either structural power or strategy. Both bases should affect the strength of the relations observed.

First, reward power should have a stronger effect than punishment power on perceptions of fairness, just as it has on behavior. Punishment power affects the capacity to inflict harm and the risk of retaliation, but it is the dependence of actors on others for rewards that motivates the use of both reward and coercive power strategies (see Chapters 6 and 7). Because reward power provides the incentive to use both bases of power, it is also more likely to influence actors' expectations about their partners' use of power.

Second, although reward power is more likely to influence perceptions of the fairness of power strategies, judgments about coercion are more likely to *be* influenced, by either base of structural power, than judgments about reward withholding. Because coercion is viewed as more intentional than reward withholding and provokes stronger affective responses, evaluations of its fairness are more likely to be affected by conditions that justify or fail to justify its use (Eckhoff 1974; Folger 1986). Consequently, the structure of power should have a stronger effect on the perceived fairness of coercion than on the perceived fairness of reward withholding. This implies that the difference in the perceived fairness of the two strategies should be greatest when the power user is disadvantaged (and coercion is perceived as most unfair), and should decrease when the power user is advantaged.

Behavioral reactions to injustice

Actors in structurally advantaged positions should be more likely than those in disadvantaged positions to resist or retaliate a partner's use of power. Two factors make independent contributions to this prediction. First, if behavioral reactions are mediated by perceptions of injustice, as Figure 8.1 proposes, then advantaged actors – who are predicted to perceive their disadvantaged partners' use of power as more unjust – should be more likely to react against it. This prediction is an extension of the one already tested in Experiment 10. Second, regardless of feelings of injustice, advantaged actors should retaliate more often than disadvantaged actors simply because they have greater capacity to do so. Actors in disadvantaged positions may comply with their partners' use of power, no matter how unfair, because it is too costly to do otherwise (Blalock and Wilkin 1979; Burgess and Nielsen 1974). But those in power-advantaged positions have little reason to tolerate the influence strategies of partners who lack the structural power to support them.

Hypotheses

Experiment 11 tested five hypotheses derived from this analysis:

H1. The structure of power will modify the perceived fairness of
     exchange partners' power strategies; strategies that are congruent
     with structural power will be perceived as more fair than those that
     are incongruent.
H2. Replicating the finding of Experiment 10, actors will perceive their
     partners' coercive strategies as more unfair than their reward power
     strategies.
H3. The difference in actors' perceived fairness of their partners' re-
     ward and coercive strategies will decrease with the partners' rela-
     tive power.
H4. The effects of structure on perceived fairness (Hypotheses 1 and
     3) will be greater for reward power than for punishment power.
H5. Structural power advantage will increase actors' behavioral reac-
     tions (resistance and retaliation) to partners' power strategies both
     directly, by increasing their capacity to impose cost, and indirectly,
     by increasing their perceptions of injustice.

Design

A $3 \times 3 \times 2$ factorial design crossed three conditions of reward power
imbalance with three conditions of punishment power imbalance with two
bases of power strategy (reward or coercive).[16] Ten networks (with one
real subject in each network) were studied in each of the 18 conditions
created by this design. As in Experiment 10, subjects exchanged for 100
opportunities.

The manipulations of power imbalance varied the power relation between the subject (S) and PO_M while holding constant the relation between
S and PO_C, the other simulated actor. For each power base, the relation
between S and PO_M was either balanced, imbalanced in favor of PO_M, or

---

[16] This design included two conditions from Experiment 10, those in which the simulated
partner used either a reward strategy or a coercive strategy in a fully balanced network.
These two conditions primarily provide an additional data point that illustrates the linearity
of the relations.

Table 8.3. *The power structures, Experiment 11*

Structure of punishment power (PP)	Structure of reward power (RP)		
	Imbalanced in S's favor	Balanced	Imbalanced in PO_M's favor
Imbalanced in S's favor	S advantaged on both bases	S advantaged on PP	S disadvantaged on RP, advantaged on PP
Balanced	S advantaged on RP	Equal power on both bases	S disadvantaged on RP
Imbalanced in PO_M's favor	S advantaged on RP, disadvantaged on PP	S disadvantaged on PP	S disadvantaged on both bases

imbalanced in favor of S. In the latter conditions, the power imbalance was .4 (a level studied in many of the previous experiments). Crossing the three levels of power imbalance for each base created the nine power structures shown in Table 8.3. The power relation between S and PO_C was balanced in all conditions, although the amount they could exchange with each other varied (i.e., a higher dependency of S on PO_M necessarily meant a lower dependency on PO_C and vice versa).

Within each of the nine structures, PO_M used either a reward strategy or a coercive strategy. These strategies were identical to the two studied in Experiment 10 (i.e., the middle strategies in Table 8.1). As in Experiment 10, PO_C always used a reciprocal, modified tit-for-tat strategy, which was consistent with the balanced power relation between PO_C and the subject.

Measures. Summing subjects' responses to the same three items used in Experiment 10 produced a justice scale with an alpha reliability of .87. Subjects also evaluated the fairness of the earnings schedule, and two items again measured subjects' assessments of their partners' behavior as intentional–unintentional and active–passive.

Measures of subjects' behavioral reactions were identical to those in Experiment 10. As in that experiment, I adjusted the measure of resistance for the difference between the strategies in their expected returns from

Table 8.4. *Mean perceptions of the fairness of PO_M's behavior, Experiment 11*

Structure of punishment power	Structure of reward power		
	Imbalanced in S's favor	Balanced	Imbalanced in PO_M's favor
Imbalanced in S's favor			
Reward strategy	13.4	13.9	15.4
Coercive strategy	6.1	7.4	16.2
Balanced			
Reward strategy	12.6	14.6	15.0
Coercive strategy	7.8	10.2	15.3
Imbalanced in PO_M's favor			
Reward strategy	14.8	14.5	14.6
Coercive strategy	8.1	12.4	15.1

Note: Scale values for the fairness of PO_M's behavior range from 3 to 21.

rewarding PO_M. These adjustments now took into account the different reward values created by the variations in structural power, but the computations of expected value and resistance were the same (see notes 14 and 15).

Tables 8.4 and 8.5 show the mean values for perceptions of fairness and behavioral reactions.

Results

Perceptions of fairness. Let us first examine the effects of structure and strategy on subjects' perceptions of the fairness of PO_M's behavior. Hypotheses 1 through 3 predict a main effect of structure (Hypothesis 1), a main effect of strategy (Hypothesis 2), and an interaction between structure and strategy, with structure modifying the size of the strategy effect (Hypothesis 3). Hypotheses 1 and 3 propose the greatest perceived injustice and strongest strategy effect when PO_M is disadvantaged, and the least injustice and weakest strategy effect when PO_M is advantaged.

An analysis of variance on the mean perceptions in Table 8.4 shows, as predicted, a main effect for reward power ($F_{2,162} = 15.99$, p $<$ .01), a main effect for strategy ($F_{1,162} = 37.24$, p $<$ .01), and a significant inter-

Table 8.5. *Mean behavioral reactions toward PO$_M$, Experiment 11*

Structure of punishment power	Structure of reward power		
	Imbalanced in S's favor	Balanced	Imbalanced in PO$_M$'s favor
a. Mean frequency of resistance			
Imbalanced in S's favor			
Reward strategy	.05	.02	.09
Coercive strategy	.16	.14	.10
Balanced			
Reward strategy	.08	.02	.06
Coercive strategy	.20	.12	.16
Imbalanced in PO$_M$'s favor			
Reward strategy	.07	.03	.06
Coercive strategy	.20	.14	.25
b. Mean frequency of retaliation			
Imbalanced in S's favor			
Reward strategy	.05	.02	.04
Coercive strategy	.10	.10	.04
Balanced			
Reward strategy	.02	.05	.02
Coercive strategy	.12	.06	.05
Imbalanced in PO$_M$'s favor			
Reward strategy	.04	.01	.00
Coercive strategy	.06	.05	.02

action between the two ($F_{2,162} = 9.89$, $p < .01$). The structure of punishment power, in contrast, has no main or interactive effects on subjects' perceptions of the fairness of PO$_M$'s behavior. This supports Hypothesis 4, but somewhat more strongly than expected. The main effect of strategy replicates the finding of Experiment 10 that a coercive strategy is perceived as more unfair than an equally nonreciprocal reward strategy.

Our primary interest in this experiment is in the direction of the main and interactive effects of reward power. T-tests of the differences in mean fairness among the three levels of reward power, both across and within strategy conditions, provide strong support for the hypotheses. As Hypothesis 1 predicts, subjects' perceived fairness of PO$_M$'s strategy increases with PO$_M$'s power advantage in the relation. Each level of greater power produces a significant increment in perceived fairness: mean fairness increases from 10.47 when PO_M is power disadvantaged, to 12.17 when power is equal (t = 1.93 for the increase), to 15.27 when PO_M is power advantaged (t = 4.01).

The interaction between structural reward power and power strategy indicates that this effect occurs only when PO_M uses coercion (the respective means are 7.33, 10.00, and 15.53). When PO_M withholds rewards, the increases in evaluations of fairness are in the same direction, but are smaller and nonsignificant (the respective means are 13.6, 14.3, and 15). In support of Hypothesis 3, the difference between the perceived fairness of PO_M's reward strategy and the perceived fairness of PO_M's coercive strategy decreases with PO_M's reward power, becoming nonsignificant when PO_M is advantaged on reward power (t = 5.97 when PO_M is power disadvantaged, 4.23 when PO_M is equal in power, and .52 when PO_M is power advantaged).

These results show that structural power legitimates the use of coercion by the advantaged, rather than justifying its use by the disadvantaged. The effect of power is substantial. Varying the power position of the coercer produces a fundamental shift in perceptions of fairness, from the judgment that coercion is unfair (below the midpoint of the scale) when disadvantaged actors use it to the judgment that it is quite fair (well above the midpoint of the scale) when the user is advantaged.

As in Experiment 10, subjects perceived the coercive strategy as significantly more intentional and active than the reward strategy ($F_{1,162}$ = 45.19 and 132.09, respectively, with p < .001). Attributions of intentionality increased the effect of reward power imbalance on perceptions of fairness, supporting the logic underlying the predicted interaction between reward power structure and strategy.[17]

Subjects correctly judged differences in "objective" fairness between balanced and imbalanced structures and between reciprocal and nonreciprocal strategies. Both bases of structural power significantly affected subjects' perceived fairness of the earnings schedule ($F_{2,162}$ = 5.22, p < .01 for reward power; $F_{2,162}$ = 3.90, p < .05 for punishment power). Subjects

---

[17] In multiple regression analyses, the addition of multiplicative interaction terms between perceived intent and two dichotomous variables representing reward power significantly increased the R^2 for perceived fairness (F change = 7.21; p < .001). Coefficients for the interaction terms were positive, indicating that the effect of reward structure on perceived fairness increased with perceived intent.

judged the structure to be fairer to participants when both reward and punishment power were balanced than when they were imbalanced, in either direction. As in Experiment 10, subjects' evaluations of PO_C's fairness were well above the midpoint value of 12 in all conditions (overall mean = 18.55), and there was no overlap between the condition means for PO_M and PO_C (the highest condition mean for PO_M was 16.2, and the lowest mean for PO_C was 16.3).

Behavioral reactions. Analyses of variance on subjects' resistance and retaliation replicate, with one exception, the effects of strategy observed in Experiment 10. In this experiment, unlike the first, coercion provoked more resistance *and* more punitive retaliation than reward withholding ($F_{1,162}$ = 28.58 for resistance and 17.05 for retaliation, p < .001 for both). The effect of coercion on retaliation is strongest in the conditions in which the subject is advantaged on at least one base of power, with no opposing imbalance on the other base (see Table 8.5). Changes in these behaviors support the patterns observed in the first experiment: resistance to coercion decreased over time, while resistance to reward withholding increased ($F_{1,162}$ = 17.61, p < .001 for the strategy × trial interaction). Retaliation decreased for both ($F_{1,162}$ = 45.10, p < .001), although the decline was steeper for coercion ($F_{1,162}$ = 6.69, p < .01 for the strategy × trial interaction).

Structural power does not modify the effects of strategy on behavior, however, as it modifies its effects on perceived justice. Reward power advantage increased retaliation ($F_{2,162}$ = 5.38, p < .01), and over time it also increased resistance – but in response to both strategies, regardless of base ($F_{2,162}$ = 12.11, p < .001 for reward power × trial). Punishment power had no effect on resistance and only a borderline effect on retaliation (p = .06), despite the fact that it directly affected subjects' capacity to retaliate.

The absence of an interaction between reward power and strategy suggests that the effects of reward power had more to do with power per se than with reactions to injustice. Examining these effects after controlling for perceived fairness confirms this suspicion. As in Experiment 10, the effect of coercion on resistance is mediated by perceived fairness (controlling for fairness reduces the eta for coercion by 32%), but none of the other effects of strategy or reward power appear to operate through concerns with justice. As Hypothesis 5 predicts, structural power affects resistance both directly and indirectly, but it has only a direct effect on retaliation.

Implications

This experiment shows that coercion is perceived as most unjust when used by the very actors who have the greatest incentive to use it: disadvantaged actors in relations of imbalanced reward power. At the same time, the results of this experiment, like the first, question the thesis that perceptions of fairness mediate behavioral reactions to coercion. In imbalanced structures, actors are more likely to resist and retaliate against partners who use coercive strategies and against partners who are disadvantaged on reward power. But only the relation between coercion and resistance is mediated to any extent by perceptions of injustice.

Nevertheless, the combination of these effects, however causally linked, confirms the potential risks of using coercion that were proposed in the last chapter: actors perceive coercion as unjust, they perceive it as more unjust when used by a partner disadvantaged on reward power, they both resist and retaliate against coercive strategies in power-imbalanced structures, and they are more likely to do so when their partner is disadvantaged on reward power.

One of the more interesting findings to emerge is that *only* reward power, and not punishment power, affects both perceptions of the injustice of coercion and reactions to coercion. The processes of expectation and legitimation that make those who are advantaged on reward power more distressed to find themselves targets of coercion do not apply to those advantaged on punishment power. Nor does punishment power advantage increase the probability that an actor will retaliate against a partner's coercion. These findings show, once again, the failure of the *capacity* to punish to act as a causal agent in social exchange. The power to punish does not provide the incentive to use punishment (Chapter 6), it only minimally constrains the partner's use of punishment (Chapter 7), and, as we see here, it does not affect perceptions about the just use of coercion. Instead, it is reward dependence that induces and constrains the use of coercion and that affects perceptions of when coercion is more or less just.

The absence of an effect of reward power on perceptions of reward withholding is rather unexpected. In a sense, though, this finding also supports the theoretical argument. Disadvantaged actors were hurt far more by their partners' reward withholding than were their advantaged counterparts, yet they evaluated this behavior as no more unfair than did actors in positions of advantage.

Summary and conclusions

This chapter investigated whether norms of justice help to explain the low use of coercive power. I tested a theoretical model which proposed that the use of power, perceptions of justice, and reactions to injustice are connected to each other through a set of causal relations that control, rather than amplify, the use of power. Power use provokes feelings of injustice in an exchange partner, the partner responds with resistance or retaliation, the costs of power use increase, and its further use is constrained. This model links justice norms with the analysis of risk in Chapter 7, by proposing that concerns with justice constrain the strategic use of power by increasing its costs.

According to this model, forms of power use that are perceived as less fair should be used less often because they are riskier. Drawing on the principle of loss aversion and attributions of intentionality, I argued that coercion is more likely than reward withholding to be judged unfair and to provoke retaliation or resistance. Two experiments supported this prediction and the logic underlying it. They also showed that perceptions of fairness are strongly influenced by actors' relative positions of reward power, in a direction that legitimates coercion by the powerful but condemns its use by the weak.

The results are strongest for *perceptions* of justice. Evidence for the relation between perceptions of injustice and behavioral reactions to injustice is more mixed. Feelings of injustice do increase an actor's tendency to resist a partner's use of power, but some punitive retaliation is likely regardless of justice sentiments. Both reactions are relatively short-lived; over time, the instrumental effects of power strategies tend to overcome reactions to injustice.

Nevertheless, even temporary reactions are likely to inhibit the use of coercion by loss-averse actors. As we saw in Chapter 7, the source of risk that most constrains coercion is the potential loss of the partner's rewards. Thus, if coercion does increase the partner's resistance to reward exchange, and perceptions of injustice mediate that relation, then justice concerns contribute to the risks that constrain the use of coercion. These constraints are strongest for the actors who have the greatest incentive, and need, to use coercion – the reward disadvantaged.

Although these experiments examined only the reactions of exchange partners, actors outside of the exchange relation can also punish norm violators. If past experience teaches individuals that norm violations typically *are* punished, by either the recipient or the collectivity that enforces norms, they may eventually refrain from acts that violate justice norms even when the risk of the partner's retaliation is low (Homans [1961] 1974; Walster et al. 1978). They may also develop a preference for using reward rather than coercive power (see Experiment 8, Chapter 7) – a preference rooted in risk but maintained by norms.

The analysis of justice bridges the focus of the two preceding chapters on actors' *use* of coercive power and the focus of the next chapter on the *effects* of coercion. In Chapter 9, I turn to the final question in the theoretical puzzle: does the low and inconsistent use of coercion, which I have sought to explain in Chapters 6 through 8, account for the weak effects of coercive power? Would stronger, more consistent coercion overcome the reactions that increase risk, or would it instead provoke even stronger resistance?

9. The effects of coercion: compliance or conflict?

The three preceding chapters have sought to explain why coercive power is used so infrequently in social exchange relations. We have seen that coercion is not structurally induced by a punishment power advantage, and that the strategic use of coercion is constrained by fear of loss, structural dependence, and norms of fairness. As a result, even when actors who are disadvantaged on reward exchange have the power to coerce more rewards from their partners, they seldom use it.

In this chapter I examine whether the low use of coercive power accounts for its weak effects on social exchange. Chapter 6 showed that both bases of power have equal effects when either is the sole source of power. And Chapter 7 showed that coercive power is more effective when the risk of retaliation is removed and its use increases. But an important question remains: how effective is coercion in the networks that are the focus of this research – networks in which all actors have both reward and punishment power, and retaliation is possible? If actors in these networks used coercion more frequently and consistently, would their coercive power be more effective?

As we saw in Chapter 3, many theories – from macro analyses of political power to micro analyses of social interaction – contend that it would not. The exchange theorists who excluded punishment from their analyses, as well as many theorists who explicitly study the use and effects of coercive power, argue that it will be *less* effective the more it is used. Rather than increasing compliance, they propose that coercion inhibits cooperative behavior and leads to escalating conflict and social disruption. Rather than enhancing the effects of structural power, they argue that the actual use of that power will destroy any positive effects that the potential to punish might otherwise have.

In this chapter I develop and test an opposing argument. I argue that the weak effects of coercive power result solely from its low use, not from its ineffectiveness. I contend that coercive power will be *more* effective when it is used frequently and consistently, to punish a partner's failure to provide rewards in exchange, and that increasing the use of coercion will increase the effects of structural variations in punishment power. A series of experiments, using computer-simulated actors who are programmed to use the kinds of coercive strategies that real actors have failed to use, test competing predictions derived from these different positions.

Theoretical approaches to the effects of coercion

The learning model that underlies exchange theory (see Chapter 2) assumes that actors respond to the actual consequences of their behaviors. They increase actions that are more rewarding or less costly and decrease those that are less rewarding or more costly. Structural power – if used – affects exchange through its effects on these behavioral consequences. Thus, coercive power has little effect on exchange because actors use it so infrequently that its consequences are trivial.

This logic implies, however, that if coercive power were used more frequently, its effectiveness should increase as a linear function of the probability of punishment for the partner's nonrewarding. As nonrewarding becomes more costly, relative to rewarding, it should decrease (and rewarding increase). More frequent use of coercion should also increase the effects of structural power: actors' absolute and relative power to coerce should have stronger effects when their use of that power increases.

Underlying this argument is the assumption that positive and negative consequences – rewards and punishments – act in parallel ways. If so, the target of coercion should comply to avoid greater loss, even if it means settling for lower rewards, just as a reward-disadvantaged actor should be willing to pay higher opportunity costs to obtain more valuable rewards. This is essentially what Heath (1976) was arguing when he proposed that voluntary and coerced exchanges follow the same principles, and that individuals will enter into exchanges if the outcomes of the exchange leave both actors better off than they would have been without it. Heath contended that whether the choice was between greater or lesser rewards, or greater or lesser losses, the same principle applies: individuals will choose a better outcome over a poorer one.

As we have seen, however, the distinction between gains and losses is not irrelevant. Avoiding loss is a *stronger* motivation than seeking gain, a phenomenon that Tversky and Kahneman (1991) call "loss aversion." The two preceding chapters have shown that loss aversion constrains actors' use of coercion, by making it riskier and more unjust. But the implications of this principle for the *effects* of coercion, when coercive power *is* used, are exactly the opposite. The same factor that makes coercion too risky to use should make it highly effective when it is used.

As we saw in Chapter 3, these predictions are at odds with numerous theories that argue that the actual use of punishment provokes hostility and retaliation, reduces cooperative behavior, and eliminates any positive effects of punishment power as a potential. Two main issues underlie these competing predictions. One is the psychological issue of whether reward and punishment affect individual behavior through similar mechanisms; the second is the social issue of how actors respond to another's use of punishment in relations of bilateral power.

The psychology of punishment

Early behavioral studies by Estes (1944), Thorndike (1932), and Skinner (1938) suggested that punishment does not weaken behavior through a process parallel to reinforcement's strengthening effect on behavior, but only suppresses it temporarily. Skinner and Estes contended that these temporary effects are emotional: punishment arouses an emotional state in the organism, through a classical (not operant) conditioning procedure, and the emotional reaction interferes – temporarily – with performance of the punished response. Skinner also argued that punishment produces negative side effects (i.e., effects other than those intended), such as fear, hostility, and withdrawal from the agent of punishment.

The classical exchange theorists were strongly influenced by this research (see Chapter 3). Both Blau (1964) and Homans ([1961] 1974) argued, on the basis of this evidence, that punishment is ineffective, that it arouses hostile emotional reactions, and that it leads to the eventual termination of exchange relations in which it is used.

Since the sixties, however, contemporary research has strongly refuted the conclusions of these early studies (for reviews, see Axelrod and Apsche 1983; Azrin and Holz 1966; Walters and Grusec 1977). In sharp contrast to the views of the early behaviorists, psychologists now contend that punishment is highly effective, that it influences behavior through a process that is directly parallel to reinforcement, and that it produces positive side effects as often as negative ones. Emotional reactions to punishment sometimes occur, but they are usually short-lived. There is no support for the theory that the effects of punishment are the product of a conditioned emotional response (Van Houten 1983), or that emotion mediates the effects of punishment, either positively or negatively. The effectiveness of punishment depends on the same parameters as the effectiveness of reinforcement – intensity, the schedule of punishment, and so forth. Punishment is most effective when combined with rewards, just as reinforcement is most effective when it is combined with punishment (i.e., by punishing undesirable behaviors and rewarding desirable behaviors). Withdrawal and social disruption are unlikely as long as reinforcement outweighs punishment in the situation.

If punishment departs from reinforcement principles in any respect, it is on the dimensions suggested by the principle of loss aversion. A number of behavioral studies show that punishment suppresses behavior faster (sometimes in a single trial) and to a greater extent than reinforcement strengthens it, and that its effects often endure longer than those of reinforcement (see Patterson 1982 and Van Houten 1983 for reviews). These findings support Tversky and Kahneman's (1991) assertion that loss aversion applies to reactions to past experiences as well as to choices of future behaviors.

In summary, contemporary research on punishment provides no support for the views of the early exchange theorists that punishment is ineffective or that it produces detrimental side effects for exchange relations. Instead, by showing that reward and punishment act in parallel ways, it supports the assumption that is necessary for extending exchange theory to coercive power and for predicting that the effectiveness of coercion should increase with the contingency and strength of its use.

Punishment in social context: retaliation and conflict

Most psychological research on punishment is conducted in settings in which the power to punish is unilateral. Unlike actors in exchange relations, the targets of punishment typically have little or no capacity to retaliate. In relations of bilateral power, the effectiveness of one actor's use of punishment necessarily depends on the relative power of the other. Exchange theory predicts that the effectiveness of coercion should decrease as the target's power to retaliate increases. If punishment power is equal, each actor's use of punishment should suppress the other's attempts to coerce, and this effect should increase with the average punishment power in the relation: both actors should be more likely to reward each other, and less likely to punish each other, as their mutual power to punish increases. If punishment power is unequal, then the power-advantaged actor should be more successful in securing compliance, to the extent of his power advantage. Because punishment suppresses undesirable behavior, the eventual outcome in either balanced or imbalanced relations should be a *decrease* in punitive actions.

Numerous theories, however, predict a very different outcome. As we saw in Chapter 3, the most common position among social scientists is that coercion provokes retaliation which then becomes an end in itself, feeding an accelerating cycle of increasing hostility and mutual aggression. One actor punishes, the other retaliates, the first counters, and conflict escalates. The end result is disruption of the social relation and the reduction of mutual benefits. This is the position of Blau and Homans, of conflict spiral theorists (e.g., Deutsch 1973), of deterrence theorists (e.g., Morgan 1977; Schelling 1960; Tedeschi et al. 1973), of most bargaining researchers (e.g., Lawler 1992; Pruitt 1981; Rubin and Brown 1975), and of numerous political theorists (e.g., Boulding 1969; Etzioni 1968). For convenience, I will call this general position the "conflict escalation perspective."

Empirical support for this position is most fully developed in the bargaining and negotiation literature. The two dominant perspectives on punishment power in bargaining are theories of bilateral deterrence (e.g., Morgan 1977; Schelling 1960) and conflict spiral (Deutsch 1973). As I discussed in Chapter 3, these two approaches are primarily concerned with how the capacity to punish (punishment power) affects the use of punishment. They make opposite predictions on that score, with deterrence theory arguing that greater capacity to punish deters the use of punishment, and conflict spiral theory arguing that it increases it. But as Lawler's (1986) explication of these two theories shows, *both* predict that once punishment is used, it leads to retaliation, reduces concessions in bargaining relations, and obstructs conflict resolution (see also Bacharach and Lawler 1981; Lawler 1992; Lawler et al. 1988). Research on explicit bargaining, as well as some gaming research, generally supports these predictions (e.g., Bacharach and Lawler 1981; Deutsch 1973; Deutsch and Krauss 1962; Michener and Cohen 1973; Pruitt 1981; Rubin and Brown 1975).[1]

Underlying these theories is the assumption that emotional reactions and impression management concerns (saving face, appearing tough) lead actors to retaliate a partner's punishment, regardless of the cost, and that retaliation leads to an escalating cycle of mutual conflict. Although only conflict spiral theory explicitly makes this argument, deterrence theory's emphasis on preventing the "first strike" reflects the same logic: deterrence is important because once punishment is used, conflict escalates. Numerous studies examine ways to promote conciliation in the face of this conflict, either through reciprocal strategies (e.g., Axelrod 1984; Patchen 1987) or unilateral initiatives combined with tit-for-tat retaliation (e.g., Boyle and Lawler 1991; Lindskold 1978; Lindskold and Collins 1978; Lindskold, Betz, and Walters 1986).

Research in applied settings also provides support for the conflict escalation hypothesis. Many family researchers, for example, believe that family violence is the result of an escalation process, in which fairly innocuous aversive events tend over time to escalate into high-intensity aggression, fueled by the tendency for attack to provoke counterattack (e.g., Burgess et al. 1981; Patterson 1982; Straus 1973). Others document a similar process in some encounters between police and criminal suspects (e.g., Berkowitz 1978; Toch 1969). And military conflicts are often considered the exemplar of conflict escalation.

A critique of the conflict perspective

The conflict escalation perspective suggests that when the power to punish is bilateral, increasing the strength and frequency of coercion should not increase compliance. Instead, coercion is likely to increase mutual punishment, decrease mutual reward exchange, and produce lower benefits for both actors. My predictions, of course, propose the opposite: that the ef-

---

[1] In contrast, Tedeschi's research on threat and punishment in *unilateral* power relations (e.g., Horai and Tedeschi 1969; Tedeschi et al. 1973) shows that compliance with threats (to punish noncooperation) increases with the credibility of threats – that is, with the contingency of punishment on noncompliance. However, Tedeschi et al. (1973) also propose that when punishment power is bilateral, its actual use is likely to lead to conflict rather than compliance.

fectiveness of coercion will be a direct function of its strength and frequency, and that increasing the use of coercion will also increase the effects of structural variations in punishment power.

My argument should not be construed to imply that individuals do not react emotionally to coercion, however, or that they do not try to hurt those who hurt them. The analyses in the preceding chapter show quite clearly that both of those assertions are true. Coercion provokes both negative affect (Molm 1991) and feelings of injustice, and punishment is typically retaliated.

But exchange theory, unlike the conflict perspective, does not predict that retaliation leads to the escalation of conflict. The psychological research on punishment suggests, instead, that retaliation and negative affect are side effects of coercion, relatively short-lived, and independent of the long-term relation between coercion and social exchange. As we have seen in repeated experiments, the frequency of retaliatory punishment is low and relatively constant across a range of conditions. While coercive punishment varies with structural conditions that affect the costs and benefits of using coercion, retaliatory punishment does not (see Chapter 5). It is unaffected by the capacity to retaliate or the magnitude of punishment inflicted, and it declines over time. These findings support the view that retaliatory punishment is a temporary, emotional response to punishment. Regardless of its consequences, it is unlikely to persist.

In short, social exchange theory offers no basis for predicting that retaliation should result in an escalation of conflict that obstructs the development of stable, mutual reward exchange. Nevertheless, the conflict escalation perspective is backed by a substantial body of empirical research. How do I reconcile my predictions with the findings of this literature?

The conflict perspective attributes the escalation of conflict to the use of punishment and the capacity to retaliate.[2] But the results of many studies that report negative effects of punishment can be explained by influences other than punishment per se. Common to most of these studies are three factors that transform punishment from a behavioral consequence

---

[2] Behavioral decision theorists also emphasize the role of "sunk costs" in the escalation of conflict in negotiations (e.g., Bazerman 1983). That is, once individuals have invested resources in a particular course of action, such as a strike, they resist conceding even if it fails to work. Rather than backing out of the conflict and avoiding further loss, they escalate the action and commit additional resources.

that suppresses undesirable behavior into a symbolic challenge that provokes and encourages it: (1) the noncontingent use of punishment, (2) the use of threats that are not backed up by actual punishment, and (3) scope conditions that increase the likelihood that actors will interpret punishment as hostile and competitive.[3]

The use of punishment. The effects of punishment should depend, first and foremost, on how it is used (see Chapter 5). Patterson (1982), for example, has argued that the most important factor in explaining the escalation of conflict in abusive families is not punishment, per se, but how family members use it. But most of the research that reports negative effects of punishment simply measures the punishment frequency of experimental subjects, whose use of punishment is uncontrolled and unanalyzed. Subjects who punish frequently may be contingently punishing a partner who fails to cooperate, retaliating another's punishment, or punishing noncontingently or offensively to project an image of strength or toughness.

Ford and Blegen's (1992) experimental comparison of the effects of offensive (noncontingent) and defensive (retaliatory) punishment on bargaining supports this argument. They found that noncontingent punishment increased the partner's punishment, producing a conflict spiral effect, while retaliatory punishment decreased it.[4] Boyle and Lawler (1991) also found that retaliatory punishment decreased a partner's punitive tactics. These findings suggest that punishment that is contingent on a partner's undesirable behaviors – either retaliatory punishment or coercive punishment (which neither Ford and Blegen nor Boyle and Lawler studied) – does not lead to an escalation of conflict. But noncontingent punishment does.[5]

Some studies also suggest that punishment which is used only to exploit, rather than to increase cooperation or mutual exchange, is more likely to

---

[3] Other experimental conditions that might affect responses to punishment include the type and magnitude of punishment, the history of interaction between actors, whether interaction is face-to-face or computerized, and so forth. But on these dimensions, the experiments in this program are very similar to experiments that support the conflict escalation hypothesis. Therefore, they cannot account for the different findings.

[4] In Ford and Blegen's study, neither defensive nor offensive punishment affected the magnitude of bargaining concessions, but neither was contingent on concession behavior. The focus of their study, like most bargaining experiments, was on reducing the use of punitive tactics rather than on the effectiveness of these tactics as a bargaining tool.

[5] Psychologists have observed that emotional reactions to punishment are also more likely when punishment is noncontingent (Van Houten 1983).

provoke retaliation and resistance (e.g., Youngs 1986). Thus, one of the most important principles of effective punishment is to combine contingent punishment for undesirable behaviors (punishment and nonexchange) with contingent rewards for reward exchange (Axelrod 1983). Purely coercive strategies, such as those studied in Chapter 7, should be less effective.[6]

The use of threats. The negative reactions in many experiments may be reactions to threat rather than punishment. Most bargaining experiments give subjects the capacity both to threaten and to punish, but provide more opportunities to do the former than the latter.[7] Not surprisingly, threats in these settings typically exceed punishments (e.g., Lawler and Bacharach 1987).

As Tedeschi's work on threat credibility shows, threats that are not backed up become ineffective (Horai and Tedeschi 1969; Tedeschi et al. 1973). But they may also acquire different symbolic meanings. Lindskold et al. (1986) suggest that in addition to verbally communicating punishment contingencies (i.e., if you don't do X, I will punish you), threats – unlike purely behavioral strategies – may insult, challenge, and raise concerns with saving face. Patterson (1982) suggests that these meanings are most likely to arise when threats are not backed up, and that this process is directly involved in the escalation of violence in abusive families. He shows that members of such families more frequently use aversive communications that are not supported by more powerful sanctions. These communications lose their function as signals of impending punishment, and instead acquire a different cultural meaning: insult or humiliation. Rather than stopping undesirable behavior, they provoke counterattack.

The implications of this analysis are ironic. As I discussed in Chapter 3, many theorists argue that coercion is ineffective without threat, or that threats are less costly than actual punishment. My analysis suggests, instead, that the more likely effect of threat is to weaken or alter the effects

[6] Although Experiment 9 in Chapter 7 indicated that even pure coercion can be effective, those results were obtained in relations in which the coercers had no power to reward and the targets of coercion could not retaliate with punishment. Whether they generalize to structures like those studied here remains to be seen.

[7] In the setting that Lawler and his associates have used, for example, subjects can threaten on any bargaining round but can punish on no more than five (e.g., Bacharach and Lawler 1981; Lawler and Bacharach 1987; Lawler et al. 1988). Similarly, in Michener and Cohen's (1973) setting, subjects could threaten on any turn during a round of negotiations, but could punish only once. Michener and Cohen also required subjects to precede punishment with threat, but – obviously – did not require them to follow threats with punishment.

of coercion and to *increase* costs in the long run, by transforming a simple coerced exchange into a symbolic confrontation in which saving face becomes more important than avoiding other costs. It was because of these potential effects that I excluded threats and other verbal communications from my analysis (see Chapter 3). Noncontingent punishment, because of its lack of association with behavior, probably acquires the same meaning: because it does not "punish" anything, in the psychological sense, it instead insults, challenges, and provokes.

The scope conditions of bargaining experiments. Much of the research supporting the conflict perspective is conducted in bargaining settings. But punishment that occurs within the scope conditions of explicit bargaining is likely to elicit different responses than punishment in reciprocal exchange. Many bargaining theories assume, as a scope condition, a high level of explicit conflict. It is this conflict (in addition to the potential for mutual gain) that provides the impetus for actors to come to the bargaining table in the first place. To meet this assumption, subjects in bargaining experiments typically begin with clearly defined, opposing positions (e.g., Deutsch 1973; Lawler and Ford 1993), or they are given the role of adversaries with a history of conflictual relations (e.g., Michener and Cohen 1973). Exchange theories, in contrast, do not assume that actors begin with opposing positions or an awareness of conflict. Although the conflict of interests is objectively the same (i.e., actors can always realize their highest payoffs if their partners give unilaterally), conflict in reciprocal exchange becomes salient only through the unequal dependencies of imbalanced relations. In balanced relations, most subjects perceive their interests to be the same.

But despite the conflict of interests that creates the need for bargaining in the first place, the structure of formal bargaining relations is in some respects more cooperative than the structure of reciprocal exchange. When actors come to the bargaining table, they have agreed to work together to try to resolve conflict and reach a mutually satisfactory settlement. Some theorists argue that punitive tactics violate this initial agreement and create a climate of distrust that makes continued cooperation difficult (see Bacharach and Lawler [1981] for a discussion and critique of this view). This reaction is likely to be intensified by the high conflict that precedes the bargaining and that can increase expectations of hostility (Tedeschi et al. 1973). In short, this unusual combination of conditions – high explicit conflict and a normative framework that assumes a cooperative effort to resolve that conflict – may create a setting in which punishment is more likely to be perceived as hostile and competitive than instrumental.

In summary, the conflict escalation observed in many experiments may result not from the use of punishment in its technical sense – that is, an aversive consequence contingent on an undesirable behavior – but from aversive actions that insult, challenge, and provoke attack, and a setting that increases the tendency to interpret any punishment in those terms.

Hypotheses

The exchange and conflict escalation perspectives offer competing hypotheses about three issues: (1) the effects of coercion on compliance, (2) how the use of coercion affects the relation between punishment power and compliance, and (3) the "side effects" of coercion.

The effectiveness of coercion. My analysis, derived from the behavioral principles that underlie exchange theory, predicts that coercion will be more effective if it is used more: the partner's reward exchange should increase as a linear function of the probability of contingent punishment. In contrast, the conflict escalation perspective contends that the use of punishment provokes hostility and reduces cooperative behavior in social relations; thus, higher probabilities of punishment should decrease rather than increase reward exchange.

Both predictions may be partially correct within certain ranges of punishment, of course. Compliance may increase with the probability of punishment until very high probabilities are reached, at which point emotional reactions set in and a backlash occurs. Or, the opposite could occur: concerns with impression management may dominate when probabilities of punishment are low, but at high probabilities, the costs of noncompliance may overcome these concerns and compliance may increase. The analysis will examine these possibilities as well.

The interaction of coercion with structural power. I predict that structural variations in punishment power will have more effect on exchange as the use of that power increases. At higher frequencies of contingent punishment, the effects of average punishment power and punishment power imbalance (which have been weak to nonexistent in previous experiments) will increase. Compliance will be greater when average power is high and power is imbalanced in favor of the coercer.

The conflict theories do not explicitly address this issue, but if the negative effects of punishment on compliance are the result of efforts to save face and appear tough, then these should be intensified at higher and more unequal magnitudes of punishment. If so, the combination of high use of punishment and high punishment power should produce particularly high levels of noncompliance. That is, in fact, what Bacharach and Lawler (1981) found: punitive tactics decreased bargaining concessions only at higher levels of punitive capability.[8] Thus, both perspectives predict an interaction between structural power and the use of coercion on compliance, but of opposite signs.

Side effects: retaliation and negative affect. Conflict escalation predicts that punishment provokes animosity, which is manifested both affectively (in negative feelings toward the partner) and behaviorally (in retaliation for the partner's punishment). Both should increase as the probability of contingent punishment increases. In addition, retaliation should increase over time, as conflict escalates.

My analysis also implies that more frequent punishment will increase negative affect and initial retaliation. But I predict that retaliation will decline over time rather than increase, and that emotional reactions will not impede the effect of coercion on the partner's rewarding.

Experiment 12: testing the effects of coercive strategies

I tested these alternative predictions in exchange relations in which reward power is imbalanced and the disadvantaged actor tries to coerce the advantaged partner to reward more frequently. This structure provides the strongest incentive for the use of coercion – reward power disadvantage (see Chapter 6) – but it also provides a conservative test of my predictions. As we saw in the preceding chapter, the use of coercion by an actor disadvantaged on reward power, against an advantaged partner, provokes more retaliation and stronger perceptions of injustice than the use of coercion by an advantaged actor against a disadvantaged partner, or by an

---

[8] Both reward and punishment power were balanced (equal) in this experiment (Bacharach and Lawler 1981: ch. 5).

actor in an equal-power relation. Therefore, if strong coercion is effective in these relations, it should be even more effective in relations in which the targets of coercion are more dependent on the coercer for rewards.

Design

The experiments in this chapter are similar in structure to those introduced in the previous chapter. All study exchange networks in which one real subject interacts with two computer-simulated actors, both of whom ostensibly can exchange with a hypothetical fourth actor in the network. The programmed strategy of one of the simulated actors is manipulated (PO_M) and the strategy of the other is held constant (PO_C). As before, the analytic focus is the exchange relation between the subject and PO_M. The relation between the subject and the alternative partner, PO_C, is always balanced, and PO_C is always programmed to use a reciprocal (tit-for-tat) strategy, identical to the one used in the experiments in Chapter 8.

Because these experiments tested the effects of coercion on behavior, however, the actors exchanged for 200 opportunities, not 100 as in the experiments in Chapter 8. The learning model that underlies the predictions requires sufficient time for the effects of coercion to develop and stabilize. At the end of the exchange period, subjects evaluated both of their partners on a series of semantic differential scales to test affective responses.

In the relation between the subject (S) and PO_M, reward power was always imbalanced in favor of the subject. Thus, PO_M is an actor disadvantaged on reward power who uses coercion to try to increase the frequency with which S rewards him. The more often S rewards PO_M, of course, the more often S must forgo exchange with S's more valuable partner, PO_C. The structure of imbalanced reward power provides the incentive for PO_M to *use* coercion and, at the same time, it provides the incentive for S to *resist* that coercion. Complying with PO_M's coercion requires the subject to act contrary to his or her own interests in order to benefit the coercive partner.

The particular structure of reward power used should be familiar; several of the previous experiments have studied it: S's reward power over PO_M was .8 and PO_M's reward power over S was .4, producing a power imbalance of .4 in S's favor, and the relation between S and PO_C was balanced (see Figure 9.1). In both relations, average reward power was .6. As we have seen, a reward power imbalance of .4 (with average power at

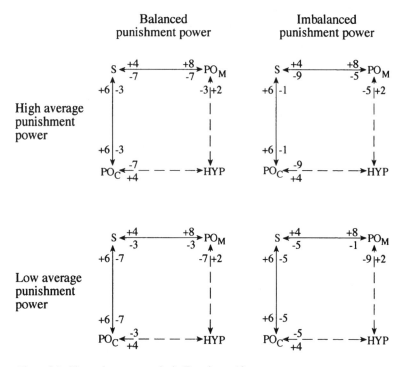

Figure 9.1. The exchange networks in Experiment 12

.6) produces predictable exchange asymmetry and substantial inequality in earnings in exchange relations between real actors. It also constrains the use of coercion, however, and, as a result, punishment power has had little effect in past experiments on this structure.

Within this basic structure of reward power, I manipulated the structure of punishment power and the level of coercion that PO_M used against S. A $3 \times 2 \times 2$ factorial design crossed three levels of coercion by PO_M (low, moderate, and high) with two levels of punishment power imbalance (balanced at 0 or imbalanced at .4, in favor of PO_M) and two levels of average punishment power (high, .7, or low, .3). Ten networks were studied in each of the 12 conditions.

Figure 9.1 shows the four structures produced by manipulating both dimensions of punishment power (average power and power imbalance) in the relation between S and PO_M. Average punishment power affects the magnitude of loss that PO_M can inflict on S on a single opportunity, hold-

Table 9.1. *The manipulation of coercion, Experiment 12*

| Experimental condition | Probability of PO$_M$'s behavior, conditional on S's prior behavior | | |
	Conditional on reward	Conditional on nonexchange	Conditional on punishment
p(P|N) = .1	R|R = 1.0 N|R = 0 P|R = 0	R|N = 0 N|N = .9 P|N = .1	R|P = 0 N|P = .1 P|P = .9
p(P|N) = .5	R|R = 1.0 N|R = 0 P|R = 0	R|N = 0 N|N = .5 P|N = .5	R|P = 0 N|P = .1 P|P = .9
p(P|N) = .9	R|R = 1.0 N|R = 0 P|R = 0	R|N = 0 N|N = .1 P|N = .9	R|P = 0 N|P = .1 P|P = .9

Note: p(i\|j) = the probability of PO$_M$'s behavior i at time t, given the occurrence of S's behavior j at time t − 1, where i and j = R (reward), N (nonexchange), and P (punishment).

ing power imbalance constant, and punishment power imbalance affects S's capacity to retaliate against PO$_M$'s punishment. When punishment power was imbalanced, PO$_M$'s punishment power advantage was equal to S's reward power advantage. The exchange relation between S and the other PO, PO$_C$, was balanced in all conditions, although the amount they could subtract from each other (the average punishment power in their relation) necessarily varied with the manipulation of punishment power in the relation between S and PO$_M$ (i.e., S's higher dependency on PO$_M$ implied a lower dependency on PO$_C$, and vice versa).

The three levels of coercion studied are shown in Table 9.1. PO$_M$ was programmed to punish S's failure to reward PO$_M$, with the probability of punishment for S's prior nonexchange (P\|N) set at .1, .5, or .9. On the remaining opportunities, PO$_M$ responded with reciprocal nonexchange (N\|N). PO$_M$ always reciprocated S's prior rewards (as a more dependent actor would be expected to do) and reciprocated S's punishment .9 of the time. The strategy of moderate coercion (.5) is almost identical to the coercive strategy studied in the experiments in Chapter 8 (the only difference is that PO$_M$ reciprocates S's rewards with a probability of 1.0 rather than .9), the weak coercion (.1) is comparable with the behavior of most real subjects in similar structures,

Table 9.2. *Mean behavioral reactions to coercion, Experiment 12*

Structure of punishment power	Probability of PO$_M$'s punishment for S's nonexchange		
	.1	.5	.9
a. Subjects' compliance (rewarding)			
High punishment power			
Balanced	.26	.26	.75
Imbalanced in PO$_M$'s favor	.17	.45	.76
Low punishment power			
Balanced	.17	.30	.47
Imbalanced in PO$_M$'s favor	.19	.43	.54
b. Subjects' retaliation (punishing)			
High punishment power			
Balanced	.02	.09	.06
Imbalanced in PO$_M$'s favor	.05	.07	.05
Low punishment power			
Balanced	.07	.06	.09
Imbalanced in PO$_M$'s favor	.01	.03	.06

and the strong coercion (.9) represents near-maximum coercion, not studied in any of the previous experiments.

The manipulation of coercion simultaneously varied the probability with which PO$_M$ punished S's nonexchange and the contingency of PO$_M$'s punishment on S's nonexchange, with contingency defined as the difference between the probability that PO$_M$ punishes S's nonexchange [p(P|N)] and the probability that PO$_M$ punishes S's rewarding [p(P|R)] (see Chapter 7). Because p(P|R) was constant (zero) in all conditions, the contingency of PO$_M$'s punishment on S's nonexchange varied directly with p(P|N): both equaled .1, .5, or .9.

Results

The effectiveness of coercion: subjects' compliance. Subjects' compliance with PO$_M$'s coercion was measured by the frequency with which S rewarded PO$_M$; mean frequencies are shown in Table 9.2a.

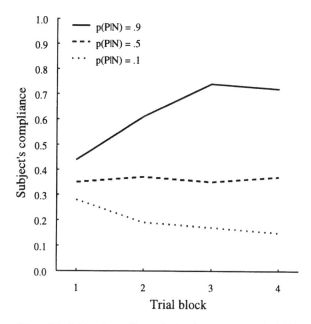

Figure 9.2. Subjects' compliance, by level of coercion and trial block, Experiment 12

To examine the effects of time as well as structural power and coercive strategy on compliance, I divided the exchange period into four 50-trial blocks and treated the trial block as a within-subject variable in an analysis of variance. Results of the analysis showed a strong main effect for PO_M's coercive strategy, in a direction that supports my predictions ($F_{2,108}$ = 60.34, p < .001). The frequency with which subjects rewarded PO_M increased with the probability of PO_M's contingent punishment of subjects' nonrewarding, from a mean of .20 to .36 to .63, when p(P|N) equaled .1, .5, and .9, respectively.

A significant interaction between coercive strategy and trial block ($F_{6,324}$ = 18.27, p < .001), graphed in Figure 9.2, shows that compliance *increased* over time when the probability of contingent punishment was .9, *did not change* when it was .5, and *decreased* when it was .1. The highest level of coercion produced a rapid increase in subjects' rewarding during the first three trial blocks that stabilized in the fourth trial block.

The predicted interactions between the use of coercion and dimensions of punishment power are also significant. The interaction between PO_M's coercive strategy and average punishment power indicates that the increased use of coercion enhanced the effects of average power ($F_{1,108} = 6.27$, $p < .01$). Average power had no effect on subjects' compliance until the probability of contingent punishment increased to .9; when both the capacity to punish and the probability of contingent punishment were high, subjects' rewarding was also at its highest: a mean of .75. This effect was strong enough to produce a significant main effect for average punishment power as well ($F_{1,108} = 8.27$, $p < .01$).

The results also show a weaker but significant interaction between punishment power imbalance and PO_M's use of coercion ($F_{1,108} = 3.13$, $p < .05$). As expected, the effect of power imbalance increased as coercion increased from low to moderate – subjects with equal power were less likely to comply than those with a power disadvantage – but this effect disappeared when coercion increased to the near-maximum (.9) level, particularly when punishment power was high.

A polynomial analysis shows that, overall, the form of the relation between PO_M's coercive strategy and S's compliance is linear. The relation departs from linearity when average punishment power is high, because of the greater increase in subjects' rewarding when the probability of coercion is .9, and it also departs when punishment power is balanced, because of the lower compliance when the probability of punishment is .5.

These findings show that coercive strategies can be highly effective, and that their effectiveness increases with both the probability and the magnitude of contingent punishment. But what are the costs of the apparent success of strong coercion? Does PO_M secure S's compliance while provoking S's wrath? To answer that question, I examined the possible side effects of coercion: retaliation and negative affect.

Side effects: retaliation. Subjects' retaliation against PO_M's coercion was measured by the frequency with which S punished PO_M (see Table 9.2b for the means). An analysis of variance on these means found only one significant effect, a main effect for trial block. The frequency of S's punishment decreased over time ($F_{3,324} = 19.71$, $p < .001$), with most of the decrease occurring between the first and second trial blocks. None of the manipulated variables had any effect on subjects' punishment.

Across all conditions, subjects punished PO_M .06 of the time on the average. Both that frequency and the tendency for punishment to decline over time, particularly after the first trial block, are typical of the punitive behavior observed in nearly all of the experiments in this program. Thus, in contrast to theories which predict that strong coercion leads to retaliation and the escalation of conflict, these findings show that high levels of coercion produce no more retaliation than very low levels, and that retaliation decreases rather than escalating into mutual conflict.

In short, the high magnitudes and probabilities of contingent punishment that are so effective in securing compliance do not affect the likelihood of retaliation one way or the other. Retaliation and compliance are, in fact, unrelated to each other ($r = .17$, n.s.). Subjects who complied more did not retaliate less, or vice versa. Clearly, these are separate dimensions of behavior, affected by different variables.

Side effects: affect. The high compliance and low retaliation that subjects displayed are both rational responses to the situation in which they found themselves: compliance was rewarded and noncompliance and retaliation were punished. That subjects behaved in ways that decreased their losses does not mean they liked doing so, however.

I measured subjects' affective evaluations of PO_M by summing their responses to four 7-point semantic-differential items: good–bad, helpful–unhelpful, nice–awful, and satisfied–dissatisfied.[9] Values on the resulting scale, which has an alpha reliability of .90, range from 4 (very negative) to 28 (very positive), with a neutral midpoint of 16.

As the mean values in Table 9.3 show, subjects tended to evaluate PO_M's behavior negatively (below the neutral point of .16) in all conditions. An analysis of variance on these means found both a significant main effect of the probability of PO_M's coercion and a significant interaction of PO_M's coercion with average punishment power, paralleling the effects of these variables on subjects' compliance ($F_{2,108} = 3.19$ and 3.27, respectively, $p < .05$). However, subjects' evaluations of PO_M become *less* negative, not more negative, as the probability of PO_M's coercion increases. This effect occurs only when average punishment power is high ($F_{2,57} = 7.03$, $p < .01$), and it results from the significantly higher evaluations in the high (.9) coercive condition than in either the .1 or .5 conditions.

---

[9] For the first three items in the scale subjects were instructed, "Please evaluate Person X's behavior toward you," followed by a labeled bipolar scale. For the fourth item, subjects were asked, "Overall, how satisfied are you with Person X's behavior toward you?" again followed by a labeled bipolar scale.

Table 9.3. *Mean affective evaluations of PO$_M$'s behavior, Experiment 12*

Structure of punishment power	Probability of PO$_M$'s punishment for S's nonexchange		
	.1	.5	.9
High punishment power			
Balanced	10.1	9.4	15.6
Imbalanced in S's favor	9.5	6.8	12.8
Low punishment power			
Balanced	8.7	11.3	10.1
Imbalanced in S's favor	12.4	10.7	11.6

Note: Scale values for evaluations of PO$_M$'s behavior range from 4 (very negative) to 28 (very positive), with a neutral midpoint of 16.

In short, the combination of structure and coercive strategy that produces the greatest compliance – a high probability of contingent punishment, combined with the power to inflict high losses – also produces the *least* negative affect. Remember, subjects in this condition have been coerced, through repeated strong punishment, into exchanging with a *less* valuable partner the majority of the time. Nevertheless, they feel less negatively about their coercers than do subjects who are punished only occasionally and less severely.

How can we explain these results? Are subjects who volunteer for these experiments more masochistic than the rest of the population? Intriguing as that possibility is, the correct explanation is probably quite simple: strong and consistent coercion works; weak and inconsistent coercion does not. And, when coercion is used in combination with rewards for compliance, coercion that works produces more rewarding and fewer punishing interactions than ineffective coercion. Subjects who were the targets of strong coercion soon became engaged in mutually rewarding exchanges with their coercer: 75% of the time, they experienced PO$_M$ as a partner who always reciprocated their rewards (albeit with lower value). Subjects who were the targets of weak coercion did not increase their giving to PO$_M$ (some decreased it) and, consequently, they continued to receive punishment from PO$_M$, even if weakly and infrequently.

Analyses of PO_M's net frequency of rewards to the subject (i.e., the frequency of rewards *minus* punishments) illustrate this point effectively. When average punishment power was high and PO_M used a strong (.9) coercive strategy, the mean net frequency with which PO_M rewarded the subject was .54. Under the other five combinations of average punishment power and coercive strategy, this mean was below .12, and the average across these conditions was .06. Furthermore, entering net reward frequency as a covariate in the analysis of subjects' evaluations showed that its effect is far stronger than the effects of any of the experimental variables, regardless of whether it is estimated before or after the main effects of the experimental variables ($F_{1,107} = 18.67$ when entered after the main effects, and 22.30 when entered before, $p < .001$ for both). When the covariate is entered first, the effects of the experimental variables become nonsignificant, indicating that these variables affect evaluations through their effects on net reward frequency. Thus, subjects' more positive evaluations of PO_M under conditions of the most intense coercion reflect their overall experiences with PO_M, which were more positive than negative because strong coercion worked.

Implications

These results show that punishment power, when used consistently and contingently to coerce rewards from a less dependent partner, can be a potent form of influence in social exchange relations. The effectiveness of coercion increases with both the probability of contingent punishment and the magnitude of punishment power, with the combination of the two producing the strongest compliance. There is no evidence of an escalation in conflict or hostility, and no indication that retaliation or animosity reduced compliance with coercion.

Although subjects did retaliate, as expected, their retaliation was low and unrelated to either the strength of punishment power or its use. These findings, which replicate the results of many of the previous experiments in this program, strongly support the thesis that retaliation is a temporary emotional reaction to another's punishment. It is independent of compliance with coercion, and it declines rapidly – even when the other's coercion continues.

Although subjects evaluated their coercers negatively, they regarded a partner who used strong and consistent punishment *more* favorably than one who sporadically and ineffectively punished. The analysis suggests that strong punishment provoked less hostility because it quickly produced compliance, allowing the relation to change from one of coercion to one of mutually beneficial exchange. This explanation supports Lawler and Yoon's (1993) theory of affect in bargaining relations, which argues that the experience of completing agreements, however beneficial, produces positive affect. It also supports psychological research showing that positive affect increases with the relative frequency of positive to negative experiences (see Patterson 1982). In this study, even though strong coercion resulted in subjects' exchanging more often with a less valuable partner, the very frequency of that reward exchange, relative to the frequency of punishment, made them feel more positive toward the less valued partner.[10]

As predicted, the effects of structural variations in punishment power increased with more frequent and consistent coercion, with one exception: a significant effect of power imbalance on reward exchange appeared when the probability of contingent punishment increased to .5 but disappeared when it increased further, to .9. Although this effect was unexpected, it is an understandable response to the unswerving toughness of our robot coercer. Resisting a partner who continues to punish at very high levels – no matter what – is simply too costly. It is likely that the capacity to retaliate with equal harm becomes irrelevant under these conditions. Real actors, unlike this PO, would be expected to vary the contingency of their punishment as the structure and their partners' behavior changed.

Nevertheless, these results, like those of the experiments in Chapters 5 and 7, suggest that how actors use punishment is more important than their power to punish. Perhaps because loss aversion enhances the magnitude of any punishment, one actor can successfully coerce another even in the absence of a punishment power advantage.

Experiments 13, 14, and 15: exploring the limits of the findings

I conducted three additional experiments to test the theoretical generalizability of the findings. Are these results restricted to the particular strate-

---

[10] Alternatively, these findings might be explained by cognitive dissonance or self-perception theories (e.g., Bem 1967). That is, subjects who comply with coercion may later explain or justify their behavior by evaluating their coercer more positively.

gies and structures examined in Experiment 12, or do they hold under different conditions as well – conditions that might be expected to affect either compliance to coercion or emotional reactions to coercion?

Experiment 13: unilateral versus bilateral power

As we have seen, the distinction between unilateral and bilateral power is central to the predictions of the conflict escalation perspective. Because retaliation drives the escalation of conflict, coercion is expected to be more effective when punishment power is unilateral than when it is bilateral (Tedeschi et al. 1973).

Even though Experiment 12 found little retaliation and no evidence of an escalation of conflict, we can still ask whether the effects of coercion on compliance are even stronger when punishment power is unilateral. To answer that question, Experiment 13 examined the effects of the same coercive strategies (.1, .5, and .9) under both high (.7) and low (.3) values of PO_M's punishment power over S. But in contrast to Experiment 12, the subjects in this experiment had no punishment power and, hence, no capacity to retaliate against PO_M's coercion.

Analyses compared the effects of these unilateral power conditions with the effects of the corresponding bilateral power conditions in Experiment 12. The combined data set replicated the effects of coercive strategy and average punishment power on compliance and affect that were found in Experiment 12. S's ability to retaliate, however, had no main or interactive effects on either S's behavior or S's evaluations of PO_M. Removing S's ability to retaliate did not increase S's compliance, with one exception: when power was unilateral, compliance no longer decreased over time when PO_M used the lowest probability (.1) of coercion.

Experiment 14: probability versus contingency of punishment

By simultaneously varying both the probability and the contingency of PO_M's punishment, the manipulations in Experiment 12 confounded these two variables. Theoretically, it is the contingency of punishment – not its probability or frequency – that is expected to increase compliance with coercion. Increasing the probability of punishment while holding contingency constant should, if anything, decrease coercion's effectiveness.

Experiment 14 sought to determine the independent effects of these two variables by comparing both high and low probabilities of punishment for two of the punishment contingencies (.1 and .5) studied in Experiment 12. Two new high probability conditions were created by changing some of the probabilities in the .1 and .5 strategy conditions of Experiment 12 (see Table 9.1). Both p(P|R) and p(P|N) were increased by .3, thus increasing the overall probability of punishment while maintaining its contingency – that is, [p(P|N) − p(P|R)] – in the original conditions.[11] The simulated actors used these strategies in the high, imbalanced power network from Experiment 12.

A statistical comparison of these two conditions with the corresponding conditions with lower punishment probabilities in Experiment 12 indicates that increasing the probability of punishment had no effect on S's compliance or on S's affective evaluations; only the contingency of punishment was significant. However, the higher probability of punishment did provoke greater retaliation (a mean of .11 rather than .06) than in Experiment 12. This finding is consistent with the earlier arguments. Punishing a partner's "good" behaviors along with the bad is a form of offensive punishment (Ford and Blegen 1992), unwarranted by the target's behavior, and such actions are more likely to provoke retaliation. The amount of retaliation remained relatively low, however, and again declined over time.

Experiment 15: varying the punishment for retaliation

Several analyses suggest that retaliation should increase if the probability with which it is punished decreases (e.g., Boyle and Lawler 1991; Ford and Blegen 1992). Experiment 15 investigated the effects of decreasing p(P|P) (i.e., the probability of PO_M's punishment given S's prior punishment) from .9 to .5 while increasing p(N|P) from .1 to .5. This change in strategy decreased the negative consequences of S's retaliation for PO_M's coercion: half the time, PO_M punished S's retaliation, and half the time, PO_M ignored it. The new probabilities were studied in combination with two of the contingency levels (.5 and .9) from Experiment 12, using the structure of high balanced punishment power from that experiment.

---

[11] In the .1 contingency condition, the overall probability of punishment was increased by increasing p(P|R) from 0 to .3 and p(P|N) from .1 to .4 (and, at the same time, decreasing p(R|R) from 1.0 to .7, and decreasing p(N|N) from .9 to .6). In the .5 contingency condition, p(P|R) increased from 0 to .3 and p(P|N) from .5 to .8, while p(R|R) decreased from 1.0 to .7, and p(N|N) from .5 to .2.

A statistical comparison of these two conditions with the corresponding conditions in Experiment 12 found no significant effects of the decrease in punishment on S's retaliation. A borderline interaction between the probability of punishment for retaliation and the contingency of punishment on nonexchange is in the predicted direction, however ($F_{1,36} = 3.60$, $p = .07$). Decreasing the punishment for S's retaliation increased retaliation in the high-contingency (.9) condition, from .06 to .14, but not in the moderate-contingency (.5) condition. Retaliation still declined over time in all conditions.

The most interesting finding of this experiment is that reducing p(P|P) from .9 to .5 eliminated the effects of the contingency of punishment on S's compliance and on S's affective reactions. While not anticipated, this result is quite logical. Reducing p(P|P) to .5 created an inconsistent strategy when contingency was high (i.e., when p(P|N) was .9). In this condition, PO_M was more likely to punish S's nonexchange than S's punishment, even though S's punishment was clearly a less desirable behavior. These results underscore the importance of using consistent strategies of punishment. For coercion to be effective, both retaliation and nonexchange must be punished at levels that reflect their relative cost to the coercer.

Implications

The variations in coercive strategy and structure tested in these experiments show that the findings of Experiment 12 are quite robust. The effects of coercion on compliance and affect hold when the partner has no capacity to retaliate, and they hold when the probability of punishment is increased without changing the contingency.

The conclusion that emerges from these systematic variations is that the most important factor for the effectiveness of coercion is its contingency: the probability of punishment for undesirable responses (punishing and not exchanging with the partner) must be greater than the probability of punishment for desirable responses (giving rewards to the partner). The greater the difference, the more effective the coercive strategy. In addition, the probability of punishment for undesirable responses must be consistent; that is, punishing a partner's failure to reward while ignoring her punishment sends mixed signals.

Two of the manipulations – increasing the overall probability of punishment while holding contingency constant, and decreasing the punishment for retaliation – produced some increase in retaliation, as expected. However, the level of retaliation remained low and, as always, it declined over time.

Conclusions

The analyses in this chapter show that the weak effects of punishment power on social exchange cannot be explained by the ineffectiveness of coercion as an influence technique. When coercion is applied consistently and contingently, it is a powerful means of obtaining greater benefits from an exchange partner, even when that partner is advantaged on reward power. As the earlier studies suggested, how punishment power is used is more important than the structure of power, although the use of power also enhances structural effects. By demonstrating that weak coercion actually *decreases* reward exchange (at least when used against a reward-advantaged partner), while strong coercion increases it, the results support the argument that it is the infrequent use of coercion, not the ineffectiveness of coercive power per se, that accounts for its weak effects.

As these experiments show, even though weak, inconsistent coercion is ineffective, it produces just as much retaliation (and more negative affect) as stronger, more consistent coercion. Because it does not work, the behavior that provokes it continues, and the coercion continues – sporadic and ineffectual, but highly irritating. Examples abound: the nagging spouse, the critical boss, the distracted parent with the misbehaving child. These results help to explain why punishment is both so common *and* so ineffective in social relations. Ironically, the reluctance of individuals to use strong coercion, whether from concerns with risk or justice, may actually increase its use in the end.

10. A theory of coercion in social exchange

The five preceding chapters developed and tested a theory of coercion in social exchange. Because one of my aims was to show how a program of cumulative experimental research can be used as a tool for building and testing theory, I constructed the theoretical puzzle piece by piece. This chapter provides an overview of the finished picture. Here, I summarize the development of the theory, offer a more formal statement of its logic, and discuss the findings that support it. I then examine the implications of the work for social exchange theory, and revisit the advantages and disadvantages of integrating the study of coercive power within the framework of social exchange.

Logic and development of the theory

Scope conditions

The five conditions that limit the scope of Emerson's theory of reward exchange (Table 2.1) also restrict the scope of coercive exchange theory. The boundaries of the research project were further set by the additional conditions specified in Chapter 3. Several of these are clearly *theoretical* scope conditions, restricting coercive exchange theory to (1) relations in which actors can reward as well as punish each other, (2) negatively connected networks, (3) nonnegotiated (reciprocal) exchanges, and (4) settings in which actors can neither change the structure nor avoid a partner's rewards or punishments.[1] The logic of the theory rests on the assumption that these conditions are met. The other conditions limit the situations

---

[1] The portion of Emerson's theory on which I draw is also restricted to negatively connected networks, although his theory as a whole is not.

under which coercion was studied, but they are not essential for the logic of the theory.

Reward power and social exchange

My development of coercive exchange theory began with power-dependence theory's analysis of reward power. Whether that analysis could be generalized directly to coercive power, without modification, was the question that occupied the first phase of the research. Four assumptions and three theorems summarize the formal logic of the theory (all terms are defined in Appendix I):

> *Assumption 1.* A's power over B derives from, and is equal to, B's dependence on A; that is, $P_{ab} = D_{ba}$.
>
> *Assumption 2.* B's dependence on A increases with the *value* of the outcomes that A can produce for B, and decreases with B's *alternative* sources of outcomes within the same domain.
>
> *Assumption 3.* Actors initiate exchanges of benefits by giving rewards to other actors on whom they are dependent.
>
> *Assumption 4.* Actors increase patterns of exchange that are relatively more rewarding or less costly, decrease those that are relatively less rewarding or more costly, and change behaviors (i.e., engage in exploratory behavior) when rewards decline or costs increase.

When actors engage in recurring exchanges with partners in negatively connected networks, these assumptions imply three key predictions about the relations between structural power and the frequency and distribution of exchange:

> *Theorem 1.* A's initiations of exchange with B increase with A's dependence on B (and B's power over A).
>
> *Theorem 2.* The average frequency of exchange in a relation increases with the average power and dependence in the relation.
>
> *Theorem 3.* The asymmetry of exchange in a relation increases with power imbalance, in favor of the more powerful (less dependent) actor.

These patterns of exchange are structurally induced by the power-dependence relations among the actors. Actors initiate exchange with those on whom they are dependent (Assumption 3); the greater their dependence, the more frequent the initiations (Theorem 1), and the greater their *mutual* dependence, the more frequent the exchange of benefits (Theorem 2). Power advantage leads to power use (Theorem 3) because power-advantaged actors have access to more or better alternatives (Assumptions 1 and 2); when they pursue exchange with these alternatives (Assumption 3), they inadvertently withhold rewards from their more dependent partners – that is, they "use power" over them. In the process, they drive up the costs of obtaining the rewards they control, while lowering their own cost of obtaining their partners' rewards. Thus, as long as actors follow the behavioral principles in Assumptions 3 and 4, those actions, combined with the relations between power and dependence stated in Assumptions 1 and 2, will produce the relations predicted in Theorems 1 through 3.

The early research, described in Chapter 5, tested whether Theorems 1–3 also apply to coercive power. Do equivalent structures of power, differing only on whether power is based on the capacity to produce gains or losses for other actors, have equivalent effects on social exchange? Results of the first five experiments showed that the answer to that question is clearly no. Not only did equivalent structures of reward and coercive power have unequal effects on exchange, but in these experiments, coercive power had almost no effects on exchange. The mere potential for punishment did not induce exchange partners to reward more to prevent the other's punishment (Theorem 1), and average punishment power and punishment power imbalance had almost no effects on either the frequency or the distribution of exchange (Theorems 2 and 3).

When coercive power *did* affect exchange, however, its effects were always similar in direction to those of reward power. In addition, the structural conditions that increased the use of coercive power were ones that affected the costs and benefits of using punishment in ways consistent with exchange theory. These findings suggested that it should be possible to use exchange principles to explain the use and effects of coercive power, but that the theory, in its current form, was inadequate for the task.

Structure and power use

The logic for extending Assumptions 1–4 to punishment and coercion rested on the argument that dependence on another for avoiding punishment provides the same basis for power as dependence on another for obtaining rewards (Assumption 1). Both determine the potential cost that one actor can impose on another. I also argued that under the scope conditions of the project (networks in which actors can both reward and punish each other, with relations negatively connected on the domain of rewards), dependence varies as a function of value and alternatives for both rewards and punishments (Assumption 2). Actors who are dependent on one another for either obtaining rewards or avoiding punishments should initiate exchange with those on whom they are dependent by giving rewards to them (Assumption 3), and their subsequent interaction should be governed by behavioral principles of both reward and punishment; that is, actors should seek to increase rewards and decrease punishments (Assumption 4).

There is nothing wrong with these assumptions, per se. But they do not lead to the same implications for coercive power as they do for reward power. They imply an effect of coercive power on the initiation of *reward* exchange (i.e., a relation between disadvantage on coercive power and giving rewards to the partner), but not an effect of coercive power on the *use of coercion* (i.e., a relation between coercive power advantage and punishing the partner). The logic works as long as more dependent actors give rewards to their power-advantaged partners to *prevent* their punishment (Assumption 3, extended to punishment). But if actors engage in exploratory behavior with alternative partners, as they are expected to do, then the effects of coercive power rest on the use of that power and the consequences it produces for actors (Assumption 4). Unless actors punish their partners' defections from reward exchange, their potential power will soon lose its potency. Like reward power, coercive power is effective only if it is used, but unlike reward power, the use of coercion is not inherent in a coercive power advantage.

As we saw in Chapter 6, the reason for this difference lies in the different role that alternatives play for the two bases of power. Access to alternative sources of reward increases an actor's power relative to another's, by reducing her dependence, *and* induces the use of that power. The more (or better) alternatives A has to B, the more likely A is to withhold rewards from B – that is, to "use power" over B. It was for this reason that Emerson proposed that a concept of power use as a distinct, voluntary mode of action was unnecessary; whenever actors initiate exchange with one partner in negatively connected networks, they simultaneously "use power" against another partner.

But alternative sources of punishment reduce dependence and increase relative power without providing any incentive to use that power. They affect an actor's *capacity* to withstand cost imposed by the other, but not the actor's *incentive* to impose cost on the other. In short, the link between power advantage and power use that is at the heart of Emerson's theory is missing. The logic of the theory implies that actors should *reward* those who have the power to punish them (Assumption 3), not punish those who fail to reward them.

The experiments in Chapter 5 offered repeated evidence that, indeed, actors did not punish those who failed to reward them, even when they were on the losing end of an exchange relation. But neither did actors consistently reward those with the power to punish them. Only one experiment (in Chapter 6) found that the capacity to punish, per se, increased reward exchange, and then only in power-balanced networks. Instead, experiments repeatedly found that variations in the structural power to punish had little influence on any exchange behaviors.

In short, these experiments showed that the differences between reward power and coercive power are not limited to differences in how rewards and punishments affect behavior, as many social scientists have assumed. Their most important difference is in the relation between the *structure* and *use* of power. The use of power is inherent in a reward power advantage, as Emerson proposed, but not in a punishment power advantage. Consequently, a punishment power advantage fails to have similar effects on social exchange.

Chapter 6 developed and tested this important insight, showing that when conditions are created so that punishment power advantage *does* structurally induce the use of punishment, just as reward power advantage structurally induces reward withholding, the two bases of power have virtually identical effects on the frequency and distribution of exchange. Actors who are faced with the task of simply distributing rewards or punishments among alternative partners, in networks based solely on reward or punishment power, follow the same principles in doing so: they provide more frequent benefits (rewards or the withholding of punishment) to those on whom they are most dependent, while at the same time inflicting greater cost (reward withholding or punishment) on those on whom they are less dependent.

The absence of a direct relation between coercive power and power use is one of the primary factors that accounts for the low rate of coercion in social exchange relations. But it also makes prediction of the *use* of coercive power a separate and distinct problem. That task required three related components: (1) a conception of strategic power use and a set of assumptions that govern it, (2) an analysis of how the structure of power and dependence affects strategic power use, and (3) an examination of how justice norms affect reactions to strategic power use under different structural conditions.

Strategic power use

The use of power can be structurally induced by power advantage, as Emerson proposed, but it can also be *strategic*. The distinction between these two forms of power use is central to the distinction between reward power and coercive power. Whereas structurally induced power use requires only that actors follow Assumptions 3 and 4 (initiating exchange with those who control rewarding outcomes, and responding to the consequences of those initiations in accord with behavioral principles of reinforcement and punishment), strategic power use requires actors to create contingencies of reward or punishment that produce consequences for other actors' behaviors – that is, to use their exchange resources selectively to reward or punish their exchange partners' behaviors. Such actions are typically purposive attempts to change the partner's behavior and improve the actor's benefits from exchange. As a form of strategic power use, coercion is a behavioral solution to an unsatisfactory exchange relation – an effort to increase the partner's rewarding by contingently applying punishment. Predicting the strategic use of coercion was the task of Chapters 7 and 8.

For that task, I drew on two theories of strategic action and decision making under conditions of risk and uncertainty: Axelrod's (1984, 1986) work on the evolution of cooperation and Kahneman and Tversky's (1979) prospect theory. These theories and the empirical work on which they are based suggested four new assumptions for deriving predictions about strategic power use:

Assumption 5. Actors initiate strategic power use by imposing cost on other actors who fail to provide rewards in exchange.

Assumption 6. Strategies are dynamic and adaptive; once initiated, they are shaped by the consequences produced by other actors' responses.

Assumption 7. The potential consequences of strategic power use include both gain (from compliance) and loss (from retaliation); the probabilities of both are unknown but greater than zero.

Assumption 8. Actors evaluate exchange outcomes (both anticipated and experienced) by a value function that has three main characteristics: referent dependence, diminishing sensitivity, and loss aversion:

(a) *Referent dependence.* Outcomes count as *gains* (or rewards) if they improve an actor's current outcome level (the status quo), and as *losses* (or punishments) if they worsen it.

(b) *Diminishing sensitivity.* The marginal value of gains and losses decreases with their distance from the reference point (i.e., the status quo).

(c) *Loss aversion.* The negative subjective value of a loss is greater than the positive subjective value of an equivalent gain.

Assumption 5 is parallel to Assumption 3. It recognizes that strategic power use is based not on the expectation of reciprocity that underlies Assumption 3 and the inadvertent use of structurally induced reward power, but on an application of the behavioral principles in Assumption 4. Rather than giving rewards to obtain benefits in return, actors impose cost (by administering punishment or withdrawing rewards) on partners who fail to provide sufficient benefits. Once initiated, strategies – like other patterns of exchange behavior – should increase or decrease according to their consequences; thus, Assumption 6 is parallel to Assumption 4.

Assumption 7 makes explicit the risk and uncertainty involved in strategic power use. Partners may respond with either compliance (increased reward exchange) or retaliation (decreased rewards or punishment). I assume that the probabilities of the partner's compliance or retaliation are unknown to the actor, but that both are greater than zero. As I argued in Chapter 7, both responses are reasonable and rational, depending on the time frame of the partner: complying with coercion produces the immediate benefits of a decrease in punishment, but in a continuing relation, retaliating against coercion can reduce the likelihood of coercion in the future.

To the extent that actors anticipate the consequences of power use, the relative gains or losses attached to these alternative outcomes can affect decisions to initiate power strategies. And once power strategies are initiated, the actual gains and losses experienced can affect subsequent power use.

Assumption 8 specifies the value function, taken from Kahneman and Tversky's (1979) prospect theory, that describes how actors evaluate gains and losses (both actual and anticipated) under conditions of risk and uncertainty. The first two properties of this value function are already implied, respectively, by my definitions of reward and punishment and by the second scope condition of exchange theory (see Table 2.1). The third property – loss aversion – is new and important. It produces the phenomenon known as the status quo bias (Kahneman and Tversky 1984), applied here to strategic power use:

> *Theorem 4 (The Status Quo Bias)*. When the potential gains from compliance are no greater than the potential losses from retaliation, strategic power use is unlikely. Actors will accept the status quo of a relation rather than risk the use of power to change it.

As long as actors stand to lose as much as they might gain, and both outcomes are uncertain (Assumption 7), the subjective overweighting of losses relative to gains (Assumption 8c) will constrain the strategic use of either reward power or coercive power in social exchange relations. Loss-averse actors will opt for the certainty of the status quo, accepting their current position in a relation rather than risking the use of power to improve their outcomes.

As potential gains increase and potential losses decrease, the status quo bias should decrease and the use of coercion should increase. These gains and losses vary with the structure of power and dependence.

Dependence, risk, and coercion

Actors' dependencies affect both the probabilities of coercion and its likely consequences (retaliation or compliance), and the magnitudes of gain and loss attached to those alternative outcomes.

Actors' *relative* dependencies – that is, their positions of power advantage or disadvantage – influence both the *probability of coercion* and the *probability of retaliation* against coercion.

Theorem 5. The probability that B initiates a coercive power strategy to influence A increases with B's reward power disadvantage in the relation.

This theorem follows directly from Theorem 3 and Assumption 5. Reward power disadvantage provides the behavioral motivation to use coercion to improve one's outcomes from exchange. A structural imbalance in reward power reduces the advantaged partner's reward frequency, which in turn motivates the disadvantaged actor to try to change that behavior and increase the partner's rewarding. In contrast, actors who are advantaged on reward power have little need to use coercion to get what they want. We saw some support for this theorem in Chapter 5; regardless of their punishment power, actors who were disadvantaged on reward power were more likely than advantaged actors to use coercion, even though the frequency of their punishment was still low.

At the same time that reward power disadvantage provides the incentive to use coercion, however, it also increases risk. Power-advantaged actors stand to gain more by retaliating, and to lose more by complying, than power-disadvantaged actors. Consequently, the probability of the partner's retaliation should increase with the partner's power advantage:

Theorem 6. The probability that A retaliates rather than complies in response to B's use of coercion against A increases with A's power advantage in the relation.

Theorem 6 applies to both bases of power; that is, a partner who is advantaged on *either* reward power or punishment power is more likely to retaliate. A partner who controls rewarding outcomes can retaliate by withdrawing those rewards; a partner who controls punishing outcomes can retaliate by administering punishment.

Together, Theorems 5 and 6 imply the same result as Theorem 4: a bias *against* coercive power use and in favor of the status quo. B's reward power disadvantage provides the incentive for B to use coercion against A, but it also increases the risk that A will retaliate, by decreasing her reward exchange with B rather than increasing it. This conflict between incentive and risk, which exists for coercive power but not reward power, is the second primary cause of the low use of coercion (the failure of a coercive power advantage to structurally induce the use of coercion is the first).

Punishment power advantage should also reduce risk, by reducing the probability of punitive retaliation, but it provides no incentive to use coercion. As Chapter 8 showed, the effect of punishment power advantage on punitive retaliation is much weaker, empirically, than the effect of reward power advantage, even though it directly affects the capacity to retaliate.

While actors' relative positions of reward power affect the *probabilities* that one will initiate coercion and the other will either comply or retaliate, their absolute dependencies affect *how much* the coercer stands to gain or lose from the partner's compliance or retaliation. First, B's reward dependence on A determines the *range of potential outcomes* that A can produce for B by either increasing or decreasing the frequency of her rewarding. The value that B places on those rewards and B's alternative sources of them (i.e., B's dependence on A) determine how much A can affect B's outcomes by varying her behavior. Second, holding B's dependence on A constant, A's reward dependence on B affects the *current* frequency with which A rewards B – that is, the higher A's dependence on B, the more frequent A's rewarding; the lower A's dependence, the less frequent her rewarding (Theorem 1). The current level of A's rewarding constitutes the "status quo" of the relation for B – that is, the reference point that B uses to evaluate the potential consequences of coercion. Increases from that level count as potential gains and decreases as potential losses (Assumption 8a).

Consequently, the potential gains from coercion increase and the potential losses decrease as B's current outcomes from exchange decline. When A's rewarding becomes low enough for potential gains to outweigh potential losses – taking loss aversion into account – coercion should increase:

> *Theorem 7.* The positive effect of reward power disadvantage on both the incentive to use coercive power and the risk of retaliation will constrain B's use of coercion against A unless the proportion p of opportunities on which A rewards B, multiplied by the coefficient for loss aversion c, is less than $1 - p$: $pc < (1 - p)$. As p declines below that level, B's use of coercive power should increase.

If c equals 2 to 2.5, as a number of analyses suggest, then Theorem 7 implies that B is unlikely to use coercion against A unless the frequency with which A rewards B falls below .3 (i.e., if c equals 2, then p equals

.33; if c equals 2.5, then p equals .29). Below that level, the probability of coercion should increase as A's reward frequency decreases. At very low reward frequencies, the amount that B could lose from A's reward withdrawal becomes trivial, even if the probability of A's retaliation is high and B's reward dependence on A is high.

Because punishment power affects only the risk of using coercion, and not the incentive, its predicted effects on the use of coercion are more straightforward (and weaker). A punishment power advantage reduces the probability of the partner's punitive retaliation, while the partner's absolute punishment power increases the cost of the partner's retaliation. Therefore:

> *Theorem 8.* The frequency with which B uses coercion against A, given B's incentive to do so, increases with B's punishment power advantage and decreases with A's punishment power over B.

While strongly supporting Theorem 7, the experiments in Chapter 7 showed that the effects of punishment power predicted in Theorem 8 become apparent only when the conditions in Theorem 7 are met. The primary constraint on the use of coercion is not the risk of the partner's punitive retaliation, but the risk of her reward withdrawal. Because the partner's insufficient rewarding motivates coercion in the first place (Theorem 5), the prospect of changes in those rewards is the strongest influence on the use of coercion. Over time, the actual consequences of coercion, including punitive retaliation, determine its persistence or decline (Assumption 6). Thus, the experiments in Chapter 7 showed increased support for Theorem 8 over time, but only when the risk of reward withdrawal was reduced enough to increase coercion.

Justice, power, and coercion

While Chapter 7 examined how the structure of dependence affects risk, Chapter 8 showed that norms of justice can lead to behaviors that also increase risk and further constrain the strategic use of power. Because power use violates norms of reciprocity and fair exchange, it is inherently unjust. The more unjust a partner's perceptions of an actor's power use, the more likely that the partner will resist or retaliate, thus increasing the potential costs of power use for the actor.

Incorporating justice judgments into a theory of power and exchange also required new assumptions. Despite the exchange roots of justice theories, their predictions are derived from assumptions taken from theories of social comparison and cognitive consistency, not the assumptions of learning or rationality that underlie the predictions of exchange theory. Perceptions of justice, like evaluations of outcomes, are referent dependent. But the reference standard (i.e., the justice standard) is some function that *compares* the actor's own outcomes with those of another actor, group, or referential structure – not the status quo.

I made two assumptions about the justice standard in relations of reciprocal exchange. First, I assumed that the basic standard of justice is derived from the scope condition that defines social exchange; "benefits obtained ... are contingent on benefits provided" (Emerson 1981:32). Second, I assumed that actors' structural positions affect their expectations of the process and outcomes of exchange. In imbalanced relations, these expectations can shift the standard of justice away from reciprocity, in a direction that is congruent with actors' relative positions of power.

> *Assumption 9 (The Justice Standard).* In balanced relations of direct exchange, the standard of fair exchange is defined by reciprocity, the contingency of outcomes received on outcomes given. As power imbalance increases, expectations attached to positions of power shift this standard in a direction that is consistent with actors' positions of relative power.

The next two assumptions – that departures from the justice standard will produce emotional distress, and that actors will attempt to reduce distress behaviorally – are based on principles of cognitive dissonance:

> *Assumption 10 (The Comparison Process).* As discrepancies between the standard of fair exchange and actual exchange increase, those who receive fewer rewards or more punishments will feel emotional distress and a sense of injustice.
>
> *Assumption 11 (The Behavioral Reaction).* Actors seek to reduce the emotional distress produced by departures from fair exchange by reducing their rewards or increasing their punishments toward the partner.

Assumptions 9 and 10, combined with the principle of loss aversion (Assumption 8c), imply the following theorem:

Theorem 9. The perceived injustice of exchange partners' power use is greater for coercive power than for reward power.

Objectively, the use of either reward power or coercive power involves equal departures from the justice standard of reciprocity, if the probabilities of contingent punishment or reward withholding are equal and the values of the rewards and punishments are equal. Because of loss aversion, however, actors should tend to perceive coercion as more nonreciprocal than reward withholding.[2] And, because power use is more consistent with the expectations attached to power-advantaged than to disadvantaged positions (Assumption 9):

Theorem 10. The perceived injustice of exchange partners' use of coercion increases with the power disadvantage of the coercer.

From Assumptions 10 and 11:

Theorem 11. The likelihood of retaliation for exchange partners' use of coercion increases with the perceived injustice of the coercion.

The results of two experiments in Chapter 8 strongly supported Theorem 9. Targets of power use judged a partner's coercion as more unfair than a partner's failure to reciprocate rewards, even when both represented equal departures from reciprocal exchange. They also supported Theorem 10 for reward power, but not for punishment power. Actors perceived an exchange partner's coercion as most unjust when the partner was *disadvantaged* in the relation, on reward power, and as least unjust when the partner was *advantaged*. The structure of reward power dominates expectations about power use, just as it dominates actual power use.

Support for Theorem 11 was mixed. Perceptions of injustice increased actors' tendencies to respond to a partner's coercion with resistance – that is, with lower-than-expected levels of rewarding. Perceptions of injustice did not affect punitive retaliation, however. Power-advantaged actors were more likely to retaliate against a disadvantaged partner's use of coercion, but these responses were not mediated by perceptions of injustice. Nevertheless, as Chapter 7 showed, the source of risk that most constrains

---

[2] Attributions of intentionality also play a role, as we saw in Chapter 7. People are more likely to attribute intent to their partners' coercion than to their partners' reward withholding, and they are more likely to judge intentional departures from reciprocity as unfair. Assumptions about attributions are unnecessary for the derivation of Theorem 10, however, and I have omitted them here.

coercion is the potential loss of the partner's rewards. Thus, if perceptions of injustice increase the likelihood of that loss, then justice concerns contribute to the risks that constrain the use of coercion.

Together, the analyses of risk and justice show that actors who have the strongest incentive to use coercion – dependent actors who are disadvantaged on reward power in a relation – also face the greatest constraints. The high reward dependence of these actors on their partners increases the value of the rewards they risk losing, and their power disadvantage and social norms increase the probability of this loss, by making the use of coercion by the power disadvantaged more unjust and more subject to sanction. As a result, the strategic use of coercion is suppressed.

The effects of coercion on social exchange

Chapters 6 through 8 developed the major portion of the theory: the logic that explains why coercive power is used so infrequently in relations of mutual reward dependence and that predicts the conditions under which use should increase. Chapter 9 tested the final argument, that it is the low use of coercive power, and not the ineffectiveness of coercion per se, that accounts for its weak effects on social exchange.

Structural power affects the frequency and distribution of exchange through its effects on the rewarding and punishing consequences of actors' behaviors. Because power-advantaged actors can impose greater costs on their partners than their partners can impose in return, actors in different positions of power produce different outcomes for one another when they use power. If they respond to the consequences of their own behaviors as the learning principles in Assumption 4 suggest (increasing actions that are more rewarding or less costly, and decreasing those that are less rewarding or more costly), then the relations predicted in Theorems 2 and 3 between dimensions of structural power and reward exchange should obtain.

When coercive power is used, these same relations should develop between the structure of coercive power and reward exchange. That is, when the two bases of power are used comparably, equivalent structures of reward power and coercive power should affect exchange in parallel ways. Actors should increase the frequency of their reward exchange either to obtain rewards or to avoid punishments. If anything, loss aversion (Assumption 8c) should make coercion *more* effective than reward withholding; that is, actors should be more motivated to reduce loss than to increase gain.

Chapter 9 tested two theorems related to this argument. The first is derived from Assumption 4 and Theorems 2 and 3, the second from Assumption 4 and the definition of coercion:

> *Theorem 12.* The effects of average punishment power and punishment power imbalance on reward exchange predicted in Theorems 2 and 3 increase with the contingent use of coercion.
>
> *Theorem 13.* Holding structural power constant, the effectiveness of coercion increases with the contingency of its use; i.e., as the contingency of A's punishment on B's nonrewarding increases, the frequency of B's rewards to A will increase.

Several experiments in the earlier chapters provided general support for the argument that reward and coercive power have equal effects on exchange when they are used equally. Chapter 6 showed that when exchange structures consist of a single base of power, and the use of either reward power or punishment power is induced by a structural advantage on that base, the effects of variations in the absolute and relative strengths of the two bases of power are virtually identical. Chapter 7 showed that when pure coercive power is compared with pure reward power, under similar conditions of low risk, high magnitudes of either base of power are equally effective in securing the rewards of a mutual exchange partner.

The research in Chapter 9 tested Theorems 12 and 13 on the focal networks of the program – networks in which all actors have both reward and punishment power, and retaliation is possible. A series of experiments strongly supported both theorems. They showed that coercion, when applied consistently and contingently, is a powerful means of obtaining greater benefits from an exchange partner, even when that partner is advantaged on reward power and has the capacity to retaliate with both punishment and reward withdrawal. The effects of the coercive strategies used by the simulated actors in these experiments increased with both the contingency of their punishment and the strength of their punishment power, reaching a maximum when high losses were imposed nearly every time the partner failed to reward. Strong and consistent coercion *increased* the partner's reward exchange over time, whereas weak and sporadic coercion actually *decreased* it. These findings support the argument that it is the infrequent use of coercion, not the ineffectiveness of coercive power per se, that accounts for its weak effects in relations with both bases of power.

In short, when coercive power is used, its effects parallel those of reward power: actors increase their reward exchange to avoid punishment just as they increase it to obtain rewards. Although coercion provoked some initial retaliation, this response was minimal and short-lived. There was no support for the prediction of some theories that coercion leads to an escalating cycle of mutual hostility and aggression. As repeated experiments in this program have shown, although all actors retaliate the use of coercion, the amount of their retaliation is quite low, it declines rapidly over time, and it is largely independent of structural power. Nevertheless, the initial tendency of all actors to retaliate punishment – regardless of their relative power to retaliate – undoubtedly contributes to the suppression of coercion by real actors, who fear loss and are uncertain how persistent their partners' retaliation might be.

Implications for social exchange theory

The results of the research program offer compelling evidence that reward power and punishment power have very different effects in social exchange relations. The theory of coercive exchange developed here can account for these differences. It departs from exchange theory's analysis of reward power in two significant ways, however.

First, one of the central tenets of power-dependence theory – the prediction that power advantage inevitably leads to power use, regardless of actors' intent to use power or awareness of power – holds only for reward power. Expanding exchange theory to include coercive power requires relinquishing, as a general principle, what many consider to be the most distinctive feature of power-dependence theory: Emerson's (1972b) argument that the use of power is inherent in structural power advantage. While a purely structural analysis has the advantages of parsimony and sociological appeal, this work shows that it also has limits. It is possible to predict the distribution of exchange benefits from the availability of alternatives only when those alternatives not only reduce dependence but also induce power use.

Second, explaining the use of coercive power requires expanding exchange theory's conception of power to include strategic power use. Coercion is a mode of power use distinctly different from reward withholding. It is not structurally induced by coercive power advantage, but behaviorally motivated by conditions that produce insufficient rewards. Consequently, extending exchange theory to incorporate coercive power requires new assumptions about actors, and new derivations from those assumptions.

The new assumptions required for strategic power use do not depart from the underlying model of the actor on which power-dependence theory was originally based, however. Power-dependence theory has always combined some assumptions of "forward-looking" actors with its basic model of a "backward-looking" actor who responds to the consequences of his own actions. Both Assumption 3, which governs the initiation of reward exchange, and Assumption 5, which governs the initiation of coercion, assume forward-looking actors who take some action – either giving rewards to another or punishing another – with the aim of increasing their own rewards. And both Assumptions 4 and 6 assume that their subsequent behavior is explained by the consequences of those actions. Assumption 3 is based on an expectation of reciprocity (one must give rewards in order to receive rewards), and Assumption 5 on the expectation that others – like self – will respond to the contingent application of both rewards and punishments. Although the two expectations can imply different behaviors, both are long-standing components of social exchange theories.

Perhaps the most important new addition to the behavioral assumptions underlying the theory is the principle of loss aversion. While behavioral psychologists have long observed that punishment tends to produce faster and more enduring effects than reward, this phenomenon was not widely known until Kahneman and Tversky (1979) incorporated it in prospect theory. Loss aversion becomes important primarily in contexts of risk and uncertainty; then, fear of loss can constrain actors from making choices that would be predicted from an analysis of expected value. Because the use of reward power entails little risk for actors advantaged on reward power, neither risk nor loss aversion has been a central concern for power-dependence theorists. If the theory is to be extended to coercive power, however, they must be.

In contrast, explaining the *effects* of coercive power, when coercion is used consistently and contingently, requires no new assumptions. As Heath (1976) argued 20 years ago, coerced exchanges and mutual reward exchanges follow the same logic in their effects: actors will increase the frequency of their reward exchange either to obtain rewards or to avoid punishments. The learning principles that underlie the effects of reward power on exchange also mediate the effects of coercive power on exchange.

The benefits of integration

As this analysis suggests, we can bring coercive power within exchange theory's scope by extending its analysis of power to include strategic power use. What are the advantages of doing so, for both exchange theory and the study of coercive power? Are there benefits to be gained from the integration, or are reward power and coercive power better approached from different theoretical perspectives?

Perhaps the strongest justification for bringing coercive power within the scope of exchange theory is the central importance of *reward dependence* for understanding both bases of power. The structure of reward dependence directly induces the use of reward power and the distribution of rewards that results, but it also both encourages and constrains the strategic use of coercive power. Thus, extending the theory to incorporate punishment and coercion broadens the mechanisms through which dependence affects behavior, and increases its significance. Dependence becomes the key to understanding both structurally induced and strategic power use.

As Cook (1990) has pointed out, a theory that attempts to link the structure of relations with the behavior of actors must have an adequate conceptualization of both. For the past 15 years, exchange researchers have concentrated primarily on the former. Stimulated by Cook and Emerson's (Cook and Emerson 1978; Cook et al. 1983) pathbreaking work on power and exchange networks, researchers have developed sophisticated mathematical theories that predict the distribution of exchange benefits from algorithms based primarily on the configuration of networks (see, in particular, the June 1992 issue of *Social Networks*). While this work has produced increasingly precise predictions of how different network structures affect exchange outcomes, it has paid little attention to the processes of interaction that link structure with outcomes, or to how those processes are affected by assumptions about actors.

In this program of research, confronting the task of explaining a different form of power has led, necessarily, to more consideration of interaction processes and actors' decision-making strategies. Other researchers have begun expanding the boundaries of work on power and exchange for similar reasons, considering, for example, how instrumental exchange relations are transformed when actors repeatedly exchange with one another (Lawler and Yoon 1993, 1996), how the risk inherent in generalized exchange affects the use of strategic action and the importance of trust (Yamagishi and Cook 1993), and how actors cope with uncertainty when the value of exchange resources is unknown and partners can actively deceive one another (Kollock 1994). These studies all suggest that under many conditions, exchange outcomes are not determined solely by structure.

Coercive power also emerges from this analysis in new light. When viewed within the context of social exchange relations, its use and effects are quite different from those suggested by most theories of coercive power. Theories that consider only the punitive capabilities of actors, such as deterrence theory and conflict spiral theory, predict far stronger effects for coercive power than I found, even though they disagree about the direction of those effects. When actors need to consider only the punishments they might receive from other actors, and not the rewards they might gain (or lose), the conflict that reward dependence imposes on the use of coercion is removed. Punitive retaliation is still an issue, but both the probability and cost of retaliation is a straightforward function of punishment power. When reward dependence is brought into the picture, however, the complexity of the situation increases; now, predictions must take into account the interactions between the two bases of power. In reality, of course, reward dependence is almost always part of the picture, regardless of whether it is theoretically ignored or not. Few, if any, relations are based purely on the mutual capacity to punish.

The systematic comparison of equivalent forms of reward and coercive power, in exchange structures in which both are available, helps to explain some of the puzzling inconsistencies and contradictions that are evident in much of the literature on coercive power. As we saw in Chapter 3, competing theories have proposed that coercion is both highly potent and ineffectual, and that greater power to coerce others both encourages and deters the use of that power. By distinguishing between different dimensions and forms of power, this analysis has shown that these seemingly incompatible conclusions can both be true, under different conditions. Another's capacity to retaliate punitively does deter the use of coercion, but a far more important factor is the reward power in the relation. Actors who are highly disadvantaged on reward power are more likely to resort to coercion, regardless of the other's coercive power. And although it is true that coercion is a potentially powerful means of influencing others, it is weak when used inconsistently or under structural conditions that fail to support it.

Among the most important conclusions that result from integrating the two bases of power are two intriguing ironies. First, the same conditions that increase the likelihood that actors will *use* coercion, by decreasing the risk of reward loss, actually decrease its effectiveness. Coercion is most effective when combined with rewards for compliance, but it is most likely to be used when the partner's reward dependence is so low that those rewards have little value. This paradox undoubtedly contributes to the perception that coercive tactics do not work in exchange relations when, in fact, they can be highly effective. In contrast, theories that analyze purely coercive or punitive relations tend to focus on the problem of *preventing* coercive power use, and to emphasize the ineffectiveness of coercion when it is used.

Second, as Chapter 9 shows, the same principle that constrains the use of coercion – a preference for minimizing loss over maximizing gain – makes it highly effective when it is used. Actors who are dependent on another for rewards fear the loss of those rewards too much to risk using coercion, but when coercion is used, loss aversion enhances the likelihood that even power-advantaged actors will comply.

Conclusions

This chapter summarized the basic logic of the theory of coercive exchange that was developed over the five preceding chapters. Like any theory, it is incomplete: it is bounded by particular conditions of exchange, and limited to derivations about a particular set of relations.

Nevertheless, it provides a fundamentally different picture of coercion than the one found in most of the literature. Many of the conclusions that typically accompany analyses of coercive power – that it is used by the powerful to subjugate the weak, that it employs extreme sanctions and inflicts grave harm, that it is morally wrong and repugnant – are derived from the study of very particular, highly visible forms of coercion, such as the use of military power by the state or the physical coercion of political prisoners. Most important, they are statements of coercion stripped of the context that describes most of social life: relations in which actors are dependent on one another for the things they need and positively value.

As a form of power in social exchange relations, coercion emerges as a far less malevolent force. In exchange relations, coercion is primarily the tool of the disadvantaged – of actors who lack the reward power to get what they want. For these actors, coercion is risky and its use is constrained by fear of loss. Not only does the reward dependence of these actors increase risk, but their use of coercion is not legitimated by positions of power advantage. It is hardly surprising, therefore, that disadvantaged actors in relations of unequal reward power rarely "fight back," or that their use of coercive tactics – which tends to be sporadic and weak – is often described by terms that capture both the negative evaluation and the impotence of their efforts (e.g., "nagging, " "whining"). Their use of coercion differs, both objectively and subjectively, from the use of institutionalized coercion by powerful actors.

The next chapter considers the implications of these conclusions for social relationships, and for different structures and conditions of exchange.

11. Conclusions and implications

I began this work with two main objectives: *theoretically*, to determine whether the scope of exchange theory could be extended to include coercive power, and *empirically*, to compare the effects of reward power and coercive power on social exchange. Chapter 10 reviewed the results of the first effort, by summarizing the theory of coercive exchange developed in the project and evaluating its implications for social exchange theory.

This chapter evaluates the empirical contributions of the project. Here, I review the major substantive findings of the research, examine their implications for social relationships, and consider their relevance for other structures, forms, and conditions of exchange.

The core findings

Six core findings summarize the main conclusions about coercive power in social exchange. Many of these findings are not only nonintuitive, but directly contrary to common beliefs about the use and effectiveness of coercion.

First, coercion is not structurally induced by a coercive power advantage, but purposively enacted as a strategy to increase rewards. While a reward power advantage directly induces the use of that power, actors who use coercion are motivated, instead, by structural conditions that make acquiring rewards problematic. Their use of punishment is not an unintended side effect of other actions or other exchanges. Rather, it is a purposive effort to change a partner's behavior, by creating contingencies that produce negative consequences for the partner's failure to reward them.

Second, in relations of social exchange, coercion is most likely to be used by actors who are disadvantaged on reward power. Although legitimated, institutionalized forms of coercion are typically used by powerful actors such as the state, noninstitutionalized forms of coercion are more common among actors who are weak on reward power. Lacking the reward power to get what they want, they must either settle for poor outcomes or resort to the use of coercive tactics. Advantaged actors, in contrast, have little need for coercive power; the market mechanisms of reward power are sufficient to provide them with greater benefits, without the costly use of coercion.

Third, the reward dependence that provides the incentive to use coercion also makes it risky. While the structural conditions that promote the use of reward power decrease the risks of retaliation, those that foster coercion increase risk. Actors with the strongest incentive to use coercion – those who are disadvantaged on reward power – also face greater loss. Their powerful partners are more likely to retaliate, and their high dependence makes retaliation costly. These actors not only risk punitive retaliation, but the loss of the relation itself. Loss aversion heightens risk, increasing the likelihood that actors will refrain from coercion and accept the status quo.

Fourth, coercion is perceived as more unjust than the failure to reciprocate reward exchange, and it is more likely to provoke retaliation. Just as loss aversion increases perceptions of risk, it increases perceptions that coercion is unjust. These perceptions of injustice increase with the reward power disadvantage of the coercer. The belief that another's behavior is unjust increases resistance to reward exchange and, consequently, increases the probability of reward loss that potential coercers fear. Thus, disadvantaged actors face greater risk of retaliation both because their partners have greater power to retaliate, and because their partners are more likely to perceive their use of coercion as unjust and deserving of retaliation.

Fifth, structural conditions that reduce the risks of using coercion also decrease its effectiveness. Risk is reduced when a relation is so unrewarding for an actor that she has little to lose from the prospect of the partner's withdrawal from the exchange. Structurally, this means that coercion becomes probable only when the partner's reward dependence is so low, and power imbalance so high, that it is difficult to sustain any pattern of mutual exchange. But the lower the partner's dependence, the more difficult it becomes to coerce the partner into reward exchange. As Chapter 9 illustrated, punishment is more effective when combined with rewards and used in a structure that supports mutually beneficial exchange.

Sixth, when used contingently and consistently in structures that support it, coercion is a highly effective means of increasing a partner's reward exchange. Whereas all of the analyses of structural power suggest that coercive power is weaker than reward power, the opposite is true when actors' *use* of the two forms of power, as well as their structural capacities, is equalized. When punishment is administered contingently and consistently, coercion is a powerful means of getting what one wants. As the first five findings imply, however, the effective use of coercion, within structures that support it, is likely to be rare in relations of social exchange.

Implications for social relationships

These six findings have important implications not only for exchange theory (Chapter 10), but for the role of reward and coercion in social interaction. Any comprehensive overview of these implications is impossible, but a brief discussion of several key findings should provide some sense of the work's broader implications for the development and maintenance of social relationships.

The strategic use of coercion

Because coercion is not structurally induced, but must be used strategically, its effectiveness depends much more on the motivation, skill, and persistence of individual actors. Consequently, we should expect greater variability in the effectiveness of coercion and more ineffective use of coercion in general. Successful coercion requires diligence in monitoring another's behavior, skill in applying punishment contingently, and the willingness to accept short-term losses (including normative censure) in return for uncertain long-term gains.

As Patterson's (1982) work illustrates, most coercive power users fall far short of this model. After studying coercive processes in families for more than a decade, Patterson concluded that the primary problem is not that people punish, but that they punish so poorly. Rather than using punishment effectively or forgoing it altogether, family members engage in what Patterson calls "nattering": they express displeasure and irritation, but without following through with any real costs and without risking more serious confrontation.[1] Like the weak, sporadic punishment studied in Chapter 9, nattering decreases the partner's rewarding rather than increasing it. Instead of promoting mutual rewarding, the low-level coercion actually extends the experience, for both parties, of an unsatisfactory exchange relation. It is not only family members who natter, of course; so do friends, employers, and heads of government.

In contrast, imbalances in reward power can create inequalities in social relationships without either party having any awareness that power is being used. No particular skill is required, and no motivation other than the desire to initiate reward exchange with those on whom one is dependent. Differences in actors' dependencies will lead to a distribution of exchange that reflects those dependencies, regardless of whether actors try to influence each other.

This distinction also contributes to differences in the perceived injustice of reward power and coercive power. The market mechanisms that underlie the use of reward power tend to make it invisible. Actors "use" reward power not by actively imposing cost on another, but through omission – by exchanging with some partners while forgoing others. Simply taking advantage of one's own opportunities is rarely seen as unjust by others, and the reward differences that result from these differences in structural opportunity are more likely to be perceived as "earned." Coercion, in contrast, is not invisible; the harm it inflicts is typically purposive and targeted. That fact, combined with loss aversion, makes its effects seem more negative and more unjust.

It is noteworthy, for example, that the literature on the distributive justice of pay for work has concentrated almost exclusively on comparisons among those in similar positions of power, rather than between the powerful and the powerless (see Cook and Hegtvedt [1983] and Hegtvedt and Markovsky [1995] for summaries of this work). Most theories assume (probably correctly) that workers compare their earnings with those of other workers, not of employers. Such comparisons highlight differences in pay and opportunity among employees (e.g., men and women, minorities and majorities) while masking the large differences in benefits that often exist between labor and management. Coercive power, in contrast, is not easily masked. It is likely, for example, that Kanter's (1977) coer-

---

[1] Patterson (1982) attributes the term "nattering" to John R. Reid.

cive but relatively powerless supervisors were viewed as more unfair by subordinates than were the corporate executives who paid low wages to a large and available labor pool.

Reward power disadvantage and the use of coercion

Some of the most intriguing and important implications of this research derive from the central argument that in exchange relations, coercion is the tool of actors who are disadvantaged on reward power. This finding strikes many people as counterintuitive, despite support from research on families, organizations, and international relations (e.g., Bueno de Mesquita 1981; Kanter 1977; Patterson 1982; Raush et al. 1974). It contradicts the traditional belief that it is the strong who coerce the weak.

The "weak" who are predicted to use coercion against the "strong" are weak on reward power, however, not coercive power. Some of the classic examples of coercion, such as master and slave or mugger and victim, consist of purely coercive relations in which one actor (the master or mugger) can only punish and the other (the slave or victim) can only reward. In these relations, we would never think of the master or mugger as "weak" (despite greater reward dependence), and the slave or victim as "strong," because the coercive power of the master or mugger is far greater than the reward power of the slave or victim. Nevertheless, it is the coercer's dependence on the other for rewards that motivates the use of coercion.

Research on coercive power has traditionally ignored how the reward power in relations affects the use of coercion. Inspired by the arms race during the cold war, the interest of both deterrence theorists and conflict spiral theorists has centered on how actors' mutual capacity to punish either deters or encourages their use of that power (Bacharach and Lawler 1981). But even in the international arena, researchers have observed that countries that are weak on reward power often initiate wars because they have less to lose from such risk taking (e.g., Bueno de Mesquita 1981), just as individuals who are weak on reward power are more likely to engage in activities of sabotage or terrorism.

Similarly, in family relations, most attention has focused on men's greater power to coerce women physically, and adults' greater power to coerce children physically. But husbands who use coercive tactics against their wives are more likely to be low on reward power in other relations

– for example, with their employer. And when physical forms of coercion are excluded, numerous studies of the family find that it is women and children – the members of families who are traditionally more dependent, and who have fewer alternatives – who are most likely to use other forms of coercion. It is their lack of reward power, not their greater coercive power, that increases their use of coercive tactics.

Reward dependence and risk

In general, actors are more likely to use coercion as their partners' reward dependence (and reward frequency) declines. The conflict between the incentive to use coercion and the risk of retaliation is most intense for actors in moderately disadvantageous relations, in which the prospects of gain or loss are roughly equal. Those in highly imbalanced relations have less to lose and more to gain. In purely coercive structures, the absence of mutual reward dependence removes risk altogether. Muggers and terrorists obtain no rewards without coercion, and so they lose nothing by using coercion.

The relation between dependence and risk implies that the use and effectiveness of coercion should vary across the developmental stages of relationships. In the exploratory stages of new relationships, actors are more likely to take risks because they have little to lose. No clear reference level has been established, and neither the value of the relationship nor its loss is as salient as it might become later. At the same time, of course, a new relationship typically provides less incentive to use coercion. But if exchange outcomes are unsatisfactory, actors are more likely to try coercive tactics to improve them in new relationships than in established ones.

Relationships are likely to become established – that is, to develop a pattern of regular and consistent exchange – only if actors' mutual reward dependence is relatively high. Consequently, once a stable relation of reward exchange has been achieved, actors should be more reluctant to use punitive tactics, even when they are dissatisfied with their outcomes. The risk of reward loss is high, and the relation is likely to be governed primarily by reward power.

Over time, however, actors' dependencies on one another can decline and they often decline unequally. As power imbalance in the relation increases, mutual reward dependence may become too low to support the more powerful actor's exchange. If so, the more dependent actor is faced with increasingly poor outcomes from a valued relationship. At this point, the potential gains of coercion can outweigh the losses. Thus, coercion is more likely to be used when relationships are in decline – by workers who are about to be laid off, by spouses whose marriages are in trouble, and so forth.

The risk of reward loss can also be reduced by social barriers that make the partner's withdrawal difficult. Various combinations of social norms, contractual obligations, and restricted alternatives tend to keep people in marriages, partnerships, and friendships, even when they are dissatisfied. When a decline in mutual dependence and an increase in power imbalance are combined with barriers to dissolving relations, coercion should be particularly likely to increase. The reduced risk of losing a valued exchange partner in a contractual relationship such as marriage may be one explanation for the finding that punitive and coercive behavior is more common among family members than among strangers or casual acquaintances (e.g., Birchler, Weiss, and Vincent 1975; Halverson and Waldrop 1970; Winter, Ferreira, and Bowers 1973).

Together, these considerations suggest that coercion is most likely to be used either very early or very late in the course of relationships. During the intermediate stages, when coercion might well restore a more equal exchange that would prevent future deterioration of the relationship, risk constrains its use. Using coercion in relations in which mutual dependence has declined markedly is unlikely to be effective, however, and may serve only to reduce any remaining chances of a mutually satisfactory relationship.

Implications for other settings

The research on which these conclusions are based was conducted under a particular set of conditions. These conditions, which were either assumed by the theory or required to meet the research objectives (see Chapters 3 and 4), necessarily restrict generalizability. Determining just how restrictive these particular conditions are – that is, the extent to which the results would hold under different conditions – is a task for future research. Here, I discuss some of the implications of the work for different structures, forms, and conditions of exchange, and consider how variations in these factors might affect the conclusions of the study.

The structure of exchange

Opportunity for escape or structural change. Two structural restrictions limited the choices of actors in these experiments. First, actors could not escape punishment. They could exit a relationship, by refusing further interaction with a partner, but they could not prevent the partner from continuing to act unilaterally toward them. Second, actors could not change the structure of the network or their relative power within it.

To the extent that actors can escape another's punishing actions, coercion becomes impossible (Azrin, Hake, Holz, and Hutchinson 1965). Thus, in one sense, preventing actors from escaping is a rather obvious restriction for the study of coercion. It is also consistent with an implicit assumption of exchange theory: that the development and maintenance of exchange relations is limited to actors who are in mutual "range" of each other's rewarding actions. But in another sense, it bears repeating and emphasizing, for the simple reason that actors are more likely to try to escape punishment than reward.

This condition is most likely to restrict the use of coercion during the exploratory stages of relations, before social barriers and contractual commitments make it difficult for people to leave relations. Even if they can leave, individuals in long-term relations are likely to be enmeshed in a network of connections that makes it difficult to escape the punitive actions of former exchange partners. As the news media testify daily, ex-spouses and fired workers can still inflict considerable harm on their former exchange partners.

Not only did the structures in the experiments remain constant, but actors had no means of changing them: they could not form coalitions, or seek out new exchange partners, or obtain new resources that might enhance their power (Emerson 1972b). If actors could change the structure of the network, of course, the very conditions that affect the incentive to coerce and the capacity to coerce could be changed.

One of the most potent forms of structural change is the formation of coalitions. If actors who were disadvantaged on reward power could form coalitions, thus restricting the alternatives of their advantaged partners, they could increase their capacity to obtain rewards without the use of coercive tactics. Or, alternatively, coalitions could be formed to increase the coercive power of actors. This mechanism underlies many forms of collective action, from union strikes to consumer boycotts to the organization of terrorist groups. As these examples illustrate, coercive coalitions are typically formed by actors who are weak on reward power. By acting in concert, they increase their coercive power and their capacity to influence powerful exchange partners.

Other exchange structures. The theory developed in this program is restricted to direct exchanges in negatively connected networks. But coercion can also be used in other structures of exchange, including productive exchange, generalized exchange, and positively connected networks (see Chapter 2).

Both generalized exchange and productive exchange represent collective forms of interaction, in which multiple actors must cooperate for the good of all. In productive exchange, actors contribute individually to a collective product (e.g., a coauthored book, or a team championship) that provides joint benefits to the actors; in generalized exchange, actors engage in unilateral giving that provides returns to self only if other actors also participate (see Figure 2.1 in Chapter 2). Both types of interaction can suffer from the presence of "free riders." In productive exchanges, free riders reduce the value of the collective product or, if contributions from all are required, prevent its production. In some forms of generalized exchange, free riders can virtually shut down the system; in others, they can impede its effectiveness (Yamagishi and Cook 1993).

In both productive and generalized exchange, coercion provides a potential means to force free riders to contribute rewards, either to the collective good or to another actor in the system. Not surprisingly, the use of punishment and the development of sanctioning systems has been a major topic of discussion in both of these literatures, for both involve social dilemmas (Yamagishi 1995; Yamagishi and Cook 1993). In these structures, however, punishment is more likely to be applied by the collectivity. Those who reward infrequently hurt the group as a whole; therefore, sanctioning low rewarders benefits the group as a whole. When coercion is applied collectively, to punish those who harm the collective welfare, it is reinforced by the weight of social norms (Heckathorn 1988). Over time, such forms of coercion are more likely to become legitimated and institutionalized than coercion in direct exchange relations.[2]

---

[2] When productive exchange is limited to two actors, there is no collectivity to punish defection by one actor. However, the failure of either of the actors to contribute to the joint

In positively connected exchange networks, resources flow *across* relations. The benefits obtained from one relation (e.g., information, money, status) have exchange value in another relation. Thus, if B–A–C is a positively connected network, B's failure to provide rewards to A not only affects A's benefits from that relation, it affects A's ability to provide rewards to C and, consequently, A's ability to obtain benefits from C. In such networks, it is the central actor – in this example, A – who is most likely to use coercion, against B. But because A's ability to extract rewards from B also benefits C, C might provide A with resources that will enhance A's coercive power against B. Thus, countries sometimes provide resources to help other countries fight wars, either because the benefits of winning will be collectively shared (in productive exchange), or because the benefits for one country (e.g., increased economic development) may be valuable resources for the other country in future exchange relations (in a positively connected exchange network).

The form of exchange

The theory developed in this book is a theory of coercion in direct, reciprocal exchanges – that is, exchanges that are not explicitly negotiated through a formal bargaining process. Coercion is certainly possible in both reciprocal and negotiated exchanges, and some of the theoretical principles and research findings may pertain to both. Nevertheless, it is likely that each of the major findings – on the use, risks, injustice, and behavioral effects of coercion – will vary, more or less, for these two major forms of exchange. I discussed some of these differences in Chapter 9.

Negotiated exchange differs from reciprocal exchange in two important ways. First, actors know the terms of an exchange before they agree to it. Because actors know what they are getting for what they are giving, it is unlikely that coercion will be used in response to a partner's unequal or insufficient rewarding. Instead, coercion is more likely to be used during the *process* of bargaining, in an effort to secure greater concessions from the other party and obtain a better deal (e.g., Lawler 1992). In relations in which agreements are nonbinding, coercion might also be used to extract rewards from a partner who fails to uphold her end of the bargain,

---

product will prevent both from obtaining rewards. Thus, there is a built-in incentive to contribute, and less need for punishment.

who is deceptive about the value of her resources, or who delivers less than the agreed-upon amount.

Second, when actors bargain, they engage in a process that resembles productive exchange more than direct exchange (see Figure 2.1 in Chapter 2). The agreement to negotiate a settlement transforms the structure of exchange from one in which each actor is dependent on the other's behavior for valued outcomes, to one in which *both* actors are dependent on their *joint* actions (Molm 1994b). If actors fail to reach an agreement, neither receives any benefit from the relation. How much that matters to them will vary with their relative and absolute dependencies. But regardless of differences in power, the agreement to engage in negotiation increases the dependence of both actors on the relation (Lawler and Yoon 1993) and creates a normative expectation of a form of cooperation.

Because the relation between these actors is nevertheless one of conflict, that transformation of the structure of the relation could have two opposing effects. On the one hand, it might increase hostile, emotional reactions to coercion, perceptions of injustice, and the likelihood of retaliation (see Chapter 9). On the other hand, the greater dependence of both actors on the relation may reduce the likelihood that the partner will withdraw from the relation as a form of retaliation. The question of which of these effects actually occurs can only be settled by research that systematically compares negotiated and nonnegotiated exchanges. As this brief discussion suggests, analyzing the theoretical and empirical differences between these two forms of exchange is long overdue.

Assumptions about rewards, punishments, and costs

The bases of power. In this research, I studied coercion in the context of relations in which all actors have some capacity to both reward and punish their exchange partners. Most important, I assumed that the primary goal of all actors was obtaining benefits from others, either through mutual reward exchange or coercive exchange.

Coercion minimally requires one actor who can reward, and one who can punish. Making either of those unilateral bases of power bilateral increases the risks of using coercion. The risk of retaliatory punishment increases with the punishment power of the target of coercion, and the risk of reward loss increases with the reward power of the coercer. If *both* coercer and coercee are dependent on each other for rewards, then the potential for mutual reward exchange exists, and coercion risks the loss of that relation.

In contrast, in purely coercive relations (i.e., relations in which the target of coercion has no punishment power and the coercer has no reward power, such as muggers and victims or masters and slaves), the risks that constrain the use of coercion in social exchange are absent. Nevertheless, coercers often face another source of risk that I have not considered – retaliation by third parties on behalf of the target of coercion. If the use of coercion violates either social norms or laws, the coercer may be punished by other members of the collectivity or by the state.

The costs of exchange. In this research, the only direct costs to actors of performing either rewarding or punishing actions were opportunity costs. This restriction made the costs of reward exchange and coercive exchange comparable. When the rewards exchanged are tangible goods that are transferred from one actor to another, however, reward exchange entails actual losses as well as opportunity costs. Under those conditions, reward exchange may be more costly than coercive exchange, and actors may be more likely to use coercion. Slavery may replace paid labor, for example, because it is cheaper. If, on the other hand, coercion involves costly investments (raising armies, buying weapons, building prisons or concentration camps), then the opposite may be true. (Often, of course, these ''costly investments'' are costly to some, but profitable to others.)

The critical point is that the relative costs of performing reward exchanges and coercive exchanges can affect the likelihood that one or the other will be used. For this analysis, I assumed these costs were equal and focused solely on variations in the cost of the partner's retaliation for coercion. Changes in these assumptions could lead to different conclusions.

Conditions of punishment. The restriction of the research to a particular type of punishment (the removal of rewards), applied without threats and with fixed value, may also affect responses to a partner's use of coercion. Some forms of punishment are more likely than others to provoke emotional reactions or to be interpreted as insult or challenge. Psychological research suggests such reactions occur more frequently in response to physical punishment or intense levels of punishment, although this generalization is by no means always supported (Newsom et al. 1983). More important than the type of punishment is the use of punishment; noncontingent punishment is most likely to produce these effects (e.g., Ford and Blegen 1992).

This research excluded two factors that are commonly believed to make punishment more effective: the use of threats that specify contingencies of punishment (e.g., "if you don't do X, I will punish you"), and control over the magnitude of any single act of punishment. Because the value of punishment was fixed, actors could not begin with mild punishment, signaling displeasure, and work up to more intense levels if mild punishment failed to work. Nor could they signal their intent to punish with verbal threats.

Rather than increasing the effectiveness of punishment, however, these two factors likely decrease it. Because the actual use of coercion is riskier than mere threat, and because strong punishment is more apt to provoke retaliation than weak punishment, actors are likely to threaten more than punish and to use weak punishment before strong. But threats that are not carried out begin to signal insult and challenge rather than impending punishment (e.g., Lindskold et al. 1986; Patterson 1982). And gradual increases in the intensity of punishment reduce its normal effects, requiring more – not less – punishment to produce the same result (Van Houten 1983).

In short, the type of punishment I have studied and its surrounding conditions may have been particularly conducive to producing compliance rather than retaliation and conflict escalation. In natural settings, actors have access to threats and to a range of different types and intensities of punishment. Threats and punishments may be used in many ways, and escalations of conflict should be more common. In addition, because coercion is particularly risky for disadvantaged actors, they are more likely to make threats they fail to carry out, and to use mild rather than strong forms of punishment.

Exchange information

In all experiments, actors had full information about the values governing the relative dependencies in their own exchange relations. While the reciprocal form of exchange meant that the consequences of exchange behaviors were uncertain, actors did know the values of the rewards and punishments that each of their partners could give and receive in exchange.

Consequently, they could derive inferences about power, even though those inferences were incomplete (i.e., actors did not know the dependence of the fourth actor in the network on their partners). In both experimental and natural settings, these conditions of information can vary.

The amount of information actors have is most likely to affect exchange processes that rely, at least partially, on cognition: evaluations of risk and fairness. Certain assumptions about information are fundamental to theories of justice, and the kind and amount of information that actors have necessarily affects their perceptions of fairness. Obviously, actors' perceptions of the injustice of coercion cannot be influenced by the relative power of the coercer if they lack knowledge of that power. And judgments of reciprocity are more difficult, or more likely to be biased, if actors do not know the values of their behaviors for their partners.

Because information is the primary variable affecting estimates of subjective probabilities, variations in information about the power structure, the partners' outcomes, and so forth can also affect assessments of risk, by providing information about either the value or the probability of both compliance and retaliation. For this analysis, I assumed that actors considered the probability of these two responses to be roughly equal, if they estimated probabilities at all. Restricting actors' information about the power structure might have either of two effects. On the one hand, disadvantaged actors might be more likely to use coercive power if they were unaware of their partner's power advantage. On the other hand, any reduction in information increases uncertainty and, as a result, might further inhibit risk taking. Whatever the effects of information on assessments of risk, they are more likely to be variations in the strength of relations rather than qualitative changes in the basic findings themselves.

Concluding comments

Although the scope and setting conditions of this program necessarily restrict the generalizability of the theory, I hope they also provide the impetus for further research. The use of a single setting facilitated the cumulation of results and the development of theory. But determining the robustness of the findings and understanding the conditions that modify or change the use and effects of coercive power require a different strategy.

The value of moving back and forth between these two strategies – of standardized experimentation and control, and of variations that push the current boundaries of exchange theory – is an implicit but important theme of this work. Exchange researchers have made remarkable advances in the past two decades by pursuing the first strategy. Systematic research in several experimental laboratories has greatly expanded our knowledge of power in exchange relations under fairly narrow, clearly defined conditions. But it is important to balance the goal of increasingly precise predictions of power relations, under very restricted conditions, with the equally valuable goal of a broader understanding of power and exchange under a wider range of conditions.

As this analysis has illustrated, expanding the bases, forms, and structures of power studied can lead to new theoretical insights. In this research, broadening the scope of power-dependence theory to include coercive power led to a reexamination of the nature and causes of power, particularly the distinction between structurally induced and strategic power use. This distinction became crucial for explaining the different effects of reward power and coercive power. Similarly, analyzing coercive power that was stripped of the legitimacy of the state, but embedded in the context of social exchange, revealed the vulnerability of this highly potent form of power to dependence and risk. Finally, in contrast to most contemporary work on exchange, I studied relations in which the terms of exchange are unknown and the reciprocity of partners uncertain. Under these conditions – in which exchanges are secured not by negotiated agreements but by each actor's stake in an ongoing relation – the relations that develop depend not only on the structure of power but on the evolving strategies of interdependent actors. How much power actors have, and how they use that power, both matter.

Appendix I. Definitions of basic concepts of social exchange

Actors. Individual persons or corporate groups who engage in exchange.

Alternatives. Alternative sources (typically, alternative exchange partners) for obtaining valued outcomes within a single exchange domain.

Average power. The average of two actors' dependencies on each other. **Average reward power** refers to the average of the actors' dependencies on each other for rewards, and **average punishment power** to the average of their dependencies on each other for punishments.

Dependence. An actor is dependent on another to the extent that outcomes valued by the actor are contingent on exchange with the other. Dependence is a function of both value and available alternatives.

Exchange. The mutual giving and receiving of valued outcomes by two actors.

Exchange costs. Defined broadly as any negative value obtained through exchange (including punishments), but used specifically to refer to the negative value incurred by the actor who performs an exchange behavior (i.e., opportunity costs, investment costs, actual loss of resources, and costs intrinsic to the behavior).

Exchange domains. A class of outcomes that are functionally equivalent in the sense that the receipt of one outcome in the class reduces the value of all outcomes within that class.

Exchange network. A set of two or more connected exchange relations.

Exchange opportunity. An occasion on which an exchange can be initiated.

Exchange outcomes. The positive or negative value received from another actor through exchange. An outcome with positive value is a **reward**; an outcome with negative value is a **punishment.**

Exchange relation. A continuing series of interdependent transactions between the same actors. Two exchange relations are **connected** if the frequency or value of exchange in one relation affects the frequency or value of exchange in another; connections are **positive** if exchange in one relation increases exchange in the other, and **negative** if exchange in one decreases exchange in the other.

Power. The level of potential cost that an actor can impose on another. **Reward power** refers to the level of opportunity costs that an actor can impose on another; **punishment (or coercive) power** refers to the level of actual losses that an actor can impose on another. A's power over B = B's dependence on A; thus, A's reward power over B = B's dependence on A for rewards, and A's punishment power over B = B's dependence on A for punishment.

Power advantage. The difference between the power of the less dependent and more dependent actors in a power-imbalanced relation – that is, the net potential power of the more powerful actor. **Reward power advantage** refers to the difference between the reward power of the less and more dependent actors in a reward-power imbalanced relation, and **punishment power advantage** to the difference between the punishment power of the less and more dependent actors in a punishment-power imbalanced relation.

Power imbalance. The difference between two actors' dependencies on each other. **Reward power imbalance** refers to the difference between the actors' dependencies on each other for rewards, and **punishment power imbalance** to the difference between their dependencies on each other for punishments.

Power use. The behavioral exercise of potential power to obtain increased rewards or decreased costs (both opportunity costs and punishment) in an exchange relation. **Strategic power use** refers, more specifically, to the selective giving or withholding of rewards or punishments, contingent on the exchange partner's prior behavior.

Primacy. The number of exchange domains that a relation mediates.

Resources. Possessions or behavioral capabilities of an actor that are valued by others, when considered in the context of a relation with those others.

Transaction. A single exchange of mutual value between two actors. Transactions can be **negotiated** or **reciprocal** (nonnegotiated).

Value. Across domains, an actor's preference ordering of those domains. Within a domain, the magnitude of outcomes that an actor potentially can receive in a relation.

Appendix II. The experimental instructions for the standardized setting

With the exception of minor modifications required for certain experiments (e.g., those in which subjects controlled either rewards or punishments for one another), the instructions shown here were used for all experiments in the program. Each subject was referred to by a particular letter. To avoid the evaluative connotations that student subjects might attach to the letters normally associated with academic grades (i.e., A, B, C, and D), the four actors in the network were instead labeled W, X, Y, and Z. These instructions are written for Person X; consequently, they refer to the subject's two interaction partners as Persons W and Y – the partners for Person X.

Screen 1

WELCOME TO THE SOCIAL INTERACTION EXPERIMENT!

You are participating in this experiment with 3 other students. Like you, they volunteered for the experiment to earn money. During the experiment, you will interact with one another by using the computers on your desks. The choices you make will affect how much money you earn.

Because we don't want your interaction to be influenced by personal characteristics like sex or appearance, you will not meet or talk to each other either during or after the experiment. You will interact only through the computers, which are connected to a larger computer in the control room. The computer records your responses for future data analysis.

During the experiment, you will use the computer mouse on your desk to make choices that will affect each other's earnings. We are interested in the choices that people make about whom they interact with and how they behave toward them under various conditions.

To continue the instructions, please press any one of the buttons on your mouse. The next screen will appear when all four of you are ready to continue.

Screen 2

At the top of your computer is a label indicating that you are Person W, X, Y, or Z. We will refer to you by these letters during the experiment.

We will now explain how the experiment works, and give you a chance to practice making choices with the mouse. The instructions will take about half an hour. Make sure you read each screen of the instructions carefully. You won't be able to go back to previous screens. After the instructions, you will be able to ask questions.

PAY ATTENTION TO THE INSTRUCTIONS.
YOU MUST UNDERSTAND THEM COMPLETELY
TO MAKE MONEY.

If you wish, you can write down questions as you are reading, on the notepad on your desk. Each screen has a page number on it, in the lower right-hand corner, that you can refer to in your questions if you wish.

PLEASE DON'T USE YOUR NOTEPAD FOR OTHER WRITING. IN PARTICULAR, PLEASE DON'T KEEP A WRITTEN RECORD OF CHOICES MADE BY YOU AND THE OTHER PARTICIPANTS DURING THE EXPERIMENT. We want you to respond to the interaction as you experience it.

To continue the instructions, please press your mouse button.

Screen 3

In the experiment you will use your computer mouse to make choices on your screen. We'd like you to get familiar with doing that before we continue with the instructions. You may have used a computer mouse before to make choices from a "menu" presented on a computer screen. If not, it's very easy to learn.

Place your hand on the mouse, with the mouse flat on your desk. (If you are left-handed, you'll first want to move the mouse to the left side of your desk.) Try moving the mouse up and down, and sideways, while keeping it flat on your desk. Moving the mouse moves the cursor on your screen. The cursor moves up or down, or sideways, as you move the mouse in those directions. Try moving the mouse around while watching the cursor move to see how this works.

When you are ready to continue the instructions about using the mouse, please press your mouse button.

Screen 4

During the experiment, you will be asked to make choices by using your mouse. The choices will be presented on the screen, in boxes. You will choose the response you want by first using your mouse to move the cursor on top of the box containing your choice, and then pressing one of your mouse buttons to select the choice. When you make a choice by pressing a mouse button, the name of the choice will light up in the box you have selected. As long as you have your cursor WITHIN the box, or ON THE LINE around the box, pressing your mouse button will select that choice. If the cursor is outside of any of the boxes, pressing a mouse button won't do anything.

To see how this works, please press your mouse button to continue the instructions.

Screen 5

Here are four choices. Try moving the cursor to different boxes by moving your mouse around. Then, to select the choice in one of the boxes, press your mouse button while the cursor is on the box. Watch the choice light up when you press the mouse button.

[CHOICE BOXES DISPLAYED HERE]

Try it one more time.

Screen 6

Okay, now we're going to give you a brief overview of what you will be doing in the experiment. Then we'll describe the procedures in more detail.

During the experiment, each of you will be able to interact with TWO of the three other participants in the experiment. Each of you will begin the experiment with a "bank account" consisting of a number of points. Then, during the experiment, each of you will make choices that will either

ADD TO or SUBTRACT FROM the points of one of the two persons with whom you can interact. The amount of money you make in the experiment will depend on how many points you have at the end of the experiment; one point equals 1 cent.

In other words, your earnings in the experiment depend on the choices that other participants make. Their earnings depend on the choices that you make. YOU CANNOT GIVE ANY POINTS TO YOURSELF. When you subtract points from others, those points are not added to your earnings. Similarly, when you add points to others' earnings, those points are not subtracted from your own earnings.

Please press your mouse button to continue the instructions.

Screen 7

The experiment will consist of a large number of choice opportunities. On each of these opportunities, you will make two choices:

First, you will choose which person you wish to act toward on that opportunity.

Second, you will choose whether to add to or subtract from that person's points.

You will make these choices by using your mouse to select options presented on your computer screen.

The number of points that you can add to or subtract from each person's earnings on any single choice opportunity will be displayed on your computer screen throughout the experiment. The number of points that each of the other persons can add to or subtract from your earnings will also be shown.

To continue the instructions, please press your mouse button.

Screen 8

All of you will make your choices at the same time, without knowing what the others are intending to do. The person you choose to act toward may or may not choose to act toward you; you will NOT know that ahead of time.

After you make your choices on each opportunity, your computer screen will show you the choices made by each of the two persons with whom you can interact. You will be told that each person added to your points, subtracted from your points, or did not act toward you. If a person does not act toward you, that means that he or she chose to act toward another person instead.

Your total points will be shown on the screen at all times, and changed whenever you gain or lose points. You will NOT be shown the total points of the other participants. On any choice opportunity, it is possible to gain or lose points from one, both, or neither of the two persons with whom you can interact.

To continue the instructions, please press your mouse button.

Screen 9

YOU SHOULD TRY AT ALL TIMES
TO MAKE AS MUCH MONEY AS YOU CAN.

Because your earnings depend on what the other participants choose to do, you must try to influence THEIR choices in order to make money. Your ability to affect their earnings gives you the means to influence them. But how you use it is up to you; there are no right or wrong responses in the experiment.

To continue the instructions, please press your mouse button.

Screen 10

With that brief overview, let us turn to a more detailed description of how you will actually use the computer to interact with one another.

First, the two persons with whom you can interact are Y and W. Y and W can interact with you, and with Z. Y and W CANNOT INTERACT WITH EACH OTHER.

Throughout the experiment, the number of points that you, Y, and W can add to or subtract from each other's earnings will be displayed on the top of your screen. Those values will be called the "earnings schedule" for the experiment. To see what the format of the earnings schedule looks like, please press your mouse button.

Screen 11

[EARNINGS SCHEDULE DISPLAYED HERE]

Right now, the numbers of points in the earnings schedule are all shown as zeros. When the experiment begins, the earnings schedule will show actual point values.

To continue with the display and instructions about the earnings schedule, please press your mouse button.

Screen 12

[EARNINGS SCHEDULE DISPLAYED HERE]

The earnings schedule tells you how many points you can GAIN from Y and W, on a single choice opportunity, and how many points you can LOSE from Y and W if they subtract from your points. It also tells you how many points Y and W can gain and lose from you and from Z, the other person with whom they can interact. It does not tell you how much Z can gain and lose from Y and W.

To continue the instructions, please press your mouse button.

Screen 13

Pay careful attention to the earnings schedule when making your choices. THE EARNINGS SCHEDULE WILL NOT CHANGE DURING THE EXPERIMENT. IT WILL STAY THE SAME THE ENTIRE TIME.

The Total Points that you have made in the experiment will also be shown on the screen at all times, in the lower right-hand corner. One point equals 1 cent. To see this display, please press your mouse button.

Screen 14

You will begin the experiment with a number of points. You can then gain or lose points as a result of Y's and W's choices. Whenever you gain or lose points, your total points will change. Each time they change, they will blink for several seconds.

At the end of the experiment, you will be paid the monetary value of your Total Points: 1 cent for every point you have, or $1.00 for every 100 points. AT ALL TIMES, YOUR OBJECTIVE SHOULD BE TO MAKE AS MUCH MONEY AS YOU CAN.

[TOTAL POINTS BOX DISPLAYED HERE]

To continue the instructions, please press your mouse button.

Screen 15

The experiment consists of a large number of choice opportunities. Each choice opportunity begins with a request that you choose which person you want to act toward: Person Y or Person W. You should use your mouse to move your cursor on top of the box with the name of the person you wish to choose, and then press your mouse button. The name of the person you have chosen will light up on the screen.

To see how this works, press your mouse button. Then, on the next screen, select either Person Y or Person W by using your mouse. The name of the person you select will light up. After observing it, press your mouse button to continue the instructions.

[PRACTICE: CHOOSING A PARTNER]

Screen 16

Once you choose a person to act toward, the screen will immediately show a new request, asking you to choose an action toward that person: Add points to, or subtract points from, that person's total. Using your mouse again, you will select one of these two actions on your computer screen.

To see how this works, please press your mouse button. When the next screen appears, respond to the first request by using your mouse to choose either Person Y or Person W, and then respond to the second request by using your mouse to choose to add or subtract points.

[PRACTICE: CHOOSING A PARTNER AND CHOOSING
AN ACTION]

Screen 17

Remember, the person that you choose to act toward will not necessarily choose you. Similarly, a person can choose to act toward you – and add to or subtract from your points – even if you have not chosen to act toward that person on that choice opportunity. Over the course of the experiment, you can choose different persons on different opportunities, or the same person on all opportunities. The choice is up to you.

The requests to choose a person and an action will always remain on your screen until you select one of the options. It doesn't matter how fast you make a choice. THE SPEED OF YOUR RESPONSE DOES NOT AFFECT YOUR EARNINGS. The experiment has the same number of choice opportunities regardless of how quickly or slowly you respond.

To continue the instructions, please press your mouse button.

Screen 18

As soon as you and the other participants have made your choices, you will learn what choices others made. The computer screen will show your own choices (as a reminder), and it will show what Y and W chose: whether each person added to your points, subtracted from your points, or did not act toward you. It will also show your net gain or loss. The screen will not show you Z's choices.

If your net gain or loss is other than zero, your Total Points will change accordingly. The changed points will blink for several seconds.

Let's try the full sequence now. For this demonstration, let's assume that each of you can add 3 points to or subtract 3 points from each other's total points. When the next screen appears, respond to the first request by choosing either Person Y or Person W with your mouse, and then respond to the second request by choosing either to add to or subtract from that person's points. Then, watch carefully when the information about the choices that each of you has made appears, and your Total Points are changed. You will begin with a total of 10 points.

To start this demonstration, please press your mouse button.

[PRACTICE: FULL CHOICE (EXCHANGE) OPPORTUNITY
SEQUENCE]

Screen 19

We have now gone through the sequence of events on each choice opportunity. After each opportunity ends, a new choice opportunity begins. The computer screen will signal the start of a new opportunity by once again requesting that you choose Y or W. This sequence of events will be repeated a large number of times during the experiment.

To continue the instructions, please press your mouse button.

Screen 20

Before we start the experiment, we're going to have a short practice exercise. It will consist of nine choice opportunities in a row. This will give you a chance to become more familiar with making choices with your mouse, and then reading what choices Y and W have made.

Because this is just a practice, it won't be realistic. We want each of you to try out all of the different choices you make: adding to Y's points, subtracting from Y's points, adding to W's points, and subtracting from W's points. We want you to become familiar with reading the information on everyone's choice. But because all of you will be trying out different choices, just for practice, you won't be interacting with each other as you will be in the experiment. So, the practice exercise won't tell you how others are likely to respond to you during the experiment. It will just give you practice making choices and reading the screen.

To continue the instructions, please press your mouse button.

Screen 21

Each of you will begin the practice exercise with 40 points. You will be able to add 3 points to or subtract 3 points from each other's earnings. THESE POINT VALUES ARE JUST FOR THE PRACTICE EXERCISE. THE POINT VALUES USED IN THE EXPERIMENT WILL BE DIF-FERENT. Also, since this is just a practice exercise, you won't be paid for any points you have at the end of it.

During the practice exercise, the screen will automatically change after your choices, just as it will in the experiment. You won't need to press your mouse button to produce a new screen.

Okay, to start the nine choice opportunities, press your mouse button. When all of you are ready, the practice exercise will begin.

[PRACTICE: NINE CHOICE (EXCHANGE) OPPORTUNITIES]

Screen 22

Okay, that was very good. As you've just seen, your task in the experiment is really very simple. You just use your mouse to select persons and actions toward them over repeated opportunities. Try to make as much money as possible. Carefully study the earnings schedule before you be-gin. Then, pay close attention to how the others act toward you.

That concludes the instructions for the experiment. If you have any questions about the instructions, please write them on the notepad on your desk. We will collect the questions, and read and answer them over the intercom system. When you are ready, please select one of the boxes below to indicate either that you have no questions and are ready to begin the experiment, or that you have a question for the experimenter to collect and answer.

[QUESTIONS]

Screen 23

We're now ready to start the experiment. When all four of you have pressed your mouse buttons, the screen will change and begin the exper-iment. Before you respond to the first choice request, carefully study the earnings schedule and make sure that you understand it.

REMEMBER, THE SAME EARNINGS SCHEDULE WILL BE IN EFFECT FOR THE ENTIRE EXPERIMENT. THE POINT VALUES WILL NOT CHANGE.

Please press your mouse button to start the experiment. It will begin when all participants are ready.

References

Adams, J. Stacy. 1965. "Inequity in Social Exchange." *Advances in Experimental Social Psychology* 2:267–299.

Ainslie, George, and Nick Haslam. 1992. "Self-Control." Pp. 177–209 in *Choice over Time*, edited by George Loewenstein and Jon Elster. New York: Russell Sage.

Allais, Par M. 1953. "The Behavior of Rational Man in Risk Situations: A Critique of the Axioms and Postulates of the American School." *Econometrica* 21:503–546.

Allison, Paul D., and Jeffrey K. Liker. 1982. "Analyzing Sequential Categorical Data on Dyadic Interaction: A Comment on Gottman." *Psychological Bulletin* 91:393–403.

Anderson, Bo, and David Willer. 1981. "Introduction." Pp. 1–21 in *Networks, Exchange and Coercion: The Elementary Theory and Its Applications*, edited by David Willer and Bo Anderson. New York: Elsevier.

Arendt, Hannah. 1970. *On Violence*. London: Allen Lane, Penguin Press.

Aronson, Elliott, Marilynn Brewer, and M. Merrill Carlsmith. 1985. "Experimentation in Social Psychology." Pp. 441–486 in *Handbook of Social Psychology*, vol. 1, edited by Gardner Lindzey and Elliott Aronson. 3rd ed. New York: Random House.

Austin, William, and Elaine Hatfield. 1980. "Equity Theory, Power, and Justice." Pp. 25–62 in *Justice and Social Interaction*, edited by Gerald Mikula. New York: Springer-Verlag.

Austin, William, Elaine Walster, and Mary K. Utne. 1976. "Equity and the Law: The Effect of Harmdoer's Suffering in the Act on Liking and Assigned Punishment." *Advances in Experimental Social Psychology* 9:163–190.

Axelrod, Robert. 1984. *The Evolution of Cooperation*. New York: Basic Books.

——— 1986. "An Evolutionary Approach to Norms." *American Political Science Review* 80:1095–1111.

——— 1992. "How to Promote Cooperation." *Current Contents* 24:10.

Axelrod, Robert, and Douglas Dion. 1988. "The Further Evolution of Cooperation." *Science* 242:1385–1390.

Axelrod, Saul. 1983. "Introduction." Pp. 1–11 in *The Effects of Punishment on Human Behavior*, edited by Saul Axelrod and Jack Apsche. New York: Academic Press.

Axelrod, Saul, and Jack Apsche (eds.). 1983. *The Effects of Punishment on Human Behavior.* New York: Academic Press.

Azrin, Nathan H. 1956. "Some Effects of Two Intermittent Schedules of Immediate and Nonimmediate Punishment." *Journal of Psychology* 42:3–21.

Azrin, N. H., D. F. Hake, W. C. Holz, and R. R. Hutchinson. 1965. "Motivational Aspects of Escape from Punishment." *Journal of the Experimental Analysis of Behavior* 8:31–44.

Azrin, N. H., and W. C. Holz. 1966. "Punishment." Pp. 380–447 in *Operant Behavior: Areas of Research and Application,* edited by Werner K. Honig. New York: Appleton.

Bacharach, Samuel B., and Edward J. Lawler. 1980. *Power and Politics in Organizations: The Social Psychology of Conflict, Coalitions, and Bargaining.* San Francisco: Jossey-Bass.

——— 1981. *Bargaining: Power, Tactics, and Outcomes.* San Francisco: Jossey-Bass.

Bachrach, Peter, and Morton S. Baratz. 1963. "Decisions and Nondecisions: An Analytical Framework." *American Political Science Review* 57:641–651.

Barbalet, J. M. 1987. "Power, Structural Resources and Agency." *Perspectives in Social Theory* 8:1–24.

Bazerman, Max H. 1983. "Negotiator Judgment: A Critical Look at the Rationality Assumption." *American Behavioral Scientist* 27:211–228.

Bem, Daryl. 1967. "Self-Perception: An Alternative Interpretation of Cognitive Dissonance Phenomena." *Psychological Review* 74:183–200.

Berger, Joseph, Bernard P. Cohen, and Morris Zelditch Jr. 1972. "Structural Aspects of Distributive Justice: A Status Value Formation." Pp. 119–146 in *Sociological Theories in Progress,* vol. 2, edited by Joseph Berger, Morris Zelditch Jr., and Bo Anderson. Boston: Houghton Mifflin.

Berger, Joseph, and Morris Zelditch Jr. (eds.) 1993. *Theoretical Research Programs: Studies in the Growth of Theory.* Stanford, CA: Stanford University Press.

Berkowitz, Leonard. 1978. "Is Criminal Violence Normative Behavior?" *Journal of Research in Crime and Delinquency* 15:148–161.

Bienenstock, Elisa Jayne, and Phillip Bonacich. 1992. "The Core As a Solution to Exclusionary Networks." *Social Networks* 14:231–243.

Bierstedt, Robert. 1950. "An Analysis of Social Power." *American Sociological Review* 15:730–738.

——— 1965. "Review of Blau's 'Exchange and Power.' " *American Sociological Review* 30:789–790.

Birchler, Gary, Robert L. Weiss, and John P. Vincent. 1975. "Multimethod Analysis of Social Reinforcement Exchange between Maritally Distressed and Nondistressed Spouse and Stranger Dyads." *Journal of Personality and Social Psychology* 31:349–360.

Blalock, Hubert M., Jr. 1987. "A Power Analysis of Conflict Processes." Pp. 1–40 in *Advances in Group Processes,* vol. 4, edited by Edward J. Lawler and Barry Markovsky. Greenwich, CT: JAI Press.

1989. *Power and Conflict: Toward a General Theory*. Newbury Park, CA: Sage.

Blalock, Hubert M., Jr., and Paul H. Wilkin. 1979. *Intergroup Processes: A Micro–Macro Perspective*. New York: Free Press.

Blau, Peter M. 1964. *Exchange and Power in Social Life*. New York: Wiley.

Bonacich, Phillip. 1992. "Power in Positively Connected Exchange Networks: A Critical Review." Pp. 21–40 in *Advances in Group Processes*, vol. 9, edited by Edward J. Lawler, Barry Markovsky, Cecilia Ridgeway, and Henry A. Walker. Greenwich, CT: JAI Press.

Borgatta, Edgar R., and George W. Bohrnstedt. 1974. "Some Limitations of Generalizability from Social Psychological Experiments." *Sociological Methods and Research* 3:111–120.

Boulding, Kenneth E. 1969. "Toward a Pure Theory of Threat Systems." Pp. 285–292 in *Political Power: A Reader in Theory and Research*, edited by Roderick Bell, David V. Edwards, and R. Harrison Wagner. New York: Free Press.

1989. *Three Faces of Power*. Newbury Park, CA: Sage.

Boyle, Elizabeth Heger, and Edward J. Lawler. 1991. "Resolving Conflict through Explicit Bargaining." *Social Forces* 69:1183–1204.

Bueno de Mesquita, Bruce. 1981. *The War Trap*. New Haven: Yale University Press.

Burgess, Robert L., Elaine A. Anderson, Cynthia J. Schellenbach, and Rand D. Conger. 1981. "A Social Interactional Approach to the Study of Abusive Families." Pp. 1–46 in *Advances in Family Intervention, Assessment and Theory*, vol. 2, edited by John P. Vincent. Greenwich, CT: JAI Press.

Burgess, Robert L., and Joyce M. Nielsen. 1974. "An Experimental Analysis of Some Structural Determinants of Equitable and Inequitable Exchange Relations." *American Sociological Review* 39:427–443.

Cairns, Robert B. 1979. *Social Development: The Origins and Plasticity of Interchanges*. San Francisco: W. H. Freeman.

Chamberlain, Neil W. 1955. *A General Theory of Economic Process*. New York: Harper and Row.

Cheney, John, Thomas Harford, and Leonard Solomon. 1972. "The Effects of Communicating Threats and Promises upon the Bargaining Process." *Journal of Conflict Resolution* 16:99–107.

Clegg, Stewart R. 1989. *Frameworks of Power*. London: Sage.

Cohen, Bernard. 1989. *Developing Sociological Knowledge: Theory and Method*. 2nd ed. Chicago: Nelson-Hall.

Cohen, Ronald L. 1982. "Perceiving Justice: An Attributional Perspective." Pp. 119–160 in *Equity and Justice in Social Behavior*, edited by Jerald Greenberg and Ronald L. Cohen. New York: Academic Press.

1986. "Power and Justice in Intergroup Relations." Pp. 65–84 in *Justice in Social Relations*, edited by Hans Werner Bierhoff, Ronald L. Cohen, and Jerald Greenberg. New York: Plenum Press.

Coleman, James S. 1973. *The Mathematics of Collective Action*. Chicago: Aldine.

1990. *Foundations of Social Theory*. Cambridge, MA: Harvard University Press.

Cook, Karen S. 1975. "Expectations, Evaluations, and Equity." *American Sociological Review* 40:372–388.

(ed.) 1987. *Social Exchange Theory*. Newbury Park, CA: Sage.

1990. "Linking Actors and Structures: An Exchange Network Perspective." Pp. 113–128 in *Structures of Power and Constraint: Essays in Honor of Peter M. Blau*, edited by Craig Calhoun, Marshall W. Meyer, and W. Richard Scott. Cambridge: Cambridge University Press.

1991. "The Microfoundations of Social Structure: An Exchange Perspective." Pp. 29–45 in *Macro–Micro Linkages in Sociology*, edited by Joan Huber. Newbury Park, CA: Sage.

Cook, Karen S., and Richard M. Emerson. 1978. "Power, Equity and Commitment in Exchange Networks." *American Sociological Review* 43:721–739.

Cook, Karen S., Richard M. Emerson, Mary R. Gillmore, and Toshio Yamagishi. 1983. "The Distribution of Power in Exchange Networks: Theory and Experimental Results." *American Journal of Sociology* 89:275–305.

Cook, Karen S., and Mary R. Gillmore. 1984. "Power, Dependence, and Coalitions." Pp. 27–58 in *Advances in Group Processes*, vol. 1, edited by Edward J. Lawler. Greenwich, CT: JAI Press.

Cook, Karen S., and Karen A. Hegtvedt. 1983. "Distributive Justice, Equity, and Equality." *Annual Review of Sociology* 9:217–241.

1986. "Justice and Power: An Exchange Analysis." Pp. 19–41 in *Justice in Social Relations*, edited by Hans W. Bierhoff, Ronald L. Cohen, and Jerald Greenberg. New York: Plenum Press.

Cook, Karen S., Karen A. Hegtvedt, and Toshio Yamagishi. 1988. "Structural Inequality, Legitimation, and Reactions to Inequity in Exchange Networks." Pp. 291–308 in *Status Generalization: New Theory and Research*, edited by Murray Webster Jr. and Martha Foschi. Stanford, CA: Stanford University Press.

Cook, Samuel DuBois. 1972. "Coercion and Social Change." Pp. 107–143 in *Coercion*, Nomos 14, edited by J. Roland Pennock and John W. Chapman. Chicago: Aldine.

Coombs, Clyde H., and George S. Avrunin. 1977. "Single-Peaked Functions and the Theory of Preference." *Psychological Review* 84:216–230.

Dahl, Robert A. 1957. "The Concept of Power." *Behavioral Science* 2:201–205.

1961. *Who Governs? Democracy and Power in an American City*. New Haven: Yale University Press.

Dahrendorf, Ralf. 1959. *Class and Class Conflict in Industrial Society*. Stanford, CA: Stanford University Press.

Dawes, Robyn M. 1980. "Social Dilemmas." *Annual Review of Psychology* 31: 169–193.

1988. *Rational Choice in an Uncertain World*. New York: Harcourt Brace Jovanovich.

Della Fave, L. Richard. 1980. "The Meek Shall Not Inherit the Earth." *American Sociological Review* 45:955–971.

Deutsch, Morton. 1973. *The Resolution of Conflict.* New Haven: Yale University Press.

Deutsch, Morton, and R. M. Krauss. 1962. "Studies of Interpersonal Bargaining." *Journal of Conflict Resolution* 6:52–76.

Easterlin, Richard A. 1974. "Does Economic Growth Improve the Human Lot? Some Empirical Evidence." Pp. 89–125 in *Nations and Households in Economic Growth*, edited by P. A. David and M. W. Reder. New York: Academic Press.

Eckhoff, Torstein. 1974. *Justice: Its Determinants in Social Interaction.* Rotterdam: Rotterdam University Press.

Elster, Jon. 1984. *Ulysses and the Sirens: Studies in Rationality and Irrationality.* Cambridge: Cambridge University Press.

Emerson, Richard M. 1962. "Power-Dependence Relations." *American Sociological Review* 27:31–41.

——— 1972a. "Exchange Theory, Part I: A Psychological Basis for Social Exchange." Pp. 38–57 in *Sociological Theories in Progress*, vol. 2, edited by Joseph Berger, Morris Zelditch Jr., and Bo Anderson. Boston: Houghton-Mifflin.

——— 1972b. "Exchange Theory, Part II: Exchange Relations and Networks." Pp. 58–87 in *Sociological Theories in Progress*, vol. 2, edited by Joseph Berger, Morris Zelditch Jr., and Bo Anderson. Boston: Houghton-Mifflin.

——— 1981. "Social Exchange Theory." Pp. 30–65 in *Social Psychology: Sociological Perspectives*, edited by Morris Rosenberg and Ralph H. Turner. New York: Basic Books.

——— 1987. "Toward a Theory of Value in Social Exchange." Pp. 11–46 in *Social Exchange Theory*, edited by Karen S. Cook. Newbury Park, CA: Sage.

Estes, William K. 1944. "An Experimental Study of Punishment." *Psychological Monographs* vol. 57, no. 3, whole no. 263.

Etzioni, Amitai. 1968. *The Active Society: A Theory of Societal and Political Processes.* New York: Free Press.

Fishburn, Peter C., and Gary A. Kochenberger. 1979. "Two-piece von Neumann-Morgenstern Utility Functions." *Decision Sciences* 10:503–518.

Folger, Robert. 1986. "Rethinking Equity Theory: A Referent Cognition Model." Pp. 145–163 in *Justice in Social Relations*, edited by Hans Werner Bierhoff, Ronald L. Cohen, and Jerald Greenberg. New York: Plenum.

Ford, Rebecca, and Mary A. Blegen. 1992. "Offensive and Defensive Use of Punitive Tactics in Explicit Bargaining." *Social Psychology Quarterly* 55: 351–362.

French, John R. P., Jr., and Bertram Raven. 1959. "The Bases of Social Power." Pp. 150–167 in *Studies in Social Power*, edited by Dorwin Cartwright. Ann Arbor: University of Michigan Press.

Galanter, Eugene, and Patricia Pliner. 1974. "Cross-Modality Matching of Money against Other Continua." Pp. 65–76 in *Sensation and Measurement*, edited by Howard R. Moskowitz, Bertram Scharf, and Joseph C. Stevens. Dordrecht, Holland: Reidel.

Galaskiewicz, Joseph. 1979. *Exchange Networks and Community Politics*. Beverly Hills, CA: Sage.

Gale, John, Kenneth G. Binmore, and Larry Samuelson. 1995. "Learning to Be Imperfect: The Ultimatum Game." *Games and Economic Behavior* 8:56–90.

Gamson, William. 1968. *Power and Discontent*. Homewood, IL.: Dorsey Press.

Garrett, James, and William L. Libby Jr. 1973. "Role of Intentionality in Mediating Responses to Inequity in the Dyad." *Journal of Personality and Social Psychology* 28:21–27.

Giddens, Anthony. 1976. *New Rules of Sociological Method*. London: Hutchinson.

Gilham, Steven A. 1981. "State, Law and Modern Economic Exchange." Pp. 129–151 in *Networks, Exchange and Coercion: The Elementary Theory and Its Applications*, edited by David Willer and Bo Anderson. New York: Elsevier.

Gottman, John M. 1979. *Marital Interaction: Experimental Investigations*. New York: Academic Press.

Gouldner, Alvin W. 1960. "The Norm of Reciprocity: A Preliminary Statement." *American Sociological Review* 25:161–178.

Gray, Louis N., and Irving Tallman. 1987. "Theories of Choice: Contingent Reward and Punishment Applications." *Social Psychology Quarterly* 50:16–23.

Griffith, W. I. 1989. "The Allocation of Negative Outcomes." Pp. 107–137 in *Advances in Group Processes*, vol. 6, edited by Edward J. Lawler and Barry Markovsky. Greenwich, CT: JAI Press.

Halverson, Charles F., Jr., and Mary R. Waldrop. 1970. "Maternal Behavior toward Own and Other Preschool Children: The Problem of 'Ownness.' " *Child Development* 41:839–845.

Hamilton, V. Lee, and Steve Rytina. 1980. "Social Consensus on Norms of Justice: Should the Punishment Fit the Crime?" *American Journal of Sociology* 85:1117–1144.

Harris, Richard J. 1976. "Handling Negative Inputs: On the Plausible Equity Formulae." *Journal of Experimental Social Psychology* 12:194–209.

Harsanyi, John G. 1962. "Measurement of Social Power, Opportunity Costs, and the Theory of Two-Person Bargaining Games." *Behavioral Science* 7:67–80.

Hassebrauck, Manfred. 1987. "The Influence of Misattributions on Reactions to Inequity: Towards a Further Understanding of Inequity." *European Journal of Social Psychology* 17:295–304.

Heath, Anthony F. 1976. *Rational Choice and Social Exchange: A Critique of Exchange Theory*. Cambridge: Cambridge University Press.

Heckathorn, Douglas D. 1985. "Power and Trust in Social Exchange." Pp. 143–167 in *Advances in Group Processes*, vol. 2, edited by Edward J. Lawler. Greenwich, CT: JAI Press.

1988. "Collective Sanctions and the Creation of Prisoner's Dilemma Norms." *American Journal of Sociology* 94:535–562.

Hegtvedt, Karen A. 1990. "The Effects of Relationship Structure on Emotional Responses to Inequity." *Social Psychology Quarterly* 53:214–228.

Hegtvedt, Karen A., and Barry Markovsky. 1995. "Justice and Injustice." Pp. 257–280 in *Sociological Perspectives on Social Psychology*, edited by Karen S. Cook, Gary Alan Fine, and James S. House. Boston: Allyn and Bacon.

Heimer, Carol A. 1985. *Reactive Risk and Rational Action: Managing Moral Hazard in Insurance Contracts*. Berkeley: University of California Press.

———. 1988. "Social Structure, Psychology, and the Estimation of Risk." *Annual Review of Sociology* 14:491–519.

Henshel, Richard L. 1980. "Seeking Inoperative Laws: Toward the Deliberate Use of Unnatural Experimentation." Pp. 175–199 in *Theoretical Methods in Sociology*, edited by Lee Freese. Pittsburgh: Pittsburgh University Press.

Herrnstein, Richard J. 1970. "On the Law of Effect." *Journal of the Experimental Analysis of Behavior* 13:143–166.

———. 1993. "Behavior, Reinforcement, and Utility." Pp. 137–152 in *The Origin of Values*, edited by Michael Hechter, Lynn Nadel, and Richard E. Michod. New York: Aldine de Gruyter.

Hershey, John C., and Paul J. H. Schoemaker. 1980. "Risk Taking and Problem Context in the Domain of Losses: An Expected Utility Analysis." *Journal of Risk and Insurance* 47:111–132.

Hickson, D. J., C. R. Hinings, C. A. Lee, R. E. Schneck, and J. M. Pennings. 1971. "A Strategic Contingencies' Theory of Intraorganizational Power." *Administrative Science Quarterly* 16:216–229.

Hogan, Robert, and Nicholas P. Emler. 1981. "Retributive Justice." Pp. 125–143 in *The Justice Motive in Social Behavior*, edited by Melvin J. Lerner and Sally C. Lerner. New York: Plenum.

Holz, W. C., and N. H. Azrin. 1962. "Recovery during Punishment by Intense Noise." *Psychological Reports* 11:655–657.

Homans, George C. [1961] 1974. *Social Behavior: Its Elementary Forms*. New York: Harcourt Brace and World.

———. 1976. "Commentary." Pp. 231–244 in *Advances in Experimental Social Psychology*, vol. 9, edited by Leonard Berkowitz and Elaine Walster. New York: Academic Press.

Horai, Joann, and James T. Tedeschi. 1969. "Effects of Credibility and Magnitude of Punishment on Compliance to Threats." *Journal of Personality and Social Psychology* 12:164–169.

Hornstein, Harvey A. 1965. "The Effects of Different Magnitudes of Threat upon Interpersonal Bargaining." *Journal of Experimental Social Psychology* 1:282–293.

Hunter, Floyd. 1953. *Community Power Structure*. Chapel Hill: University of North Carolina Press.

Jacobs, David. 1974. "Dependency and Vulnerability: An Exchange Approach to the Control of Organizations." *Administrative Science Quarterly* 19:45–59.

Jasso, Guillermina. 1980. "A New Theory of Distributive Justice." *American Sociological Review* 45:3–32.

Kahneman, Daniel, Jack L. Knetsch, and Richard H. Thaler. 1986. "Fairness and the Assumptions of Economics." *Journal of Business* 59:S285–S300.

——— 1991. "The Endowment Effect, Loss Aversion, and Status Quo Bias." *Journal of Economic Perspectives* 5:193–206.

Kahneman, Daniel, and Dan Lovallo. 1993. "Timid Choices and Bold Forecasts: A Cognitive Perspective on Risk Taking." *Management Science* 39:17–31.

Kahneman, Daniel, and Amos Tversky. 1979. "Prospect Theory: An Analysis of Decision under Risk." *Econometrica* 47:263–291.

——— 1982. "The Psychology of Preferences." *Scientific American* 246:160–173.

——— 1984. "Choices, Values, and Frames." *American Psychologist* 39:341–350.

Kahneman, Daniel, and Carol Varey. 1991. "Notes on the Psychology of Utility." Pp. 127–163 in *Interpersonal Comparisons of Well-Being*, edited by Jon Elster and John E. Roemer. Cambridge: Cambridge University Press.

Kanter, Rosabeth Moss. 1977. *Men and Women of the Corporation*. New York: Basic Books.

Kelley, Harold H., and John W. Thibaut. 1978. *Interpersonal Relations: A Theory of Interdependence*. New York: Wiley.

Keohane, Robert O., and Joseph S. Nye. 1977. *Power and Interdependence: World Politics in Transition*. Boston: Little, Brown.

Knetsch, Jack L. 1989. "The Endowment Effect and Evidence of Nonreversible Indifference Curves." *American Economic Review* 79:1277–1284.

Knetsch, Jack L., and J. A. Sinden. 1984. "Willingness to Pay and Compensation Demanded: Experimental Evidence of an Unexpected Disparity in Measures of Value." *Quarterly Journal of Economics* 99:507–521.

Kollock, Peter. 1994. "The Emergence of Exchange Structures: An Experimental Study of Uncertainty, Commitment, and Trust." *American Journal of Sociology* 100:313–345.

Kuhn, Alfred. 1963. *The Study of Society: A Unified Approach*. Homewood, IL: Irwin-Dorsey.

Lasswell, Harold, and Abraham Kaplan. 1950. *Power and Society*. New Haven: Yale University Press.

Lawler, Edward J. 1975. "An Experimental Study of Factors Affecting the Mobilization of Revolutionary Coalitions." *Sociometry* 38:163–179.

——— 1986. "Bilateral Deterrence and Conflict Spiral: A Theoretical Analysis." Pp. 107–130 in *Advances in Group Processes*, vol. 3, edited by Edward J. Lawler. Greenwich, CT: JAI Press.

——— 1992. "Power Processes in Bargaining." *Sociological Quarterly* 33:17–34.

Lawler, Edward J., and Samuel B. Bacharach. 1987. "Comparison of Dependence and Punitive Forms of Power." *Social Forces* 66:446–462.

Lawler, Edward J., and Rebecca Ford. 1993. "Metatheory and Friendly Competition in Theory Growth: The Case of Power Processes in Bargaining." Pp. 172–210 in *Theoretical Research Programs: Studies in the Growth of Theory*, edited by Joseph Berger and Morris Zelditch Jr. Stanford, CA: Stanford University Press.

Lawler, Edward J., Rebecca Ford, and Mary A. Blegen. 1988. "Coercive Capability in Conflict: A Test of Bilateral Deterrence versus Conflict Spiral Theory." *Social Psychology Quarterly* 51:93–107.

Lawler, Edward J., Cecilia Ridgeway, and Barry Markovsky. 1993. "Structural Social Psychology and Micro–Macro Linkages." *Sociological Theory* 11: 268–290.

Lawler, Edward J., and Jeongkoo Yoon. 1993. "Power and the Emergence of Commitment Behavior in Negotiated Exchange." *American Sociological Review* 58:465–481.

——— 1996. "Commitment in Exchange Relations: Test of a Theory of Relational Cohesion." *American Sociological Review* 61:89-108.

Layder, Derek. 1985. "Power, Structure and Agency." *Journal for the Theory of Social Behavior* 15:131–149.

Leik, Robert K. 1992. "New Directions for Network Exchange Theory: Strategic Manipulation of Network Linkages." *Social Networks* 14:309–323.

Lerner, Melvin J. 1980. *The Belief in a Just World: A Fundamental Delusion.* New York: Plenum.

Leventhal, Gerald S., and David Anderson. 1970. "Self-Interest and the Maintenance of Equity." *Journal of Personality and Social Psychology* 15:57–62.

Leventhal, Gerald S., Jurgis Karuza Jr., and William Rick Fry. 1980. "Beyond Fairness: A Theory of Allocation Preferences." Pp. 167–218 in *Justice and Social Interaction*, edited by Gerald Mikula. New York: Springer-Verlag.

Lévi-Strauss, Claude. 1969. *The Elementary Structures of Kinship.* Rev. ed. Boston: Beacon.

Lind, E. Allan, and Tom R. Tyler. 1988. *The Social Psychology of Procedural Justice.* New York: Plenum.

Lindskold, Svenn. 1978. "Trust Development, the GRIT Proposal, and the Effects of Conciliatory Acts on Conflict and Cooperation." *Psychological Bulletin* 85:772–793.

Lindskold, Svenn, Brian Betz, and Pamela S. Walters. 1986. "Transforming Competitive or Cooperative Climates." *Journal of Conflict Resolution* 30:99–114.

Lindskold, Svenn, and Michael G. Collins. 1978. "Inducing Cooperation by Groups and Individuals." *Journal of Conflict Resolution* 22:679–690.

Lucas, Robert E., Jr. 1986. "Adaptive Behavior and Economic Theory." Pp. 217–242 in *Rational Choice: The Contrast between Economics and Psychology*, edited by Robin M. Hogarth and Melvin W. Reder. Chicago: University of Chicago Press.

Luce, R. Duncan, and Howard Raiffa. 1957. *Games and Decisions.* New York: Wiley.

Lukes, Steven. 1974. *Power: A Radical View.* London: Macmillan.

——— 1977. "Power and Structure." In *Essays in Social Theory.* London: Macmillan.

302   REFERENCES

Machina, Mark J. 1987. "Choice under Uncertainty: Problems Solved and Unsolved." *Economic Perspectives* 2:121–154.

Macy, Michael W. 1989. "Walking out of Social Traps: A Stochastic Learning Model for the Prisoner's Dilemma." *Rationality and Society* 1:197–219.

———. 1993. "Social Learning and the Structure of Collective Action." Pp. 1–35 in *Advances in Group Processes*, vol. 10, edited by Edward J. Lawler, Barry Markovsky, Karen Heimer, and Jodi O'Brien. Greenwich, CT: JAI Press.

Malinowski, Bronislaw. 1922. *Argonauts of the Western Pacific.* New York: E. P. Dutton.

Markovsky, Barry. 1985. "Toward a Multilevel Distributive Justice Theory." *American Sociological Review* 50:822–839.

Markovsky, Barry, David Willer, and Travis Patton. 1988. "Power Relations in Exchange Networks." *American Sociological Review* 53:220–236.

Markowitz, Harry. 1952. "The Utility of Wealth." *Journal of Political Economy* 60:151–158.

Marsden, Peter V., and Edward O. Laumann. 1977. "Collective Action in a Community Elite: Exchange, Influence Resources, and Issue Resolution." Pp. 199–250 in *Power, Paradigms, and Community Research*, edited by Roland J. Liebert and Allen Imershein. London: ISA/Sage.

Martin, Michael W., and Jane Sell. 1979. "The Role of the Experiment in the Social Sciences." *Sociological Quarterly* 20:581–590.

Marwell, Gerald, and David R. Schmitt. 1975. *Cooperation: An Experimental Analysis.* New York: Academic Press.

Mauss, M. 1925. "Essai sur le don: Forme et raison de l'échange dans les sociétés archaïques." *Année Sociologie* 1:30–186.

Mayhew, Bruce H., Louis N. Gray, and James T. Richardson. 1969. "Behavioral Measurement of Operating Power Structures: Characterizations of Asymmetrical Interaction." *Sociometry* 32:474–489.

McClintock, Charles G., and Linda J. Keil. 1982. "Equity and Social Exchange." Pp. 337–387 in *Equity and Justice in Social Behavior*, edited by Jerald Greenberg and Ronald L. Cohen. New York: Academic Press.

McDonald, Gerald W. 1980. "Family Power: The Assessment of a Decade of Theory and Research, 1970–79." *Journal of Marriage and the Family* 42:841–854.

Mead, George Herbert. 1934. *Mind, Self, and Society.* Chicago: University of Chicago Press.

Michaels, James W., John N. Edwards, and Alan C. Acock. 1984. "Satisfaction in Intimate Relationships As a Function of Inequality, Inequity, and Outcomes." *Social Psychology Quarterly* 47:347–357.

Michaels, James W., and James A. Wiggins. 1976. "Effects of Mutual Dependency and Dependency Asymmetry on Social Exchange." *Sociometry* 39:368–376.

Michener, H. Andrew, and Eugene D. Cohen. 1973. "Effects of Punishment Magnitude in the Bilateral Threat Situation." *Journal of Personality and Social Psychology* 26:427–438.

Miller, Dale T., and Neil Vidmar. 1981. "The Social Psychology of Punishment Reactions." Pp. 145–171 in *The Justice Motive in Social Behavior: Adapting to Times of Scarcity and Change*, edited by Melvin J. Lerner and Sally C. Lerner. New York: Plenum.

Mills, C. Wright. 1956. *The Power Elite*. Oxford: Oxford University Press.

Mindlin, Sergio E., and Howard Aldrich. 1975. "Interorganizational Dependence: A Review of the Concept and a Reexamination of the Findings of the Aston Group." *Administrative Science Quarterly* 20:382–392.

Molm, Linda D. 1981. "The Conversion of Power Imbalance to Power Use." *Social Psychology Quarterly* 16:153–166.

———. 1985. "Relative Effects of Individual Dependencies: Further Tests of the Relation between Power Imbalance and Power Use." *Social Forces* 63:810–837.

———. 1987a. "Extending Power-Dependence Theory: Power Processes and Negative Outcomes." Pp. 171–198 in *Advances in Group Processes*, vol. 4, edited by Edward J. Lawler and Barry Markovsky. Greenwich, CT: JAI Press.

———. 1987b. "Linking Power Structure and Power Use." Pp. 101–129 in *Social Exchange Theory*, edited by Karen S. Cook. Newbury Park, CA: Sage.

———. 1988. "The Structure and Use of Power: A Comparison of Reward and Punishment Power." *Social Psychology Quarterly* 51:108–122.

———. 1989a. "An Experimental Analysis of Imbalance in Punishment Power." *Social Forces* 68:178–203.

———. 1989b. "Punishment Power: A Balancing Process in Power-Dependence Relations." *American Journal of Sociology* 94:1392–1418.

———. 1990. "Structure, Action and Outcomes: The Dynamics of Power in Exchange Relations." *American Sociological Review* 55:427–447.

———. 1991. "Affect and Social Exchange: Satisfaction in Power-Dependence Relations." *American Sociological Review* 56:475–493.

———. 1994a. "Is Punishment Effective? Coercive Strategies in Social Exchange." *Social Psychology Quarterly* 57:75–94.

———. 1994b. "Dependence and Risk: Transforming the Structure of Social Exchange." *Social Psychology Quarterly* 57:163–176.

———. 1997. "Risk and Power Use: Constraints on the Use of Coercion in Exchange." *Americal Sociological Review*.

Molm, Linda D., and Karen S. Cook. 1995. "Social Exchange and Exchange Networks." Pp. 209–235 in *Sociological Perspectives on Social Psychology*, edited by Karen S. Cook, Gary Alan Fine, and James S. House. Boston: Allyn and Bacon.

Molm, Linda D., and Mark Hedley. 1992. "Gender, Power, and Social Exchange." Pp. 1–28 in Cecilia Ridgeway (ed.), *Gender and Interaction: The Role of Microstructures in Inequality*. New York: Springer-Verlag.

Molm, Linda D., Theron M. Quist, and Phillip A. Wiseley. 1993. "Reciprocal Justice and Strategies of Exchange." *Social Forces* 72:19–43.

——— 1994. "Imbalanced Structures, Unfair Strategies: Power and Justice in Social Exchange." *American Sociological Review* 59:98–121.

Morgan, Patrick M. 1977. *Deterrence: A Conceptual Analysis.* Beverly Hills, CA: Sage.

Nagel, Jack H. 1975. *The Descriptive Analysis of Power.* New Haven: Yale University Press.

Neuman, Franz L. 1950. "Approaches to the Study of Political Power." *Political Science Quarterly* 65:161–180.

Newsom, Crighton, Judith E. Favell, and Arnold Rincover. 1983. "Side Effects of Punishment." Pp. 285–316 in *The Effects of Punishment on Human Behavior*, edited by Saul Axelrod and Jack Apsche. New York: Academic Press.

O'Brien, Jodi, and Karen S. Cook. 1989. "The Sociological Significance of Micro-Level Theories of Action." Paper presented at the annual meeting of the American Sociological Association, San Francisco.

Oliver, Pamela. 1980. "Rewards and Punishments As Selective Incentives for Collective Action: Theoretical Investigations." *American Journal of Sociology* 85:1356–1375.

Orne, M. T. 1962. "On the Social Psychology of the Psychological Experiment: With Particular Reference to Demand Characteristics and Their Implications." *American Psychologist* 17:776–783.

Parsons, Talcott. 1957. "The Distribution of Power in American Society." *World Politics* 10:123–143.

——— 1963a. "On the Concept of Influence." *Public Opinion Quarterly* 17:37–62.

——— 1963b. "On the Concept of Political Power." *Proceedings of the American Philosophical Society* 107:232–262.

Patchen, Martin. 1987. "Strategies for Eliciting Cooperation from an Adversary." *Journal of Conflict Resolution* 31:164–185.

Patterson, Gerald R. 1982. *Coercive Family Process.* Eugene, OR: Castalia.

Payne, John W., Dan J. Laughhunn, and Roy Crum. 1980. "Translation of Gambles and Aspiration Level Effects in Risky Choice Behavior." *Management Science* 26:1039–1060.

Pazulinec, Robert, Michael Meyerrose, and Thomas Sajwaj. 1983. "Punishment via Response Cost." Pp. 71–86 in *The Effects of Punishment on Human Behavior*, edited by Saul Axelrod and Jack Apsche. New York: Academic Press.

Pfeffer, Jeffrey, and Gerald R. Salancik. 1978. *The External Control of Organizations: A Resource Dependence Perspective.* New York: Harper and Row.

Pruitt, Dean G. 1981. *Negotiation Behavior.* New York: Academic Press.

Rachlin, Howard, and Richard J. Herrnstein. 1969. "Hedonism Revisited: On the Negative Law of Effect." Pp. 83–109 in *Punishment and Aversive Behavior*, edited by Byron A. Campbell and Russell M. Church. New York: Appleton-Century-Crofts.

Radlow, Robert, and Marianna Fry Weidner. 1966. "Unenforced Commitments in 'Cooperative' and 'Non-cooperative' Non-constant-sum Games." *Journal of Conflict Resolution* 10:497–505.

Raush, Harold L., William A. Barry, Richard K. Hertel, and Mary Ann Swain. 1974. *Communication, Conflict, and Marriage.* San Francisco: Jossey-Bass.

Ritov, Ilana, and Jonathan Baron. 1992. "Status-Quo and Omission Biases." *Journal of Risk and Uncertainty* 5:49–61.

Rubin, Jeffrey Z., and Bert R. Brown. 1975. *The Social Psychology of Bargaining and Negotiation.* New York: Academic Press.

Russell, Bertrand. 1938. *Power: A New Social Analysis.* London: George Allen and Unwin.

Sahlins, Marshall D. 1972. *Stone Age Economics.* New York: Aldine-Atheron.

Samuelson, William, and Richard Zeckhauser. 1988. "Status Quo Bias in Decision Making." *Journal of Risk and Uncertainty* 1:7–59.

Scanzoni, John. 1972. *Sexual Bargaining: Power Politics in American Marriage.* Englewood Cliffs, NJ: Prentice-Hall.

Schelling, Thomas C. 1960. *The Strategy of Conflict.* New York: Oxford University Press.

Scher, Steven J., and David R. Heise. 1993. "Affect and the Perception of Injustice." Pp. 223–252 in *Advances in Group Processes*, vol. 10, edited by Edward J. Lawler, Barry Markovsky, Karen Heimer, and Jodi O'Brien. Greenwich, CT: JAI Press.

Schlenker, Barry R. 1974. "Social Psychology and Science." *Journal of Personality and Social Psychology* 29:1–15.

Schmitt, David R., and Gerald Marwell. 1970. "Reward and Punishment As Influence Techniques for the Achievement of Cooperation under Inequity." *Human Relations* 23:37–45.

1972. "Withdrawal and Reward Reallocation As Responses to Inequity." *Journal of Experimental Social Psychology* 8:207–221.

Simon, Herbert A. 1955. "A Behavioral Model of Rational Choice." *Quarterly Journal of Economics* 69:99–118.

1956. "Rational Choice and the Structure of the Environment." *Psychological Review* 63:129–138.

1957. *Models of Man.* New York: Wiley.

Skinner, B. F. 1938. *The Behavior of Organisms.* New York: Appleton.

1948. *Walden Two.* New York: Macmillan.

Skvoretz, John, and David Willer. 1991. "Power in Exchange Networks: Setting and Structural Variations." *Social Psychology Quarterly* 54:224–238.

Smith, Adam. [1776] 1937. *The Wealth of Nations.* New York: Random House, Modern Library.

Solomon, Richard L. 1964. "Punishment." *American Psychologist* 19:239–254.

Spranca, Mark, Elisa Minsk, and Jonathan Baron. 1991. "Omission and Commission in Judgment and Choice." *Journal of Experimental Social Psychology* 27:76–105.

Stolte, John F. 1983. "The Legitimation of Structural Inequality: The Reformulation and Test of the Self-Evaluation Argument." *American Sociological Review* 48:331–342.

———. 1987a. "The Formation of Justice Norms." *American Sociological Review* 52: 774–784.

———. 1987b. "Legitimacy, Justice, and Productive Exchange." Pp. 190–208 in *Social Exchange Theory*, edited by Karen S. Cook. Newbury Park, CA: Sage.

Straus, Murray A. 1973. "A General Systems Theory Approach to a Theory of Violence between Family Members." *Social Science Information* 12:105–125.

Szmatka, Jacek, and David Willer. 1993. "Exclusion, Inclusion and Mixed Connection: A Scope Extension and Test between Theories." Paper presented at the 1993 annual meeting of the American Sociological Association, Miami.

Tedeschi, James T., and Thomas V. Bonoma. 1972. "Power and Influence: An Introduction." Pp. 1–49 in *Social Influence Processes*, edited by James T. Tedeschi. Hawthorne, NY: Aldine.

Tedeschi, James T., Thomas V. Bonoma, and R. C. Brown. 1971. "A Paradigm for the Study of Coercive Power." *Journal of Conflict Resolution* 15:197–223.

Tedeschi, James T., Thomas V. Bonoma, and Barry R. Schlenker. 1972. "Influence, Decision, and Compliance." Pp. 346–418 in *Social Influence Processes*, edited by James T. Tedeschi. Hawthorne, NY: Aldine.

Tedeschi, James T., Barry R. Schlenker, and Thomas V. Bonoma. 1973. *Conflict, Power, and Games*. Hawthorne, NY: Aldine.

Thaler, Richard. 1980. "Toward a Positive Theory of Consumer Choice." *Journal of Economic Behavior and Organization* 1:39–60.

Thibaut, John W., and Harold H. Kelley. 1959. *The Social Psychology of Groups*. New York: Wiley.

Thibaut, John W., and Laurens Walker. 1975. *Procedural Justice: A Psychological Analysis*. Hillsdale, NJ: Lawrence Erlbaum.

Thorndike, Edward L. 1932. *The Fundamentals of Learning*. New York: Teachers College, Columbia University.

Toch, Hans. 1969. *Violent Men*. New York: Aldine.

Tornblom, Kjell. 1988. "Positive and Negative Allocations: A Typology and a Model for Conflicting Justice Principles." Pp. 141–168 in *Advances in Group Processes*, vol. 5, edited by Edward J. Lawler and Barry Markovsky. Greenwich, CT: JAI Press.

Turner, Jonathan H. [1974] 1986. *The Structure of Sociological Theory*. Homewood, IL: Dorsey.

Tversky, Amos, and Daniel Kahneman. 1974. "Judgment under Uncertainty: Heuristics and Biases." *Science* 185:1124–1131.

———. 1981. "The Framing of Decisions and the Psychology of Choice." *Science* 211: 453–458.

1983. "Extensional versus Intuitive Reasoning: The Conjunction Fallacy in Probability Judgment." *Psychological Review* 90:293–315.

1986. "Rational Choice and the Framing of Decisions." *Journal of Business* 59:S251–S278.

1991. "Loss Aversion in Riskless Choice: A Reference-Dependent Model." *Quarterly Journal of Economics* 106:1039–1061.

1992. "Advances in Prospect Theory: Cumulative Representation of Uncertainty." *Journal of Risk and Uncertainty* 5:297–323.

Utne, Mary K., and Robert F. Kidd. 1980. "Equity and Attribution." Pp. 63–93 in *Justice and Social Interaction*, edited by Gerald Mikula. New York: Springer-Verlag.

van de Stadt, Huib, Arie Kapteyn, and Sara van de Geer. 1985. "The Relativity of Utility: Evidence from Panel Data." *Review of Economics and Statistics* 67:179–187.

Van Houten, Ron. 1983. "Punishment: From the Animal Laboratory to the Applied Setting." Pp. 13–44 in *The Effects of Punishment on Human Behavior*, edited by Saul Axelrod and Jack Apsche. New York: Academic Press.

Walster, Elaine, G. William Walster, and Ellen Berscheid. 1978. *Equity: Theory and Research*. Boston: Allyn and Bacon.

Walters, Gary C., and Joan E. Grusec. 1977. *Punishment*. San Francisco: W. H. Freeman.

Weber, Max. 1947. *The Theory of Social and Economic Organization*. New York: Oxford University Press.

Webster, Murray, Jr., and Leroy R. F. Smith. 1978. "Justice and Revolutionary Coalitions: A Test of Two Theories." *American Journal of Sociology* 84: 267–292.

Weiner, Harold. 1962. "Some Effects of Response Cost upon Human Operant Behavior." *Journal of the Experimental Analysis of Behavior* 5:201–208.

Whitmeyer, Joseph M. 1994. "Social Structure and the Actor: The Case of Power in Exchange Networks." *Social Psychology Quarterly* 57:177–189.

Willer, David. 1981. "The Basic Concepts of Elementary Theory." Pp. 25–53 in *Networks, Exchange and Coercion: The Elementary Theory and Its Applications*, edited by David Willer and Bo Anderson. New York: Elsevier.

1987. *Theory and the Experimental Investigation of Social Structures*. New York: Gordon and Breach Science Publishers.

Willer, David, and Bo Anderson (eds.). 1981. *Networks, Exchange and Coercion: The Elementary Theory and Its Applications*. New York: Elsevier.

Willer, David, and Barry Markovksy. 1993. "Elementary Theory: Its Development and Research Program." Pp. 323–363 in *Theoretical Research Programs: Studies in the Growth of Theory*, edited by Joseph Berger and Morris Zelditch Jr. Stanford, CA: Stanford University Press.

Willer, David, Barry Markovsky, and Travis Patton. 1989. "Power Structures: Derivations and Applications of Elementary Theory." Pp. 313–353 in *Soci-

ological Theories in Progress: New Formulations, edited by Joseph Berger, Morris Zelditch Jr., and Bo Anderson. Newbury Park, CA: Sage.

Winter, William D., Antonio J. Ferreira, and Norman Bowers. 1973. "Decision-Making in Married and Unrelated Couples." *Family Process* 12:83–94.

Wrong, Dennis H. 1979. *Power: Its Forms, Bases and Uses.* Oxford: Blackwell.

Wuebben, Paul L., Bruce C. Straits, and Gary I. Schulman. 1974. *The Experiment As a Social Occasion.* Berkeley, CA: Glendessary Press.

Yamagishi, Toshio. 1995. "Social Dilemmas." Pp. 311–334 in *Sociological Perspectives on Social Psychology*, edited by Karen S. Cook, Gary Alan Fine, and James S. House. Boston: Allyn and Bacon.

Yamagishi, Toshio, and Karen S. Cook. 1993. "Generalized Exchange and Social Dilemmas." *Social Psychology Quarterly* 56:235–248.

Yamagishi, Toshio, Mary R. Gillmore, and Karen S. Cook. 1988. "Network Connections and the Distribution of Power in Exchange Networks." *American Journal of Sociology* 93:833–851.

Yamaguchi, Kazuo. 1996. "Power in Networks of Substitutable/Complementary Exchange Relations: A Rational-Choice Model and An Analysis of Power Centralization." *American Sociological Review* 61:308-332.

Youngs, George A., Jr. 1986. "Patterns of Trust and Punishment Reciprocity in a Conflict Setting." *Journal of Personality and Social Psychology* 51:541–546.

Zelditch, Morris, Jr. 1969. "Can You Really Study an Army in the Laboratory?" Pp. 428–539 in *A Sociological Reader on Complex Organizations*, edited by Amitai Etzioni. New York: Holt, Rinehart, and Winston.

Name index

Subject index

actors, 13–15, 62–64, 79–81
  assumptions about, 13–15, 20, 64
  individual or corporate, 13
  strategic, 161–163, 250–251
affective reactions, 165–166, 221–222, 225, 230, 237–240
agency, 8, 35–37, 41
allocation, compared with exchange, 193–194
alternatives to exchange partners, 23–24, 29–30, 34–35, 37–38, 65–66, 73, 86–87, 107, 246–249
average power, 30–34, 67–68, 104, 113, 246
  average punishment power, 68, 70, 118–120, 122–124, 223, 236–237, 259
  average reward power, 68, 70, 107, 121–122, 130–132, 188
  defined, 30–31
  operationalized, 87–90

bargaining research, 27, 57–59, 67, 223–224, 227–229
bases of power, 48–49, 276–277; see also power
  issue of conceptual distinction, 70–71

coalitions, 37, 273–274
coercion, 44–48, 66–67; see also coercive power
  defined, 66–67
  in families, 59–60, 224, 226, 227, 268–269, 270–271
  in international relations, 270
  in organizations, 269–270
  other definitions of, 49–52
  as a reaction to exploitation, 47–48, 52
  as a type of exchange, 45
  ubiquity in everyday life, 47–48
coercive power, 2–3, 48–55, 67–68, 136–139, 247–249

critique of research on, 61–62
limitations, 8, 263–265
other theories of, 55–60, 220–229
preventing the use of, 52, 58, 118–119, 224, 264
use of, 52–53, 68–69, 130–132, 145–148, 178–179, 247–250, 253–255, 266–267
cohesion, 31
commission and omission, acts of, 137, 197, 269
compliance with coercion, 53–54, 56, 60, 220–221, 234–236
conditionalization assumption, 120–121, 124
conflict, 2, 42–43, 66, 222–224
  conflict escalation, 55–56, 125, 219, 222–224, 241, 260, 278; critique of perspective, 224–229
conflict spiral theory, 53, 58, 113, 119–122, 146, 223–224, 263, 270
connections of exchange relations, see networks
contingency, 25, 36; see also strategies
  of punishment, 126, 129–130, 185, 241–242, 243, 259, 268
  of reward, 185, 194
costs
  of exchange, 16–17, 62–63, 72, 277; see also opportunity costs
  imposed by power use, 32–33, 68–69, 136–137
cumulative research, 5–6, 100–101

dependence, 29, 64–65, 67, 189, 246–247; see also power
  defined, 29
  operationalized, 78, 87
deterrence theory, 52–53, 57–58, 117, 119–120, 121, 157, 223–224, 263, 270